Getting Started in

REAL ESTATE INVESTMENT TRUSTS

T0373448

The *Getting Started In* Series

Getting Started in
REAL ESTATE INVESTMENT TRUSTS

Richard Imperiale

WILEY

John Wiley & Sons, Inc.

Published by John Wiley & Sons, Inc., Hoboken, New Jersey.
Published simultaneously in Canada.

For general information on our other products and services or for technical support, please contact our Customer Care Department within the United States at (800) 762-2974, outside the United States at (317) 572-3993 or fax (317) 572-4002.

Wiley also publishes its books in a variety of electronic formats. Some content that appears in print may not be available in electronic books. For more information about Wiley products, visit our web site at www.wiley.com.

ISBN-13 978-0-471-76919-4
ISBN-10 0-471-76919-3

10 9 8 7 6 5 4 3 2 1

To Sue, Emily, and Mary

Contents

The Easy Way to Own a Vast Real Estate Portfolio

How do you make a small fortune in real estate? Answer: Start with a large for tune! U nfortunately that is the experience of many small r eal estate inv estors. R eal estate is a business of siz e and scale, and without a large amount of capital and kno wledge, it is a risky business. In fact, it is a risky business ev en with capital and kno wledge. So ho w is an inv estor able to get inv olved in a por tfolio of r eal estate without having a v ast fortune? The answer is *real estate investment trusts,* known best by their acronym REITs (pronounced *reets*). This book provides an explanation and analysis of r eal estate investment trusts to help the average investor get started in REIT investing.

Real estate is one of the largest and most per vasive industries in the country and w e are exposed to the business of r eal estate ev ery day. The homes and apar tments in which w e liv e, the offices and factories in which we work, the stores we shop in, the hospitals in which are children are born, even the nursing homes in which some will spend their remaining years are part of the real estate investment landscape.

This v ast landscape of r eal estate inv estment takes many forms. Large institutional investors such as pension plans and insurance companies o wn v ast por tfolios of r eal estate holdings. P rivate individuals also own large and small por tfolios of real estate. In fact, about two-thirds of all American households own their homes, which in many ways is a r eal estate investment.

In the recent past, real estate investing picked up a bad r eputation. During the inflation-pr one, tax-motivated real estate days of the 1970s, many people and institutions invested and lost money in a variety of tax-motivated real estate inv estments. Real estate dev elopers and pr omoters were often thought of as hucksters and charlatans, and many were. Devel-opers also got a bad r eputation as r eal estate co wboys who would build anything if they could get the money. This too was true.

Real estate pr omoters and dev elopers were the dot-com ex ecutives of the 1970s. They became rich as inv estors dir ected an ev er-growing stream of capital into the industry. The Tax Reform Act of 1986 changed the r eal estate landscape b y ending the tax incentiv es that w ere fueling capital formation in the r eal estate industry. The resulting bubble in r eal estate ended with the largest glut of pr operty ever seen in the U.S. r eal es-tate market. The property glut was financed in large par t by the savings and loan industry. The collapse in the r eal estate bubble pr ecipitated the savings and loan crisis as property owners defaulted on their highly lever-aged real estate holdings. With little or no equity in these pr operties and falling property values and rents, there was little incentive not to turn the keys back to the mor tgage holders. The R esolution Trust Company worked during the late 1980s to r esolve the S&L crisis. B y the early 1990s, the excesses of the 1970s had been resolved, but real estate invest-ments continued to hav e a bad r eputation among small inv estors. The Tax Reform Act of 1986 had set the stage for a mor e financially rational real estate mar ketplace. Legendar y v alue inv estors like S am Z ell and many others saw this rationalization of assets and inv ested early in what has turned out to be one of the most stable and w ell-defined real estate recoveries in modern history. Real estate investors have become far more disciplined, demanding r eturns on inv ested capital that r eflect the lev el of investment risk associated with a real estate asset. Mortgage lenders are also far mor e conser vative. They will not lend capital on pr ojects that they do not view as highly feasible. This has brought a capital market dis-cipline to the commer cial mor tgage ar ena. The net r esult has been longer, more stable real estate expansions and less severe real estate cycles. From this cr ucible of industr y r eshaping has emerged a ne w real estate paradigm. D isciplined o wners, rational lenders, and higher r eturns on capital have resulted. Among the new class of disciplined o wners are real estate investment trusts, which collectively own over 10 per cent of the investment-grade real estate in the United States. REITs offer the opportunity for small investors to participate in a broad range of real estate opportunities across most major property sectors and in most geographic locations. Disciplined real estate professionals whose financial interests are largely aligned with those of the shareholders generally manage REITs.

REITs and real estate investing have endured a checkered history. In general terms, REITs were historically a small and misunderstood part of the real estate investment landscape. Over the past decade, however, this has changed. Now REITs are major owners of investment-quality real estate and a major force in the institutional investment arena. REITs are a viable and competitive investment option for investors who are looking to broaden and diversify their investment portfolios. They provide returns that are competitive with—and independent from—stocks and bonds. This fact allows REITs to add an additional element of diversification when they become part of a portfolio along with stocks and bonds.

This book describes these features and attempts to put them into a framework that examines the critical investment aspects of REITs and the theoretical real estate principles that drive the REIT investment decision. As a professional investor in REITs, I noticed that the average investor largely misunderstood REITs. Many professional investors and portfolio managers also had little knowledge of REITs. In addition, very few books had been written on the subject of REITs. Those books that were available provided either a very simplistic overview or a highly complex academic treatment of the topic. Most did not address the fundamental real estate concepts that underlie the basics of real estate investing or the methods of integrating REITs into an investment portfolio. This book is an attempt to address these very issues.

We begin in Part One with a general discussion of real estate as an asset class. Then the legal and financial history of REITs is examined. The section ends with a discussion of how REITs behave as an investment class and how they are best integrated into an investor's portfolio. Part Two describes the fundamental economic issues that affect real estate in general and analyzes these issues in the context of the REIT investment vehicle. The section concludes with specific methods for analyzing REITs as an investment and advanced investment topics involving REITs. Part Three uses the theoretical constructs developed in the first two parts to examine each major property category within the REIT universe. I n vir tually ev ery chapter, y ou will find sidebars featuring key terms and "REIT I dea" concepts—and, at the end of the book, I hav e provided directories for both real estate mutual funds (A ppendix A) and real estate investment trusts (Appendix B). All things consider ed then, I believe this book fills a v oid in the av ailable curr ent literatur e about REITs and promotes a better understanding of an emerging asset class. It is my hope that you will feel the same.

Richard Imperiale

Union Grove, Wisconsin
May 2006

Acknowledgments

Although the author ultimately gets the cr edit for writing a book, there is an army of others who contribute to the pr ocess. I would like to r ecognize them. This book is dedicated to my wife, S ue, and our two daughters, E mily and M ary, who put up with my absence from family and school functions and during many ev enings and w eekends. Their support and encouragement made the completion of this project possible. Every day they make me realize how fortunate I really am.

Of course, it is not a book without a publisher. In the middle of the dot-com frenzy, David Pugh at John Wiley was open-minded enough to listen to my ideas about r eal estate, giv e me critical feedback, and go to bat for me on my first book pr oject about real estate. David has been an excellent coach and critic and helped me shape this book and two others into better and useful texts. I now consider him a good friend and thank him for all his help.

The book contains a fair amount of data compiled from company reports and industry trade associations. M uch of that data was pr ocessed by my assistant, Rochell Tillman, and my research associates, Farid Shiek, Tom McNulty, Jackie Hughes, Isac Malmgren, and Jeff Lenderman, who collectively reviewed the SEC filings of over 200 real estate investment trusts and real estate operating companies. Their diligence and har d work provided consolidated data that is not found in any other single place. Lastly I thank David Howard, Michael Grupe, and Tony Edwards, all from the National Association of R eal Estate I nvestment Trusts (NAREIT). They hav e each assisted me with critical comments, data, and analysis as w ell as industr y contacts who were helpful in providing insights and information.

R. I.

Part 1

Getting Started in REITs

Real Estate as an Asset Class

More money has been made in real estate than all industrial investments combined.

—Andrew Carnegie, 1902

To understand *real estate investment trusts* (REITs), an investor needs a basic understanding of the real estate asset class. The recent popularity of r eal estate inv esting has helped to bring the inv estment oppor tunities in r eal estate br oader exposure to noninstitutional inv estors. U ntil r e-cently, real estate was one of the best kept secr ets in the investment community. It is an asset that major investment institutions have formally embraced as a part of their por tfolios for the last centur y. Among institutional inv estors it is no secr et that w ell-located, high-quality real estate can provide an excellent return on investment, high current income, and a significant hedge against inflation.

> **real estate investment trust (REIT)**
>
> a tax conduit company dedicated to owning, managing, and operating income-producing real estate, such as apartments, shopping centers, offices, and warehouses. Some REITs, known as mortgage REITs, also engage in financing real estate.

Characteristics of Real Estate as an Investment

Institutional r eal estate inv estors o wn the v ast majority of the estimated $11.0 trillion of

A Brief History of REITs

REITs actually date back to the trusts and robber barons of the 1880s. Investors could avoid taxation because trusts were not taxed at the corporate level if income was distributed to the trust beneficiaries. Over time this tax advantage was reversed. In 1960, President Eisenhower signed the tax provisions into law with the Real Estate Investment Trust Act of 1960, which reestablished the special tax considerations for qualifying REITs as pass-through entities. This allowed REITs to avoid taxation at the corporate level on income distributed to shareholders. This law formed the basis for present-day REITs.

REIT investment increased throughout the 1980s as the Tax Reform Act of 1986 eliminated many real estate tax shelters. The Tax Reform Act of 1986 allowed REITs to manage their properties directly, and in 1993 REIT investment barriers to pension funds were eliminated. This history of reforms continued to increase the opportunity for REITs to make high-quality property investments. Currently there are more than 200 publicly traded REITs in the United States and the REIT structure is being adopted in many countries around the world.

Real Estate Investment Trust Act of 1960

the federal law that authorized REITs. Its purpose was to allow small investors to pool their investments in real estate in order to get the same benefits as might be obtained by direct ownership, while also diversifying their risks and obtaining professional management.

investment-grade *commercial real estate* in the United States. By comparison, the total capitalization of all public U.S. equities is estimated to be $12.9 trillion, and the nominal v alue of all non-government U.S. bonds is estimated to be $36.4 trillion. U.S. domestic r eal estate as an asset class ranks thir d, behind stocks and bonds, and r epresents 18 per cent of the total of the thr ee asset classes (see Figure 1.1).

Positive Attributes of the Real Estate Asset Class

Each institution generally has its own particular investment policy when it comes to r eal estate. Normally, institutions are attempting to match the life of assets they o wn with that of for ecast liabilities.

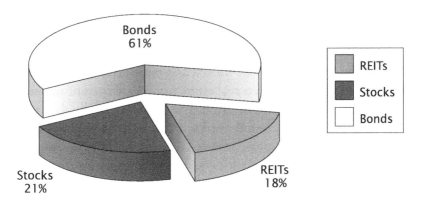

FIGURE 1.1 Commercial Real Estate versus Stocks and Bonds

Retirement funds, insurance companies, and commercial banks ar e among the major priv ate sector investors in r eal estate. They all have projected liabilities that must be met at some future date.

The consistent and r elatively pr edictable cash flows associated with real estate allow for a high degree of confidence when matching futur e liabilities. The cash flow comes in the form of rent paid to the building owner. The buildings that ar e owned by institutional investors tend to have *credit tenants*. (There will be more about credit tenants in Chapter 15.)

Consistent and pr edictable cash flo w is just one attractive featur e of the r eal estate asset class. Real estate also tends to per form better than financial assets in an inflationar y envir onment. I n r eviewing the histor y of r eal estate per formance, a number of studies hav e found that r eturns fr om real estate were higher during times of inflation and lower during periods of disinflation. Thus, a por tfolio of largely financial assets can be hedged—to

> **commercial real estate**
>
> all real estate excluding single-family homes and multifamily buildings up to four units, raw land, farms and ranches, and government-owned properties. About half of commercial real estate as defined is considered to be of sufficient quality and size to be of interest to institutional investors. This real estate is known as *investment grade*.

some extent—against the corr osive effects of inflation thr ough the ownership of real estate. Taxable investors can also derive some additional tax benefits from the real estate asset class. F or tax accounting purposes, the value of r eal estate other than land can be depr eciated at a rate that is generally greater than the actual economic life of the pr operty. In most cases, the value of a well-maintained property in a good location actually increases over time at a rate similar to inflation. This accelerated tax depreciation results in a partial sheltering of cash flow as well as the deferral of taxes, which can usually be treated as a more favorable long-term capital gain for tax purposes. S o real estate can cr eate current income in the form of cash flo w that is par tially shelter ed fr om taxation until some futur e date. I t is possible to capture some of the benefits of r eal estate's unique tax qualities for tax-ex empt investors such as pension funds. Structuring partnerships and operating agreements in ways that allo w taxable benefits to flow to those who can use them, while allocating higher levels of cash flow to tax-exempt investors, is one way tax-exempt investors can benefit fr om the tax advantages of real estate. In some instances, the tax benefits of certain real estate projects can be sold to taxable investors by tax-exempt investors, which allows incremental total return to be enhanced.

credit tenant
a tenant that has the size and financial strength to be rated as investment grade by one of the three major credit rating agencies: Moody's, Standard & Poor's, and Fitch. The investment grade rating increases the probability that the financial strength of the company will allow it to continue to pay rent even during difficult economic times.

There are some other primary reasons that large institutional investors are attracted to real estate. One factor that is often cited by institutions is that real estate r eturns behav e v ery differ ently fr om stock and bond r eturns. H ow investment r eturns behav e r elative to one another is kno wn as *correlation*. This low correlation of r eturns pr ovides an added div ersification benefit within an investor's portfolio. In general, adding real estate to a portfolio of stocks and bonds enhances r eturn and lo wers risk in a giv en portfolio. There is a large body of academic and professional work that suggests that investing 5 per cent to 15 per cent of a por tfolio in r eal estate increases the total return and lowers the portfolio risk. This is consistent with the fact that the largest 200 r etirement plans hav e an av erage total of 17 percent of their assets invested in real estate.

Attribution of Return in Real Estate

A fancy way of explaining wher e the r eturn of a par ticular investment comes from is known as the *attribution of return*. The return attribution of real estate can be identified by a number of features, some of which are unique to real estate and some of which ar e common to other classes of investments such as stocks and bonds. As discussed pr eviously, the value of w ell-maintained r eal estate in a good location will actually incr ease over time. This capital appr eciation aspect of r eal estate is similar to the long-term growth in value seen as a primar y component of return in the equity asset class. Investors buy stocks because they expect over time that the price will go up . The same is tr ue of inv estors who buy r eal estate. But, unlike stocks, most r eal estate also has some bondlike characteristics. It is the consistent and pr edictable cash flo w associated with r ents paid on r eal estate that is the primar y focus of most institutional investors. This steady str eam of r ental income attributable to a giv en property or portfolio is much like the regular interest paid as the coupon of a bond. The terms of these bondlike payments are typically detailed in a lease agr eement betw een the o wner of the r eal estate and the user or tenant of the real estate. It is the quality and completeness of these terms and conditions as stated in the lease that allo w for the analysis of the underlying cash flo ws of a giv en pr operty. The *term,* or length, of the rental payments as stated by the lease also produces duration characteristics similar to those of a bond inv estment. In a bond, the duration is, in part, a function of the term r emaining before the bond matur es. In real estate, the duration of the rental income is a function of the length of the underlying lease or r emaining period of the r ental stream. Rents derived from hotel and motel properties, which can change on a daily basis, have the shor test duration, follo wed by apar tment r ents, which ar e generally set for a term of one or two y ears (see Table 1.1). O ffice, r etail, and industrial properties tend to hav e longer duration leases that can extend for a term of 10 years to 30 years or more.

TABLE 1.1 Average Lease Duration by Property Type

Hotels	1 to 3 days
Self-storage	6 months
Apartments	1 year
Offices	5 to 15 years
Industrial	5 to 20 years
Retail	10 to 30 years

Real estate also has a credit profile, much like the credit rating of a bond. This credit profile is determined by the credit quality of the underlying tenants that pay the lease and occupy the real estate. For example, an office building with 50,000 square feet leased on a long-term basis to IBM will have a much better credit profile than the same space leased to Bob's Pretty Good Computer Company, a new enterprise with an operating history of less than five years. Similarly, an IBM bond would presumably have a better credit rating than a loan to Bob's Pretty Good Computer Company, which would most likely be considered a higher-risk proposition.

There are also return attribution features that are unique to the real estate asset class. The physical attributes of a given piece of real estate can have an impact on value. For example, visualize two suburban office buildings, of the same size and age, in a similar location. One is built of brick and stone, the other using simple wood construction. It is likely that because the brick-and-stone office building has a higher replacement cost, it may also have a higher value than the wood-frame office building. Thus a building's physical quality can have a unique impact on its value.

Location is also a unique feature that can ascribe greater or lesser value to real estate. Because any given piece of real estate can only occupy a single location, each piece of real estate is, in essence, unique. Real estate in a highly desirable location may have a much greater value than identical real estate in a different, less desirable location. This location factor can be so important in that in some cases it is the overall value determinant of a real estate parcel. That is why companies like Walgreen's will close a store on the southwest corner of an intersection and reopen the store on the northeast corner of the same intersection! Location, Location, Location—always remember how important it is in real estate.

There is also the situation of what are called *externalities* in the economics of real estate. An externality occurs when an activity or event affects (for good or bad) another that is external to it. If Donald Trump builds a shining new skyscraper in the middle of a marginal neighborhood, this is a positive externality for the owners of many adjoining properties, who see the value of their holdings increase overnight as a result of no direct activity on their part. Conversely, if the house next door to an apartment building in an urban neighborhood is converted to a homeless shelter, it is likely to be considered a negative externality that lowers the value of the apartment building.

Because the problem of externalities is so crucial to real estate value, a high degree of zoning and entitlement exists in the r eal estate mar ket-place. Normally zoning considers what is commonly referred to as *highest and best use.* This is a use that is economically and physically feasible when considered relative to other adjoining r eal estate, economic activities in the area, the size of the site, and the intended design and use of the new building. Zoning and entitlement also extend to the regulatory level when examining real estate. Many localities have low- or no-growth policies that make it difficult to dev elop ne w r eal estate. S ome localities adopt master plans that strictly limit the siz e, style, design, and use of a building in any given area of the planned community.

In some communities there is simply no more available vacant space on which to build. These are referred to as *urban infill* or *redevelopment* communities. Any *entitlement* in these areas becomes part of the removal and redevelopment of an existing site or the expansion and refinement of an existing property. The ever-growing political sentiment of "not in my backyard" among the residents of many communities often creates a situation of externalities that can hav e significant positive or negativ e impact on the v alue of a pr operty. These ar e unique aspects of the r eal estate asset class. The featur es that ar e unique to r eal estate, physical attributes, location, local externalities, zoning, and entitlement, contribute to r eal estate's low corr elation of r eturn r elative to stocks and bonds. The value of r eal estate is driv en by supply and demand in the local r eal estate mar ket. The best building imaginable might sit empty in a market where supply ex ceeds demand for that type of real estate. B ecause of its permanent physical nature, real estate cannot be moved to a market where the demand is gr eater than the supply . I n its simplest terms, real estate is a v ery local asset class driven by all the macr oeconomic and micr oeconomic factors of the local and regional marketplace.

This is not to say that r eal estate is insulated from more national economic factors. The aggregate demand for r eal estate in general is driv en b y the overall growth in the national economy. Population

entitlement
the legal right as granted by state and local real estate zoning authorities to build or improve a parcel of existing real estate, normally unimproved land. The grant of entitlement to improve property can take long periods of time and be expensive from a legal standpoint. But entitlement can create immediate value for previously unentitled parcels of real estate.

REIT Idea: *Kelo et al. v. City of New London et al.*

This supply and demand struggle was showcased in the recent Supreme Court case of *Kelo et al. v. City of New London et al.*, which was argued February 22, 2005, and decided June 23, 2005.

After approving an integrated development plan designed to revitalize its ailing economy, the city of New London, Connecticut, purchased most of the property earmarked for the project from willing sellers, but initiated condemnation proceedings when Kelo and the owners of the rest of the property refused to sell. The city claimed the proposed taking of their property qualified as a "public use."

Prior court rulings were clear that the city could not take the land simply to confer a private benefit on a particular private party. However, the property at issue here would be claimed pursuant to a carefully considered development plan, which was not adopted to benefit a particular class of identifiable individuals.

The city determined that the area at issue was distressed and that their program of economic rejuvenation was entitled to proceed. The city had carefully formulated a development plan that it felt would provide appreciable benefits to the community, including new jobs and increased tax revenue. The Supreme Court agreed with the city and the taking of the private land was allowed.

demographics, job cr eation, and the general business cy cle all hav e an impact on the final demand for real estate. However, this demand manifests itself in very local ways. For example, the Internet frenzy that gripped San Francisco and San Jose in the late 1990s had a huge impact on the final demand for real estate in those cities, driving real estate prices to unsustainable lev els. D uring the same time period, r eal estate prices in Atlanta, Georgia, remained relatively soft due to an excess supply of local property, which had to be absorbed before prices could again advance.

Real estate seems to have a litany of positive investment characteristics. It has both stock- and bond-type attributes as w ell as per formance features that enhance por tfolio diversification. It tends to per form well in an inflationary environment and achieves good outcomes in both rising and falling inter est rate envir onments. Taxable inv estors also enjo y certain tax advantages when investing in real estate. These are the beneficial features that hav e made r eal estate a fav orite among institutional investors.

Negative Attributes of the Real Estate Asset Class

Although real estate has a long list of positive investment attributes, there are also some negative characteristics related to direct investments in real estate. Lack of liquidity is the single most negative factor that goes along with owning a real estate investment portfolio. The process of buying and selling real estate can be long and involved. An investment-class property can easily take six months to a year to sell, depending on market conditions and the prevailing economic environment. The marketability of a property will often depend on the terms and conditions of a sale. The terms are often subject to negotiation at times, lengthy negotiation between any given number of potential buyers and the seller. Because real estate is often financed in part with debt, the type and amount of financing that is readily available for a given property or in a given marketplace will often affect these negotiations. This lack of liquidity, when compared to other financial assets such as stocks or bonds, adds to the potential risk inherent in the real estate asset class.

An investor in a share of IBM common stock is buying one share out of millions of identical common shares that trade freely on a daily basis. The buyer of an office building in Detroit faces an entirely unique set of facts and circumstances that are largely different from the facts and circumstances that may affect a similar office building in Denver. Furthermore, office buildings in Detroit and Denver similar to those described may only change hands every few years. At times it may be difficult to establish a relevant market price with which to compare similar real estate. This lack of liquidity, when coupled with the local market nature of real estate, can create a situation where real estate is a less efficient asset class. This is due in part to the uniqueness of each property as it is situated in each market. Local economic factors can lead to real estate values rising in one area of the country while falling in others. These same factors can lead to rising prices for industrial buildings and falling prices for office buildings in the very same market. The uniqueness of real estate causes these inefficiencies. The lack of liquidity and the less efficient local characteristics of real estate also create problems when attempting to measure the performance of real estate. Performance is most accurate when measured over the period the real estate is owned, which may be 5 to 10 years or longer. However, measuring annual or quarterly returns from a pr operty or a por tfolio can be difficult giv en the lack of market information. A ppraisals are sometimes used to estimate periodic values over shorter periods of time, but this is not as accurate as the data from actual transactions. And it still leav es unanswered the question of how a real estate por tfolio is per forming relative to other similar por tfolios. These inefficient aspects of dir ect r eal estate inv estment manifest themselves in the higher potential r eturns that result from superior mar ket kno wledge. The inefficiencies cr eate adv antages for inv estors who have cultivated local market knowledge and use it to the disadv antage of the less informed o wner. This use of material inside information that may be gleaned fr om political and business r elationships is not illegal in real estate transactions, as it is in securities transactions. O n this basis, some observers argue that r eal estate is a less than lev el playing field for the small investor. This perception may have some basis in the recent history of the small investor and real estate.

The late 1970s and early 1980s saw a confluence of events that hurt the general credibility of the real estate asset class in the eyes of the small investor. The federal tax code had cr eated a situation of positiv e incentives for the o wnership of inv estment real estate. The inflationary environment of the period led to ev er-escalating real estate prices, which, in turn, led to an excess amount of capital from small investors flowing into the r eal estate mar ket. This took the form of a large number of priv ate limited par tnerships that w ere cr eated to inv est in r eal estate. F ederally insured savings and loan institutions became lenders to the par tnerships in an envir onment where lenders had little incentiv e not to lend. There was little regulatory oversight of the situation and a great deal of leverage and liquidity. This led to a speculative real estate bubble that resulted in a real estate crash during the mid 1980s and a near collapse of the entir e U.S. savings and loan system.

It took nearly a decade for the economy to absorb the excess supply of r eal estate, and an entir e generation of small inv estors was left with painful financial losses and a negative outlook on real estate as an investment. M any small inv estors vie w r eal estate as an institutional ar ena. Given the large amount of capital r equired to buy a r eal estate por tfolio diversified by property type and geography , it is easy to understand the continuing negative sentiment of the small investor. The aftermath of the limited partnerships and the savings and loan crisis has led to a real estate market with a new sense of order. Tax law changes have resulted in more modest capital formation in the real estate markets. The increased regulation and scr utiny of lenders and their loan por tfolios has lo wered the propensity for excess leverage in the r eal estate sector by requiring more equity and higher loan under writing standar ds. This has r esulted in a mor e balanced r eal estate economy. Wall Street has also made a contribution to the r eal estate sector . The growth in *securitization* of r eal estate assets thr ough such v ehicles as *commercial mortgage-backed securities* (CMBS) and real estate inv estment tr usts has cr eated a public market discipline that has r esulted in better transparency of the real estate markets and a more moderate real estate cycle.

> **securitization**
> the process of financing a pool of similar but unrelated financial assets (usually loans or other debt instruments) by issuing to investors security interests representing claims against the cash flow and other economic benefits generated by the pool of assets.

The growth of REITs as an asset class has cr e-ated an opportunity for small investors to participate in the o wnership of institutional-quality r eal estate. REITs have created a solution to the lack of liquidity, lack of efficiency , and lack of r elevant per formance measurement that confr ont r eal estate inv estors in general. In addition, they provide an efficient mechanism for small investors to participate in r eal estate por tfolios that offer div ersity by pr operty type and geography. The advantages and benefits of REITs as an asset class and how to integrate them into a portfolio strategy are the focus of this book.

Points to Remember

- Real estate has been an impor tant component of large institutional investment portfolios for the last century.
- Well-located, high-quality real estate provides excellent return on investment, high current income, and a significant hedge against inflation.
- Real estate behaves very differently from stocks and bonds. Its value is driven by supply and demand in the local real estate market.
- Real estate per forms well in both rising and falling inter est rate environments.

- Returns in the r eal estate asset class riv al those of stocks on a long-term basis.

- Because it is a har d asset, r eal estate pr ovides an inflation hedge, but, unlike most hard assets, real estate provides current income.

- In 1960, a vehicle was created by Congress that enabled groups of investors to collectively own real estate portfolios similar to those of institutions. This vehicle was kno wn as the r eal estate inv est-ment trust (REIT).

The History of Real Estate Investment Trusts

There are two areas where new ideas are terribly dangerous: economics and sex.

—Felix Rohatyn, 1984

I n 1960, the concept of real estate investment trusts (REITs) was a new and bold adv ance. The idea was to allo w groups of small inv estors to pool their r esources to inv est in large-scale, income-pr oducing commercial pr operty, which had historically been the domain of w ealthy investors and large institutions. The enabling legislation for REIT s was modeled after the *registered investment company* (RIC), more commonly known as a mutual fund. The idea behind the enabling legislation was simple: Let shareholders create a commonly owned, freely traded portfolio of buildings just like they cr eate a por tfolio of commonly o wned stocks through a mutual fund.

The REIT Structure

A REIT begins as a simple business tr ust or corporation. If a number of requirements are met on a year-by-year basis, the business trust or corporation may elect to be consider ed a REIT for federal income tax purposes. The general requirements fall to four areas:

1. *Organizational structure.* The REIT must be organized as a business trust or corporation. M ore specifically, it must be managed by one or mor e trustees who have fiduciary duty o ver the management of the organization. The organization must hav e evidence of beneficial shar es of o wnership that ar e transferable b y certificates. The beneficial o wnership must be held b y a minimum of 100 persons, and the five largest individual shareholders in the aggregate may not own more than 50 percent of the shares outstanding.

2. *Nature of assets.* The company's assets ar e primarily r eal estate held for long-term investment purposes. The rules require that at the end of each taxable y ear, at least 75 per cent of the value of a REIT's total assets must be represented by real estate assets, cash, and go vernment securities. Also, a REIT may not o wn non-government securities in an amount gr eater than 25 per cent of the value of assets. Securities of any single issuer may not ex ceed 5 percent of the total value of the REIT's assets or more than 10 percent of the securities of any corporate issuer , other than taxable REIT subsidiaries.

3. *Sources of income.* At least 75 percent of the company's income is derived fr om r eal estate or r eal estate-r elated inv estments. A REIT must actually satisfy two income tests. F irst, at least 75 percent of a REIT 's annual gr oss income must consist of r eal property rents, mortgage interest, gain from the sale of real estate assets, and cer tain other r eal estate-r elated sour ces. S econd, at least 95 percent of a REIT's annual gross income must be derived from the income items fr om the pr eceding 75 per cent test plus other passive income sour ces such as dividends and any type of interest.

4. *Distribution of income.* Ninety per cent of net income must be distributed to shareholders. This is defined as net taxable income as determined b y the I nternal R evenue Code. I f the r equired conditions are met, a REIT may deduct all dividends paid to its shareholders and av oid federal taxation at the corporate lev el on the amount distributed.

Unlike the case for other corporations, which tend to retain most of their earnings and pay tax at the corporate lev el, the income tax bur den for REITs is substantially shifted to the shareholder level. The REIT only pays federal income tax on any of the 10 percent of undistributed net income it elects to r etain. Unlike par tnerships, REITs cannot pass losses through to their inv estors. D espite the legislativ e intent of the REIT structure, the industry experienced a tor tuous and checkered history for its first 25 y ears. In the early days, REIT s were seriously constrained b y policy limitations. They were mandated to be passiv e por tfolios of r eal estate and were allowed only to own real estate, not to operate or manage it. This early requirement dictated that REITs needed to use thir d-party independent contractors to operate and manage their investment properties. This arrangement often came with built-in conflicts of inter est, and the investment marketplace did not easily accept this passiv e paradigm. As mentioned in Chapter 1, during these early y ears the r eal estate investment landscape was driven by tax shelter-oriented investment characteristics. Overvalued properties, coupled with the use of high debt levels, created a significant ar tificial basis for depr eciation and interest expense. These interest and depreciation deductions were used to reduce or eliminate taxable income b y creating so-called paper losses used to shelter an individual taxpayer's earned income. In an era of high marginal tax rates, the idea of using these real estate tax shelters became an industry unto itself. Investment r eal estate was analyz ed, developed, packaged, and sold on the basis of its ability to str ucture and generate paper losses, which were used to shelter ordinary taxable income. This environment removed any sound economic rationale from the real estate investment equation.

Because REITs are most often geared specifically toward generating taxable income on a r egular basis, and a REIT , unlike a par tnership, is not permitted to pass losses thr ough to its o wners, the REIT industr y simply could not compete effectiv ely for inv estment capital against tax shelters. The idea of r eceiving r egular income then fr om an inv estment was not usually consider ed favorable unless there were losses available to offset that income because most individual investors were subject to high marginal tax rates.

The REIT industr y has suffer ed some debacles that r esulted fr om the tax envir onment of the early y ears. B ecause of the inability to pass losses thr ough, many REIT s focused on making mor tgages of v arious types during the tax-motivated era in real estate. A large number of mortgage REITs made loans to builders and dev elopers who in turn dev eloped pr operty that was intended for use as tax shelters. When inter est rates rose to double-digit levels in the mid-1970s, many mortgage REITs were unable to access capital and collapsed, leaving the REIT industr y with a bad reputation. The bankruptcies included many REITs that were associated with large, w ell-known (and allegedly conser vative) financial institutions.

The tax-motivated environment also led to the creation of *finite-life real estate investment trusts* (FREITs). The idea behind these was to create a type of REIT that would liquidate its property portfolio (arguably for a large gain) at some cer tain time in the futur e. The FREIT would then use a very high degree of leverage to buy properties. The high interest ex-pense would substantially reduce the REIT's current income available for distribution. Then the por tfolio would be liquidated and the capital gains would be distributed to shar eholders. Most FREITs were not able to liquidate their holdings for any meaning ful gain. In fact, most lost all the equity of the shar eholders. P erhaps the most infamous aspect of REIT history is the stor y of the pair ed-share and stapled REIT s, which were also born in the era of tax-motiv ated investing. For a more detailed discussion, see Chapter 10.

Tax Reform Act of 1986

With the *Tax Reform Act of 1986*, Congress changed the entir e dynamic of the real estate investment landscape. By limiting the deductibility of in-terest, lengthening depreciation periods, and r estricting the use of passiv e losses, the 1986 Act drastically reduced the potential for real estate invest-ment to generate tax shelter oppor tunities. This policy change at the leg-islative level meant that the new dynamic in real estate investment needed to be on a mor e economic and income-oriented footing. M ore impor-tantly, as part of the 1986 Act, Congress also modified a significant policy constraint that had been imposed on REIT s at the beginning. The new legislation modified the passiv e aspects of the original REIT r ules. The change permitted REITs not simply to own, but also to operate and man-age most types of income-pr oducing commercial properties by providing "customary" services associated with real estate ownership. This new legis-lation finally allowed the economic interests of the REIT's shareholders to be merged with those of its operators and managers. The change applied to most types of r eal estate other than hotels, health car e facilities, and some other businesses that provide a high degree of personal service.

The results of the ne w legislation in 1986 set the stage for significant growth of REITs as an asset class. From a policy standpoint, the new
legislation achieved three important milestones:

1. It eliminated the artificial tax-motivated cap-
    ital flows to the real estate sector that skewed
    the inv estment rationale and distor ted the
    economic basis for real estate activities.

2. It eliminated any artificial bias in the forma-
    tion of capital b y applying uniform policy
    guidelines to all r eal estate, ther eby leveling
    the playing field for all par ticipants in the
    real estate capital market.

3. It eliminated the inher ent conflict of inter-
    est that kept REIT pr operty o wners fr om
    managing their o wn por tfolio holdings,
    thus removing one of the key public market
    objections to the REIT structure.

Suddenly, dispassionate and rational economic
operation returned to the world of real estate.

> **Tax Reform Act of 1986**
> federal law that substantially altered the real estate investment landscape by permitting REITs not only to own, but also to operate and manage most types of income-producing commercial properties. It also stopped real estate tax shelters that had attracted capital from investors based on the amount of losses that could be created by real estate.

The New REIT Era

The Tax R eform A ct of 1986 dramatically r ealigned the economic and
legislative policy for ces that shape the r eal estate mar kets. The new economics of real estate and the positive changes to the REIT format set the
stage for the modern era of the REIT. However, as with any ne w market
dynamic, it took time for the mar ket participants to analyze and understand the new market forces. In addition, the ex cesses of the old r eal estate markets needed to be cured.

The aftermath of the change in tax policy was the r eal estate recess-
sion of the early 1990s. U ntil the late 1980s, banks and insurance companies continued r eal estate lending at a significant pace. F   oreign
investment in U.S. real estate, particularly from Japan, also continued to
distort the market dynamics in the late 1980s.

By 1990, the combined impact of the savings and loan (S&L) crisis, the 1986 Act, overbuilding during the 1980s by non-REITs, and regulatory pressures on bank and insurance lenders led to a nationwide r ecession in the r eal estate economy . D uring the early 1990s, commer cial property values dropped between 30 and 50 per cent. Market conditions largely impeded the av ailability of cr edit and capital for commer cial real estate. As a r esult of the r ecession and the ensuing capital cr unch, many real estate borrowers defaulted on loans. The resulting losses by financial institutions triggered the S&L crisis and cr eated a huge expense for the federal government. In order to maintain confidence in the banking system, the *Federal Deposit Insurance Corporation* (FDIC) undertook a massive bailout of the nearly bankr upt S&L system. U nder go vernment oversight, many insolv ent S&Ls w ere for ced to merge with str onger, better-capitalized S&Ls. I n or der to induce this consolidation, the go v-ernment guaranteed the financial performance of the insolvent S&Ls. In many other cases, insolvent S&Ls were liquidated with government oversight. The massive restructuring of the S&L system flooded the mar ket with nonperforming real estate assets during the late 1980s. This major dislocation of the real estate markets exacerbated the decline in commercial property values during the early 1990s.

The 1990s to the Present

The r eal estate mar ket ex cesses of the 1980s began to fade b y the early 1990s. A higher standard was now required of real estate lenders. M arket participants were no longer artificially motivated by tax policy to invest in real estate. This marked the starting point for what is consider ed by most industry observers to be the modern era of REIT s. Starting in N ovember 1991 against this backdr op, many priv ate real estate companies decided that it might be mor e efficient to access capital fr om the public mar ket-place utilizing REITs. At the same time, many investors, realizing that re-covering real estate markets were just over the horizon, decided that it was potentially a good time to invest in commercial real estate. This has led to a relatively long and stable sustained growth in the REIT asset class.

Since 1992, many ne w publicly traded REIT s have infused much needed equity capital into the o verleveraged r eal estate industr y. As of June 30, 2005, there were over 200 publicly traded REITs and real estate operating companies, with an *equity market capitalization* exceeding $800 billion. This compares with $16.4 billion of market capitalization at the start of 1992. The dramatic growth can be seen in Figure 2.1. Today REITs are essentially owned by individuals, with an estimated 30 percent of REIT shares owned directly by individual investors. Thirty-eight percent of REIT shares are owned by mutual funds, whose shares are in turn primarily owned by individual investors. But REITs certainly do not just benefit individual investors, nor should they be considered as investments only suited for retail-type individual investors.

The debt levels associated with new-era REITs are lower than those associated with overall real estate investment. This has had a positive effect on the stability of the REIT asset class. Average debt levels for REITs are typically 45 to 55 percent of market capitalization, as compared to leverage of 75 percent and often higher when real estate is privately owned. The higher equity capital level of REITs helps to cushion them from the negative effects of the cyclical fluctuations that have historically occurred in the real estate market. The ability of REITs to better withstand market downturns creates a stabilizing effect on the real estate industry and its lenders, resulting in fewer bankruptcies and loan defaults. Consequently, the general real estate industry has benefited from reduced real estate losses and more consistent investment returns. This has helped real estate regain credibility with the investing public. It has fostered continued capital flows to the REIT sector and real estate in general.

> **equity market capitalization**
> the market value of all outstanding common stock of a company.

REITs currently own approximately $1 trillion of commercial real estate. This represents less than 20 percent of the estimated $5.5 trillion of institutional-quality U.S. domestic real estate. Consistent with the public policy underlying the REIT rules, many industry observers believe that the trend over time will continue to show the U.S. commercial real estate economy moving toward more and more ownership by REITs and publicly traded real estate operating companies. This public securitization of real estate is the hallmark of the new REIT era. With the current trend in place, there are very few reasons to believe that the growth in public real estate will not continue.

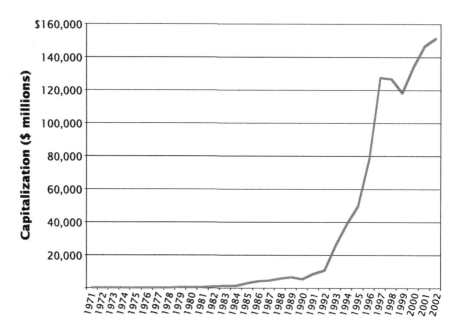

FIGURE 2.1   Equity Capitalization of REITs
Source: NAREIT.

The 1986 Act effectively married REIT management to REIT assets, and the Taxpayer Relief Act of 1997 included additional helpful REIT reforms, but members of the REIT industry still believed they were required to operate under limitations that increasingly made them noncompetitive in the emerging customer-oriented real estate marketplace. They believed that the real estate industry, like other major businesses in the United States in the 1990s, was rapidly evolving into a customer-oriented service business. REIT landlords that provide new services to their tenants, only after such services have become "usual and customary," risk losing their competitive edge in attracting and retaining top-quality tenants. Nevertheless, regulations restricted what services REITs could offer. As REITs grow larger, they automatically affect what services are considered customary in a geographic locale. Under the old rules, some services might never be considered customary because REITs are prevented from providing leading-edge services. Businesses have also discovered that providing ancillary services with good quality control produces customer loyalty. Under the law as it existed, a REIT was required to use independent contractors to provide noncustomary services to its tenants, so REIT management had little control over the quality of the services rendered by the independent contractor to the REIT 's tenants. I ncome fr om these potential r   evenue-producing oppor tunities would accrue to the benefit of a third party, not to the REIT's shareholders. The ability to pr ovide potential ne w services to tenants would hav e three key benefits for the competitiv e posture of REITs within the r eal estate industry:

1. The availability of the ne w service to the tenant would generate greater customer loyalty and allow the REIT landlor d to remain competitive with non-REIT o wners that had no limitation on the type of services they could offer.
2. The ne w ser vices (offer ed either b y the landlor d or b y a thir d party licensed b y the landlor d) could generate an additional stream of income for the REIT shareholders.
3. The REIT management could maintain better quality contr ols over the services rendered to its tenants.

Over the last decade, ne w-era REITs hav e per formed ser vices for their tenants so well that third parties began to retain REITs for that purpose. The original REIT legislation contemplated that REITs could earn up to 5 per cent of their income fr om sour ces other than r ents, capital gains, dividends, and inter est. H owever, many REIT s w ere no w being presented with the oppor tunity to maximiz e shareholder value by earning mor e than 5 per cent fr om managing joint v entures with ser vice providers and fr om selling other thir d-party ser vices. P rior to the most recent changes in REIT rules, many REITs invested in non-REIT C corporations to captur e par t of this income flo w. These corporations pr o- vided to unr elated par ties ser vices that w ere alr eady being deliv ered to a REIT's tenants, such as landscaping or the management of a shop- ping mall in which the REIT o   wned a joint v enture inter est. These arrangements often involved the use of a REIT 's management personnel and were often constr ucted in v ery complex ways in or der to maintain REIT status.

The industr y argued that these r ules w ere too r estrictive and put REIT operators (and their shar   eholders) at a distinct disadv   antage against non-REIT operators in the industr y. At the time, the REIT asset rules w ere patterned after the asset div   ersification r ules applicable to mutual funds. U nder those r ules, a REIT could not o wn more than 10 percent of the voting securities of another company (other than a "qualified REIT subsidiar y" or another REIT), and the securities of another company could not exceed 5 percent of the value of a REIT's total assets. In response to these constraints, Congr ess enacted the *REIT Modernization Act (RMA) of 1999*. The centerpiece of this legislation was the cr e-ation of r ules and guidelines for *taxable REIT subsidiaries* (TRSs). The legislation allows a REIT to own 100 percent of the stock of a company know as a TRS. The TRS can provide services to REIT tenants and third parties within cer tain limitations without jeopar-dizing the REIT status of the par ent. The limita-tions contained in the TRS r ules pr ovide for siz e limits on TRSs to ensur e that REIT s continue to focus on pr operty o wnership and operation. The key provisions are that the TRS may not exceed 20 percent of a REIT 's assets and the amount of debt and r ental payments fr om a TRS to its affiliated REIT ar e limited. The TRS r ules and a series of minor technical adjustments to the old r ules should allo w REITs to enjo y the same adv antages and benefits of service and operating strategies that non-REIT real estate competitors may employ.

REIT Modernization Act (RMA) of 1999

federal tax law change whose provisions allow a REIT to own up to 100 percent of stock of a taxable REIT subsidiary that can provide services to REIT tenants and others. The law also changed the mini-mum distribution requirement from 95 percent to 90 percent of a REIT's taxable income— consistent with the rules for REITs from 1960 to 1980.

These legislativ e initiativ es, along with the steady growth in REIT assets, have not gone unno-ticed b y the institutional inv estment community. Modern-era REIT s no w hav e sufficient siz e and history to be consider ed a viable alternativ e to di-rect r eal estate inv estments. I nstitutional inv estors have also ackno wledged the adv antage of the liq-uidity characteristic that REITs bring to the real es-tate asset class. (In Chapter 3, we explore the modern REIT as an independent asset class and the impact of REIT s in a multi-asset portfolio.)

Points to Remember

- A real estate inv estment trust (REIT) is a company dedicated to owning and managing income-pr oducing r eal estate, such as apartments, shopping centers, offices, and warehouses.

- REITs are legally required to pay virtually all of their net income (90 percent) to their shareholders each year in the form of dividends.

- REITs confer all the advantages and characteristics of owning real estate. In addition, REIT s pr ovide curr ent liquidity for shar e-holders because their shar es are freely traded on major stock exchanges. An inv estor can obtain all the benefits of o wning r eal estate and enjoy complete liquidity of the investment.

- The Tax Reform Act of 1986 radically changed the inv estment landscape for REITs. The new laws drastically reduced the potential for real estate investment to generate tax shelter opportunities by limiting the deductibility of inter est and lengthening and r estricting the use of passiv e losses. This meant that r eal estate investment had to be economic and income oriented rather than tax motivated.

- When commercial property values dropped in the early 1990s, it became difficult to obtain cr edit and capital for commer cial real estate. Many privat e real estate companies decided that the best way to access capital was thr ough the public mar ketplace using REITs.

REITs as an Asset Class

The best investment on Earth is earth.
—Louis Glickman, 1957

Behind bonds and stocks, commercial real estate is the third-largest asset class available to investors with an estimated value of $11.0 trillion in the United States. Institutional-quality real estate—real estate large enough for an institutional buyer to consider purchasing—is estimated to be worth $5.5 trillion or approximately half the value of the commercial real estate universe. Real estate investment trusts (REITs) and *real estate operating companies* (REOCs) own and operate approximately $1.0 trillion worth of institutional-quality investment real estate, or roughly 20 percent of the total.

The Real Estate Asset

As discussed in Chapter 1, real estate is an asset class that has provided institutional investors with many positive attributes over time. Real estate investment trusts are competitors with other institutional investors in the real estate market. They pool the financial resources of a large number of investors for the specific purpose of investing in real estate. In many ways, a REIT is like a mutual fund except that it invests in real estate. As discussed in Chapter 2, companies that meet certain requirements can qualify as REITs and avoid federal taxation on all net income that is distributed as dividends to their shareholders. REITs that directly own real estate share the principal investment benefits of real estate ownership that all other institutional r eal estate owners enjoy. The three key investment benefits provided by most real estate are:

1. *Cash flow.* Consistent and pr edictable cash flo w generated fr om rents paid is an attractive benefit of the real estate asset class.

2. *Inflation hedging.* Real estate tends to act as a hedge against inflation, incr easing in v alue at a rate faster than inflation o ver the long term.

3. *Portfolio diversification.* The independent local-mar ket nature of real estate produces returns that behave very independently from both stocks and bonds. This low correlation of return provides an added diversification benefit when real estate is added to a multi-asset portfolio.

Real estate is also subject to some potentially negativ e qualities. As discussed in Chapter 1, here is a brief summary of these negative attributes:

- *Real estate lacks liquidity.* Because the process of buying and selling real estate is negotiated dir ectly between buyers and sellers in local markets and often inv olves financing arrangements, transactions can be long and involved. Six months to a year is not an uncommon transaction time.

- *Real estate's performance is difficult to measure.* Because r eal estate values are determined upon sale, it is difficult to calculate total performance of a real estate portfolio prior to the sale of the properties.

- *Real estate cannot be moved.* With v ery fe w ex ceptions, such as mobile homes, it is not feasible to r elocate existing r eal estate to markets where demand is better or supply is constrained.

- *Real estate is unique.* The physical attributes of a building and its location are unique to that building. This can have both positive and negative aspects when dealing with a specific piece of real estate.

- *Real estate is subject to externalities.* Events or activities beyond the control of the pr operty owner affect (for good or bad) the v alue of a property.

As stated before, real estate is also subject to some *potentially* negative qualities. The emphasis on the word *potentially* is added because, as a substitute for the direct ownership of real estate, the unique characteristics of

REITs solve some of these pr oblems. The r emaining potential pr oblems can be effectively managed in the REIT format. These benefits give REITs a series of distinctiv e qualities that make them in many ways superior to direct real estate investment.

REIT Idea: Liquidity

The most important dilemma solved by REITs with regard to real estate is the issue of liquidity. Each market day over $800 million of REITs trade in the public markets. Compare this with the weeks or months it can take to sell a single property in the private market and the single advantage of liquidity becomes apparent.

The biggest issue solv ed b y the REIT asset class is that of liquidity . Unlike dir ect r eal estate inv estments, REITs ar e generally public compa-nies. They trade on major stock exchanges such as the New York Stock Ex-change and the American S tock E xchange as w ell as on NASDA Q and over-the-counter markets. The dramatic growth in the number of publicly traded and the r elated gr owth in public equity mar ket capitalization (see Figure 3.1) have converged to make the liquidity benefit of REITs a major

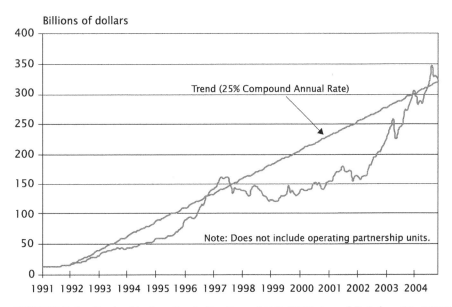

FIGURE 3.1 Equity Market Capitalization of U.S. REITs (as of October 31, 2005)
Source: Uniplan, Inc.

differentiating factor for the asset class. As seen in F igure 3.2, the av erage daily trading v olume in REITs exceeds $800 million. The public mar kets have provided between $300 million and $500 million of daily liquidity since 1996. When compar ed to a six-month liquidity windo w for dir ect real estate investment, the advantage of daily liquidity becomes apparent.

The liquidity adv antage becomes a useful tool for the REIT in vestor under a number of differ ent circumstances. The daily liquidity of REITs allows an investor to move into or out of a property category such as apartments. This can be useful to an inv estor who wants to div ersify an existing portfolio of other real estate investments. For example, an in vestor who dir ectly owns an inter est in a por tfolio of shopping centers can easily add apartments, industrial buildings, or other property sectors that are represented by REITs trading in the public mar kets. This ability to "tilt" the sector exposur e of a dir ect real estate por tfolio by adding REITs to a real estate allocation is a useful tool for all real estate investors.

The liquidity adv antage of REITs extends in the same way to the geographic diversification of a dir ect real estate por tfolio. As mentioned earlier, the physical attributes of r eal estate pr eclude mo ving pr operty from a local market where demand is falling or supply is in excess to a lo cation wher e supply-and-demand characteristics ar e better. H owever, REITs provide the direct property owner with the option of div ersifying a por tfolio b y geography. B y simply adding REIT s with exposur e in

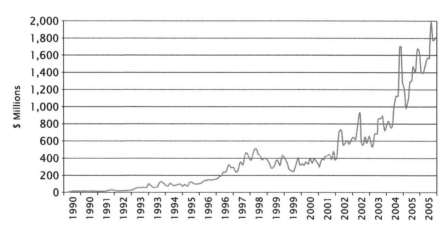

FIGURE 3.2 Monthly Average Daily Trading Volume of REITs (March 1990–October 2005)

Source: NAREIT.

other geographic r egions, additional geographic div ersification can be achieved. For example, an o wner of an inter est in a div ersified portfolio of investment real estate in the Chicago ar ea can add pr operty in other locations, such as California or N ew York City, by adding to the por tfolio REITs that have property holdings in those geographic markets. This ability to tilt the geographic exposur e of a dir ect real estate por tfolio by adding REITs to a real estate allocation allows direct real estate investors to gain exposur e in locations that hav e better fundamental supply-and-demand characteristics than those in their current portfolio.

When applied to a por tfolio made up ex clusively of REIT s, the liquidity adv antage of REIT s becomes ev en mor e pr onounced. A pur e REIT portfolio can largely eliminate the liquidity issue involved with direct real estate investments, while retaining the positive attributes of cash flow, creating an inflation hedge, and pr oviding the additional por tfolio diversification of similar dir ect r eal estate inv estments. I n addition, the liquidity advantage of REITs allows an investor to easily add sector tilt or geographic tilt within a por tfolio of REITs. The ability to migrate easily between geographic r egions and pr operty categories should not be underestimated.

Over time the pr operty types and geographic r egions most fav ored by direct institutional inv estors have shifted. These shifts ar e often dictated by changes in supply and demand, which ar e driven by local market events and macroeconomic trends. During the 1970s, r egional malls were highly sought after b y dir ect institutional inv estors. I n the late 1970s, growth in retail sales began to fall behind the rate of inflation, and the general economy began to enter a recession in 1979. This resulted in regional malls falling out of fav or with dir ect institutional inv estors. Office buildings w ent through a similar cy cle during the 1980s. S imilar local market and macr oeconomic tr ends r elated to the I nternet r evolution made San Jose and the San Francisco Bay area a highly regarded and popular geographic region for dir ect real estate investors during the second half of the 1990s. The collapse of the dot-com economy during 2000 resulted in a change in investor sentiment toward the region and a corresponding change in the v aluation levels of pr operties within the r egion. The ability to migrate easily betw een geographic r egions and pr operty categories can allow the REIT investor to capitalize on the shifts in property types and geographic r egions that ar e the r esult of local mar ket events and macroeconomic trends.

The direct institutional investor can make similar portfolio changes. However, the lack of liquidity and the high frictional cost of making those changes often pr eclude an activ e management style at the dir ect invest- ment level. For a few cents per share, a REIT investor can actively change geographic or pr operty exposures with a phone call to a br okerage firm. (Chapter 6 cr eates a frame work for the geographic and sector decision- making process that supports such real estate portfolio changes.)

The measurement of period-to-period per formance in a dir ect real estate portfolio is difficult. Information about specific r eal estate market performance is harder and more expensive to obtain than that about the performance of stocks and bonds. B ecause r eal estate v alues ar e deter- mined upon sale, the only way to kno w the true performance of a direct real estate investment is to calculate it at the time of sale of the por tfolio or a particular property within the portfolio.

Data for dev eloping performance measures over shorter periods in the direct por tfolio, such as quar terly or annual r eturns, is often the r e- sult of estimates. These estimates ar e often based on capitalization rates derived fr om examining sales of similar pr operties in the local mar ket. When used pr udently, these estimates help assess the per formance of a direct real estate por tfolio; but they tend to smooth out the fluctuations that might be observed in the actual values. For this reason, the estimate approach tends to understate the measurement of risk or the standard de- viation of returns. The true performance results will only really be known at the time of sale.

Because of the long-term policy mandates of many institutional portfolios, a periodic estimate of v alue in the r eal estate allocation is of- ten sufficient for fiduciary purposes. The real performance measurement problem begins to sur face when a fiduciar y must assess ho w a par ticular real estate por tfolio is doing r elative to other r eal estate por tfolios. B e- cause other dir ect real estate por tfolios ar e subject to the same estimate bias, it is not possible to rank the per formance of a giv en portfolio until the por tfolios in question hav e been liquidated. This makes the assess- ment of relative portfolio performance particularly difficult. By contrast, REITs pose far fe wer per formance measur ement issues. B ecause REITs and related securities trade like stocks, it is r elatively simple to calculate the periodic inv estment r eturns. In addition, the same periodic pricing data can be used to calculate risk or standard deviation of returns for any given period. The readily available pricing data makes the calculation of periodic per formance and por tfolio risk a simple matter in a por tfolio composed of REITs.

The assessment of r elative por tfolio per formance is also r eadily available for the REIT investor. There are a large number of real estate securities index es that ar e generally av ailable thr ough v arious public sources on a daily real-time basis. These indexes, which are also described in this chapter, are typically unmanaged or passiv e in constr uction and are composed of broad-based aggregates of REITs. Some also include real estate service and homebuilding companies. When used as an appr opri-ate benchmark, these indexes can help in assessing the per formance of a REIT portfolio or its manager.

There are over 70 mutual funds and sev eral exchange traded index shares that invest specifically in REITs or more generally in the real estate sector. These funds are listed in the Appendix A at the end of this book. Performance data on these funds is widely av ailable in v arious publica-tions such as the *Wall Street Journal* or through mutual fund rating ser-vices such as M orningstar and Weissenberger's. The per formance data from these funds can also be used to make comparativ e measur ements of the per formance of activ ely managed r eal estate securities por tfolios. The fund companies themselv es can also be a sour ce of additional performance-related data, including operating expenses and comparative portfolio characteristics.

The unique positiv e characteristics of the REIT asset class help it overcome the liquidity and performance issues related to direct real estate investment. As discussed, the liquidity advantage also mitigates the nega-tive issues regarding the fixed physical nature of property. Thus the issues of uniqueness and externalities r emain. These issues can have both good and bad aspects. Like any r eal estate investor, the REIT investor can at-tempt to manage the risks of uniqueness and employ strategies to defend against and monitor possible externalities. The physical attributes of a building and its location that is unique to that building can hav e both positive and negativ e aspects when dealing with a specific piece of r eal estate. S ome buildings ar e built with v ery specific objectiv es in mind. When given the right mix of cir cumstances, this can justify a higher ex-pected return from a given real estate project. Conversely, the wrong mix of circumstances can quickly create an underperforming asset.

A Wal-Mart store is physically a v ery specific type of r eal estate pro-ject. That said, owning a por tfolio of Wal-Mart stores that are leased on a

long-term basis to Wal-Mart might be a good investment. The credit quality of Wal-Mart helps to o vercome the specific physical limitations of the
actual real estate. Conv ersely, owning a por tfolio of industrial war ehouses
that were designed and built specifically to accommodate the Internet gro-
cer Web Van might not be as appealing. The credit quality of Web Van is
likely not sufficient to overcome the negative attributes of the physical real
estate. The v arious aspects of managing these types of physical issues ar e
discussed in detail in Part Three of this book, which deals specifically with
each property category available in the public REIT format.

Externalities are a group of risk factors that ar e difficult to manage.
The fact that they ar e external to the activity makes the management of
externalities a defensive process, because the causal
agent is external and bey ond the control of the affected items. The best defense against externalities
in real estate is location. The externalities that will
negatively affect a class-A high-rise office building
on P ark A venue in N ew York City ar e far fe wer
than those that could affect a class-B office building at a little kno wn intersection in suburban
Cleveland. The highest-and-best use doctrine will
likely prevent a garbage dump or chemical factor y
from appearing in Manhattan; but this may not be the case in Cleveland.
These risk factors ar e also discussed at mor e length at the pr operty-
specific lev el in each chapter of P art Three. The old r eal estate adage
cannot be str essed enough—"Location, location, location "—because it
is a key factor when anticipating external effects.

Publicly traded REITs have a par ticular type of risk that is less of a
factor in the dir ect r eal estate sector . *Systematic risk* or *market risk* is a
form of risk that the dir ect r eal estate inv estor nev er encounters. This
market risk affects REITs because they ar e part of a gr oup of companies
within a larger asset mar ket kno wn as the stock mar ket or the public
capital markets. Events that may be completely unrelated to REITs or the
local r eal estate mar kets in which they operate can hav e a negativ e
(or positive) affect on the value of publicly traded REIT shar es. The unexpected default of R ussian government bonds in 1998 caused a sev ere
dislocation in the world capital mar kets. This resulted in a sharp decline
in stock prices acr oss global mar kets, including a decline in the mar ket
price of REIT shar es. Although the default may hav e had some negative

externality

an activity or
event that affects
(positively or
negatively)
something that
is external to the
activity.

implications for the price of real estate in general, the direct real estate investor did not suffer the immediate mar ket price decline that impacted REIT shares. It could be argued that systematic risk is an externality in real estate that is specific to publicly traded REIT shares.

Public Market Real Estate Indexes

There are a large number of real estate securities indexes that are generally available through various sources on a daily real-time basis. These indexes are typically unmanaged or passiv e in constr uction and ar e composed of broad-based aggregates of REITs and other r eal estate-related companies. Some also include r eal estate ser vice companies and home building companies. The following is a brief description of the major public market real estate indexes.

The *National Association of Real Estate Investment Trusts* (NAREIT) is the primar y trade association for REIT s. I t is r ecognized as the leading public r esource on the REIT industr y and has per formance data on REITs extending back to 1972. The organization compiles and publishes a group of indexes that are composed exclusively of publicly traded REITs:

- *NAREIT Index.* This is NAREIT 's index of all publicly traded REITs. It is the best-kno wn and most r eferenced index of REIT performance. The broadest pure REIT index, it includes all publicly traded REITs in r elative mar ket w eightings. This index is available on a r eal-time basis. I t r ebalances on a monthly basis for new and merged REITs and new issuance of equity b y existing REITs.

- *NAREIT Equity Index.* This is the same as the NAREIT I ndex, except that it ex cludes mor tgage REITs to r eflect a pur e equity real estate benchmark. This index is available on a real-time basis. It rebalances on a monthly basis for ne w and merged REITs and new issuance of equity by existing REITs.

- *NAREIT 50 Index.* This is an index of the 50 largest publicly traded REITs. It is a benchmar k more suited to the institutional investor because of the liquidity issues surr ounding smaller-capitalization REITs. This index is av ailable on a r eal-time basis. It rebalances on a monthly basis for ne w and merged REITs and new issuance of equity by existing REITs.

- *NAREIT Mortgage Index.* This is an index of all publicly traded mortgage REITs. This index is available on a real-time basis. It rebalances on a monthly basis for new and merged REITs and new issuance of equity by existing REITs.

Other financial organizations also track and publish statistics on REITs and publicly traded real estate securities:

- *S&P REIT Composite Index.* This index comprises 100 REIT s, including mortgage REITs. It covers approximately 75 per cent of REIT market capitalization. This index requires high-quality financial fundamentals, good liquidity, and str ong earnings and dividend gr owth as characteristics for inclusion. I t is reweighted on a quar terly basis, and r eturns are computed on a daily basis.

- *Morgan Stanley REIT Index.* This is a tradable r eal-time market index. It is constructed by Morgan Stanley. This index has a laundry list of inclusion requirements, such as minimum market capitalization, shares outstanding, trading v olume, and shar e price. To be included, a REIT must hav e a six-month trading histor y and must be listed on a major exchange. This index is rebalanced quarterly and does not include mortgage or health care REITs. Its ticker symbol on the AMEX is RMZ.

- *Wilshire Real Estate Securities Index.* This index is composed of REITs and other r eal estate operation companies. The composition is determined on a monthly basis b y Wilshire Associates. This index includes hotel operating companies and dev elopment and homebuilding companies. I t does not include specialty, health care, or mor tgage REITs. Wilshire publishes r eturns on a monthly basis, with details av ailable on a subscription basis. There is no real-time information available on this index.

The public market real estate indexes are primarily derived from the approximately 200 publicly traded REITs—a selection of these are listed in Appendix B of this book—and other real estate-related companies that invest primarily in r eal estate but for v arious reasons have not elected REIT status (see Table 3.1). *Equity REITs* provide investment opportunities in all major property types. The large number of publicly traded REITs provides real estate exposure in most major geographic regions.

equity REIT
a REIT that owns or has an "equity interest" in rental real estate and derives the majority of its revenue from rental income (rather than making loans secured by real estate collateral).

Table 3.2 describes the distribution of properties owned by publicly traded REITs by geographic region and property type. It comes as no surprise that the distribution of REIT assets is skewed toward the largest major metropolitan markets. In fact, about 50 percent of public REIT property holdings are in the top 25 metropolitan markets. This gives the REIT investor the potential to diversify widely by geographic location and to focus on major markets with the most favorable supply and demand characteristics.

These local supply and demand factors tend to drive the performance of specific REITs. Performance is generally more of a function of local market conditions and less a function of the stock and bond markets. Because REITs have a low correlation to both stocks and bonds, they provide additional diversification to an investment portfolio. It is this diversification benefit as it fits into the framework of modern portfolio theory that REITs provide in a multiasset-class portfolio. In Chapter 4, we examine these aspects of the REIT asset class.

TABLE 3.1 Public REIT Sectors (as of June 30, 2005)

Office	16%
Industrial	9%
Residential	15%
Retail	25%
Diversified	8%
Hotels	6%
Health Care	5%
Self-Storage	4%
Specialty	4%
Mortgage	8%

TABLE 3.2 Geographic Distribution of REIT Property Ownership

Region	Apartment Units	Retail Sq. ft.	Office Sq. ft.	Industrial Sq. ft.	Hotel Rooms	Health Care Rooms
Pacific	12%	19%	20%	21%	17%	12%
Mountain	8%	16%	3%	2%	11%	9%
West North Central	2%	4%	0%	1%	7%	7%
East North Central	15%	11%	6%	28%	10%	7%
Southwest	19%	9%	19%	18%	3%	19%
Southeast	18%	19%	15%	15%	16%	20%
Mid Atlantic	14%	11%	18%	8%	14%	12%
Northeast	12%	11%	19%	7%	22%	14%
Total	100%	100%	100%	100%	100%	100%

Region 1—Pacific
Alaska
California
Hawaii
Oregon
Washington

Region 2—Mountain
Arizona
Colorado
Idaho
Montana
Nevada
Utah
Wyoming

Region 3—West North Central
Iowa
Kansas
Minnesota
Missouri
Nebraska
North Dakota
South Dakota

Region 4—East North Central
Illinois
Indiana
Michigan
Ohio
Wisconsin

Region 5—Southwest
Arkansas
Louisiana
Oklahoma
Texas

Region 6—Southeast
Alabama
Florida
Georgia
Mississippi
North Carolina
South Carolina
Tennessee

Region 7—Mid Atlantic
Delaware

District of Columbia
Kentucky
Maryland
Virginia
West Virginia

Region 8—Northeast
Connecticut
Maine
Massachusetts
New Hampshire
New Jersey
New York
Pennsylvania
Rhode Island
Vermont

Source: Uniplan, Inc.

Points to Remember

- In the public market there are about 180 publicly traded real estate investment trusts (REITs) that deal with office, industrial, apartment, shopping center, regional mall, hotel, health care, and specialty properties. Their holdings include some of the finest properties in America, such as Mall of America in Minneapolis and the Embarcadero Center in San Francisco.
- Because real estate values are driven by local supply-and-demand factors, REITs allow an investor to isolate property categories and local market conditions that are improving while avoiding markets and properties that are deteriorating.
- It is possible to gain investment exposure to most regional markets or major cities and property categories within those areas simply by investing in REITs.
- Because local supply and demand factors drive the performance of specific REITs, REITs generally behave more as a function of local market conditions and less as a function of the stock and bond markets.
- Because REITs have a low correlation to both stocks and bonds, they provide additional diversification to an investment portfolio.

REITs as a Portfolio Diversification Tool

Never have so many been paid so much to do so little.
—Anonymous investment manager on consultants

Over the past 20 years an entire industry has been born of the simple concept that the majority of the total performance of a portfolio results from the mix of investment asset classes contained in the portfolio. This simple concept is the cornerstone of *modern portfolio theory* (MPT). The industry spawned by the advent of MPT is known as the investment management consulting industry. This group of consultants stands ready to advise the investing world at large on the correct allocation of different investment vehicles that should be held in a portfolio to achieve the stated investment policy with the least risk to principal and the lowest volatility.

> **modern portfolio theory (MPT)**
>
> based on the idea that when different investments such as stocks, bonds, and REITs are mixed together in a portfolio, it improves the return and lowers the risk over time.

Asset Allocation and Modern Portfolio Theory

As is true of most objectives, there is normally a multitude of ways to achieve the stated goal. Through careful study and analysis, the investment consultant will craft a portfolio allocation model that will drive the

41

portfolio returns to the stated goal. For a modest additional fee, the consultant will assist the investor in developing a stated goal or policy that is consistent with the asset allocation model.

Large investors such as pension plans, endowments, and wealthy individuals hav e historically engaged inv estment consultants to addr ess long-term investment objectives and policy questions r elated to those issues. These large investors have a fiduciary obligation to protect the interests of their inv estors, and one way to accomplish this (as w ell as r educe their own potential liability) is to hire a consultant to monitor investment-related issues. The consultant's job is to advise the client on the corr ect mix of investments and monitor the underlying per formance of those investments to be certain they remain consistent with the objective.

In the past, the high lev el of mathematics embedded in the consultants' practice, along with the myriad of data r equired to make the analysis, limited the accessibility of investment consulting to larger institutions. The rapid growth in the power of the personal computer and the democratization of data via the I nternet and the av ailability of modestly priced software have combined to put asset allocation modeling within the reach of even the smallest investor. Websites offering asset allocation advice and online calculators hav e pr oliferated. M odestly priced financial planning and asset allocation softwar e is widely av ailable. Traditional Wall S treet brokers as well as discount brokerage firms all have asset allocation investment pr ograms available to their inv estment clients. M utual fund complexes and 401(k) pr oviders offer asset allocation advice to their clients. Although the conceptual theory of asset allocation is simple, the practical application and administration of the process is much more difficult than most people grasp. As mentioned, ther e are often many ways to arriv e at the same goal, but the devil is in the details.

Asset Allocation Theory and REITs

Total por tfolio per formance is impacted b y thr ee v ariables that can be attributed to any given investment asset class:

1. Long-term expected and historical rate of return.
2. Volatility of r eturn, often r eferred to as the *standard deviation of return.*
3. Correlation of returns.

When consultants consider an asset class as a possible investment in a por tfolio, they first study the rate of r eturn to determine if the historic and expected returns are high enough to compete with other available investments. This return analysis is tempered with a r eview of how volatile the return patterns are over time. The higher the volatility of a potential return (often called *risk*), the higher the required rate of return becomes in order to achieve a slot in the inv estment program. Finally, the pattern of returns, or the correlation of the asset class as it compares to all other asset classes in the por tfolio, must be consider ed. I f the corr elation is sufficiently differ ent fr om the other asset classes in the portfolio, the r eturns are high enough, and the v olatility is lo w enough, then the inv estment class might gain an allocation position within the portfolio.

standard deviation
measures how spread out the values in a set of data are. In the investment world, the standard deviation is the most commonly used measure of investment volatility over time. Lower standard deviation helps to moderate portfolio risk, but it also tends to provide lower returns.

The classic implementation of asset allocation is in the stock-and-bond mix of a typical balanced por tfolio. The stock-and-bond asset classes both hav e reasonable expected and historical rates of r eturn and are the two largest av ailable asset classes. Ov er the long term, bond returns are lower than stock returns, but bond returns are far less volatile than stock r eturns. And the corr elation betw een stocks and bonds is relatively lo w. When stocks underper form their historical expected rate of r eturn, bonds tend to outper form theirs. This trade-off betw een risk and return tends to lower the volatility of the entire portfolio and incr ease the *total return* per unit of risk under taken. As seen in F igure 4.1, the r eturn for real estate investment trusts (REITs) has historically been higher than that for bonds and slightly lower than that for stocks o ver most periods of time. We can conclude b y studying the numbers that the REIT asset class has historically pr ovided competitive returns when compar ed to stocks and

total return
a stock's dividend income plus capital appreciation before taxes and commissions.

bonds. I t would be expected that in the futur e REITs will continue to provide returns that are higher than bond returns and slightly lower than common stock returns.

Volatility is measur ed b y calculating the standar d deviation of the quarterly returns, as a percentage, over a given period of time for a particular asset class. The volatility of REITs is compar ed to that of large and small stocks and bonds in Table 4.1. As you would expect, because REIT returns are higher than those of bonds, the v olatility of REITs is higher than that of bonds when measured over most time periods. REIT volatility is slightly lower than that of large stocks and significantly lo wer than that of small-cap stocks, while the returns are only slightly lower.

When looking at the data in F igure 4.1 and Table 4.1, it could be concluded that REITs offer returns competitive with those of stocks, while involving substantially less risk or volatility than stocks in general. Correlation is wher e REITs clearly distinguish themselv es as an asset class when compared to stocks and bonds. The correlation coefficient of REITs compared to large and small stocks and bonds is surprisingly lo w. As summarized in Figure 4.2, REITs have a low correlation to stocks and bonds, and over the 1970s through 1990s the correlation has continued to decline.

When measured in rolling five-year periods, the correlation of REITs to small and large stocks has been steadily on the decline since the early 1990s. This roughly corresponds to the modern era in REITs as discussed in Chapter 2. Table 4.2 shows the declining trend in REIT correlation.

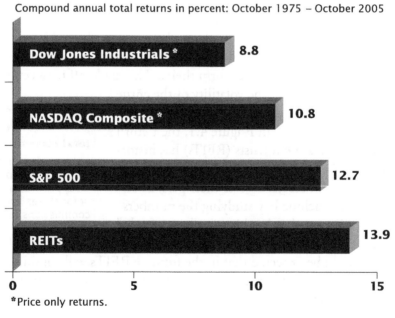

Compound annual total returns in percent: October 1975 – October 2005

Dow Jones Industrials *	8.8
NASDAQ Composite *	10.8
S&P 500	12.7
REITs	13.9

*Price only returns.

FIGURE 4.1 REITs Measure Up over Time

TABLE 4.1   Standard Deviation of Quarterly Returns

Period	REITs	Large Stocks	Small Stocks	Bonds
1972–2005	14.7	16.3	25.5	11.8
1972–1992	15.0	17.1	26.3	12.7
1993–2005	14.1	13.8	22.1	9.5

Note: REITs: NAREIT Equity Index; Large Stocks: S&P 500; Small Stocks: Russell 2000; Bonds: 20-year U.S. government bond.
Source: Uniplan, Inc.

TABLE 4.2   Monthly Correlation of REIT Total Returns to Other Assets

Period	Large Stocks	Small Stocks	Bonds
1972–2005	0.51	0.58	0.19
1970s	0.64	0.74	0.27
1980s	0.65	0.74	0.17
1990s	0.45	0.58	0.26
1993–2005	0.22	0.26	0.14

Note: REITs: NAREIT Equity Index; Large Stocks: S&P 500; Small Stocks: Russell 2000; Bonds: 20-year U.S. government bond.
Source: Uniplan, Inc.

FIGURE 4.2   Declining Equity REIT Correlation
Source: Uniplan, Inc.

When linked with competitive returns and reasonable volatility, investment return correlation provides the basic rationale for asset allocation and portfolio diversification. The highly noncorrelated nature of the REIT asset class provides a powerful means of additional portfolio diversification. In the no w-famous study "D eterminants of P ortfolio Performance" (*Financial Analysts Journal,* July/August 1986), G ary B rinson makes the case that asset allocation policy determines 91.5 percent of the investment performance of a given portfolio. In other words, the mix of assets in the underlying inv estment portfolio determines most of the investment performance. The actual security selection process, which most people consider paramount to inv estment per formance, contributes a mere 4.6 percent of portfolio return. So it is not which stocks y ou own, but the fact that you own stocks, that determines most of the return in a portfolio. Simply put, asset allocation drives portfolio return.

The Portfolio Contribution of REITs

In Figure 4.3 we return to the classic balanced por tfolio. For this example, we use a portfolio policy of 50 percent large stocks as defined by the S&P 500 I ndex, 40 per cent 20-y ear U.S. go vernment bonds, and 10 percent 30-day U.S. T-bills. From 1972 thr ough 2000, the por tfolio returns 11.8 per cent annually and has a v olatility of 11.2 per cent. When the stock and bond allocations are each reduced by 5 percent and 10 percent REITs as defined b y the NAREIT E quity I ndex are added, the r eturn over the same period rises to 12 per cent and the risk or v olatility drops to 10.9 percent. Taking the experiment one step further, when the stock-and-bond allocation are each reduced by 10 percent and a 20 percent REIT allocation is added, the r eturn over the same period rises to 12.2 percent and the risk or volatility drops to 10.8 percent.

Figure 4.4 examines the potential investment contribution of REITs in a classic bond por tfolio. In this case, w e use a por tfolio policy of 90 percent 20-y ear U.S. go vernment bonds and 10 per cent 30-day U.S. T-bills. From 1972 thr ough 2000, the por tfolio returns 9.5 per cent and has a volatility of 11.3 per cent. When the bond allocation is r educed by 10 per cent and an allocation of 10 per cent REITs as defined b y the NAREIT E quity I ndex is added to the por tfolio, the r eturn o ver the same period rises to 9.9 per cent and the risk or v olatility drops substantially to 10.6 percent. Taking the experiment one step fur ther, when the

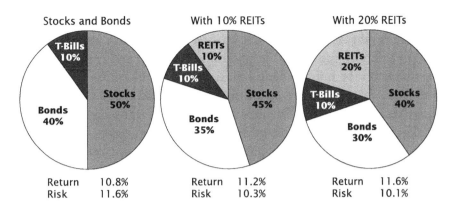

Data source: Large Stocks—Standard & Poor's 500; Bonds—20-year U.S. government bond;
T-Bills—U.S. 30-day T-Bill; REITs—NAREIT Equity Index.
This is an illustration of hypothetical results, not indicative of future returns.

FIGURE 4.3 Diversify to Reduce Risk or Increase Return: Stock and Bond Investors, 1972–2004

bond allocation is reduced by 20 percent and a 20 percent REIT allocation is added, the return over the same period continues to rise to 10.3 percent and the risk or volatility drops to 10.3 percent.

This type of what-if simulation demonstrates the beneficial effect of noncorrelated asset classes. In this instance, REITs are examined, but the analysis can extend to other noncorr elated asset classes such as small

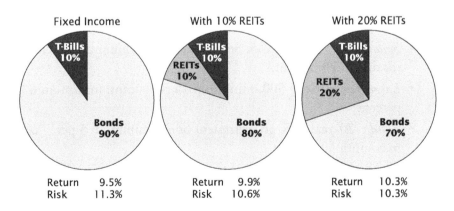

Data source: Bonds—20-year U.S. government bond; T-Bills—U.S. 30-day T-Bill; REITs—NAREIT Equity Index.
This is an illustration of hypothetical results, not indicative of future returns.

FIGURE 4.4 Diversify to Reduce Risk or Increase Return: Fixed Income Investors, 1972–2004

stocks and international stocks. The examples are designed to be simple and to prove the case that REITs as an asset class add value in a multiasset-class portfolio. In most real-life situations, investors and consultants put constraints on the minimum and maximum asset allocation for a giv en asset class. The specific inv estment policy and natur e of the por tfolio dictate these constraints. The tax status of the por tfolio has an effect on the allocation and constraints of income pr oducing assets. I n a taxable portfolio, it is normally pr eferable to minimiz e or dinary income and maximize capital gains to lo wer the curr ent tax bur den and defer tax es into the future at the lower capital gains rate. Conversely, owners of tax-exempt portfolios are more willing to hold a larger per centage of assets that produce high current income, because curr ent taxation is not a fac-tor in calculating actual net return. Total asset size is also a potential con-straining factor. Very large institutional por tfolios may not be able to effectively use smaller or more illiquid asset classes as a part of their over-all strategy due to their sheer size or need for liquidity.

A simple way to explor e the potential inv estment contribution of REITs in an allocation-constrained setting (again, while av oiding com-plex math) is to constr uct a set of what-if por tfolios using REIT s and other asset classes that ar e constrained at lev els that are common among institutional investors. These what-if simulations take constrained por t-folio allocations and add REIT s in v arying amounts o ver differing time periods in an attempt to determine their potential inv estment contribu-tion to portfolio performance. In this simulation, the following portfolio constraints are used for the following asset classes:

- *Small stocks:* Ibbotson U.S. Small Stock Series minimum 0 percent, maximum 20 percent.
- *Large stocks:* S&P 500; minimum 15 per   cent; maximum 60 percent.
- *Bonds:* 20-year U.S. go vernment bonds minimum 5 per   cent maximum 40 percent.
- *International stocks:* Morgan Stanley Capital International's Europe Asia Far East Index; minimum 0 percent; maximum 20 percent.
- *T-bills:* Minimum 0 percent; maximum 15 percent.

Using these constraints for the period from 1972 through 2000, an allocation of 10 per   cent and then 20 per   cent REIT s is added into the portfolio while adjusting all other asset allocations to create a series of return and risk (standard deviation) outcomes within the constraints de-scribed previously. This process of optimization then creates a series of outcomes while increasing risk as defined by standard deviation in 1 per-cent increments. This is the type of what-if analysis a consultant might create for an institutional client.

As can be seen in F igure 4.5, REIT s in a typical multiasset-class portfolio help add return across the efficient frontier. As discussed earlier in the chapter, measur ed in r olling fiv e-year periods, the corr elation of REITs to small and large stocks has been steadily declining since the early 1990s. This decline roughly corresponds to the modern era of REITs dis-cussed in Chapter 2. The argument could be made that as the correlation of REITs to stocks has declined, their contribution to portfolio risk reduc-tion and r eturn should become gr eater. To examine this theor y, we per-formed the same efficient frontier analysis using 10 percent and 20 percent REIT allocations. U sing the same minimum and maximum asset class constraints as in the 1972 to 2000 analysis, the risk outcomes were exam-ined for the modern REIT era of 1993 thr ough 2000. Although this is a much shorter period, due to the declining corr elation of REITs to large and small stocks, the risk and return outcomes improve dramatically.

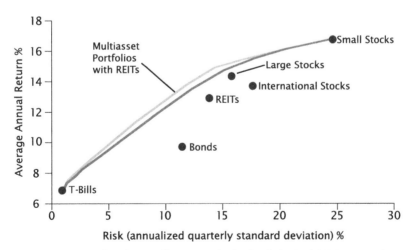

Data source: Small Stocks—Russell 2000; Large Stocks—Standard & Poor's 500; International Stocks—MSCI EAFE Index; REITs—NAREIT Equity Index; Bonds—20-year U.S. government bond; T-Bills—U.S. 30-day T-Bill.

FIGURE 4.5 Efficient Frontier with and without REITs: Stocks, Bonds, Bills, and REITs, 1972–2004

Conclusion

In reviewing the data presented in this chapter, it is easy to conclude that REITs offer an attractive risk/reward trade-off. With a risk profile slightly higher than that of bonds and a r eturn pr ofile slightly lo wer than that of stocks, REITs offer competitiv e returns for the risk assumed. F urther analysis shows that in addition to competitiv e returns, REITs as an asset class offer a lo w correlation to other financial assets, including large and small stocks, bonds, international stocks, and T-bills. This lo w corr ela-tion of r eturns to those of other asset classes has continued to incr ease over the modern REIT era of the last 12 y ears. A ttractive r eturns and low correlation help r educe risk and incr ease total r eturn when REIT s are added to a multiasset-class por tfolio. An allocation of 5 per cent to 20 percent in REITs will incr ease return and lo wer risk in most por tfo-lios, which makes o wning and understanding REIT s as an asset class important for any one who deals with inv estments within a multiasset-class setting.

REIT Idea: Diversification

After all the technical jargon, there is one thing to remember about REITs. Adding an allocation of 5 percent to 20 percent of REITs in a diversified portfolio increases returns and lowers the risk (standard deviation) of the portfolio.

Points to Remember

- Asset allocation is the cornerstone of modern portfolio theory.
- Long-term r eturns, v olatility, and corr elation of r eturns among portfolio holdings affect total portfolio performance.
- Real estate inv estment tr usts (REITs) offer competitiv e r eturns, reasonable v olatility, and lo w corr elation with other financial assets.
- REITs lower volatility and incr ease total r eturn when added to a multiasset-class portfolio.

- When considered in a constrained inv estment equation, REIT s continue to impr ove per formance outcome in multiasset-class portfolios.

- An allocation of 5 per cent to 20 per cent in REIT s incr eases return and lowers risk in most portfolios.

- Understanding REITs as an asset class is impor tant for any one who deals with inv estments within a multiasset-class por tfolio setting.

Integrating REITs into an Investment Portfolio

Real estate is the closest thing to the proverbial pot of gold.
— Ada Louise Huxtable, 1970

As the data shows, a 5 percent to 20 percent allocation of real estate investment trusts (REITs) in the typical diversified portfolio lowers volatility, increases total return, and normally increases risk-adjusted return in the portfolio over most time horizons. With that fact established, the question arises as to how to best integrate REITs into an investment portfolio. For the large institutional investor, this is an asset class decision that is often incorporated into a portfolio through the use of an investment policy statement. The policy objective gives careful consideration to the specific objectives, constraints, and goals of the investor. These same considerations apply to smaller institutional investors and individual investors as well.

Investment Policies That Utilize REITs

All investment policies, whether simple or complex and whether for large or small institutions, should reflect the needs of the people who are represented within the pool of assets. Many of the policy objectives are qualitative and some are quantitative, but the goal of both is to create an efficient portfolio that addresses the needs and objectives of the individuals who are reflected in the policy statement.

Rational inv estors always seek higher r eturns and lo wer risks in their investment portfolios. Integrating REITs creates an oppor tunity to gain higher r eturns with a lo wer risk pr ofile. There are five basic strategies for integrating REITs into a diversified portfolio:

1. *Direct investment in REITs.* For investors who wish to make their own decisions on REIT s, the pr ospect of selecting and o wning individual REITs can be of interest. This process entails the selection of an adequate number of REIT s to cr eate and maintain diversification by property type and geographic location. In most instances, this r equires a minimum 7 to 10 REIT s. Chapter 9 deals extensively with the fundamental concepts used in analyzing REITs. The direct investor uses these concepts to monitor the ongoing business activities of the REITs.

2. *Managed real estate accounts.* Under this alternative, a percentage of the v alue of a div ersified por tfolio is targeted for REIT s and that amount of money is managed b y a por tfolio manager at a firm that has a specialized real estate investment portfolio. This is typically ho w most institutional inv estors would under take the addition of REITs into their broader portfolio allocation.

3. *Real estate mutual funds.* For the smaller inv estor, this option allows the oppor tunity to invest in real estate securities in a pr o- fessionally managed por tfolio. There ar e curr ently o ver 70 mu- tual funds dedicated to r eal estate securities and the r eal estate sector. These funds usually focus on inv esting in REIT s, r eal estate operating companies, and housing-r elated stocks. I n most cases, the por tfolio is activ ely managed to take adv antage of emerging trends in the real estate markets. In the aggregate, these funds had $52.2 billion of shareholder assets as of June 30, 2005. (Appendix A contains a list of publicly traded mutual funds that focus on the real estate sector.)

4. *Real estate unit investment trusts (UITs).* Much like mutual funds, these tr usts offer small inv estors the adv antage of a large, pr ofes- sionally selected and diversified real estate por tfolio. However, un- like the case for a mutual fund, the por tfolio of a UIT is fix ed on its str ucturing and is not activ ely managed. I t is a self-liquidating pool that has a pr edetermined time span. After issue, shar es of UITs trade on the secondar y mar ket much like shar es of closed- ended mutual funds. U nder this scenario, it is sometimes possible

to buy shares of a UIT at a discount on the underlying value of the actual shares contained within the trust on the open market.

5. *Exchange traded funds (ETFs).* Much like UITs, ETFs represent a share that reflects a portfolio of stocks. Normally the shares track a market index and can be traded like a stock. ETFs represent the stocks that ar e in an index, although a fe w ETFs track activ ely managed por tfolios of stocks. I nvestors can do just about any-thing with an ETF that they can do with a normal stock, such as short selling or buying on margin. B ecause ETFs ar e ex change traded, they can be bought and sold at any time during the day . Their price will fluctuate from moment to moment just like any other stock's price. ETFs are more tax efficient than most mutual funds because y ou as the shar eholder have the final decision on when to buy and sell them. The downside is that each time y ou trade ETF shares there is a br okerage commission, which is why they do not make sense for a periodic investment plan.

REIT Idea: The Pros and Cons of REIT Investment Options

1. Direct *REIT investment*

   Pro: Low cost and total tax control

   Con: Investor must select REITs and monitor their performance

2. *Managed accounts*

   Pro: Professionally managed and usually tax controlled

   Con: Higher expenses

3. *Mutual funds*

   Pro: Professionally managed

   Con: Lack of tax control

4. *Unit investment trusts (UITs)*

   Pro: Fixed portfolio lessens tax events

   Con: Passive management prevents value-added investing

5. *Exchange traded funds (ETFs)*

   Pro: Low expenses and total tax control

   Con: Generally passive strategy with commissions on each share traded

Relevant Characteristics of REITs

Investors' por tfolio policies and strategies ar e often influenced b y their capital mar ket and economic expectations. These expectations ar e a r eflection of the relevant social, political, and economic data that are available to investors at any given time. To the extent that inv estors monitor these economic and market factors and modify their portfolio allocations according to their perceptions, it is important to consider the key factors that may impact REITs as an asset class.

Interest Rates and REITs

Because of a generally higher than average dividend yield, many investors consider REITs to be bondlike in their characteristics. To some extent, this is true with regard to the fact that REITs provide a high level of current income, as do bond investments. However, REITs are not like bonds in their response to changing interest rates. In fact, REITs tend to be less sensitive to changes in the inter est rate envir onment than both bonds and the broader stock market.

Real estate inv estment tr usts and many other high-yielding stocks, such as utility and energy stocks, are often perceived to be substitutes for fixed-income securities. Conv entional wisdom about inter est rate sensitivity suggests that, compared to fixed-income investments such as bonds and Treasury bills, high-yielding stocks ar e attractive during periods of declining inter est rates and in lo w-interest rate envir onments. M any investors believ e that during periods of incr easing inter est rates, high-yielding equity securities and REIT s are relatively less attractiv e because the rising interest rate environment might have a negative impact on the underlying value of the stock's price. Just as rising interest rates diminish the current value of a bond 's market price, inv estors perceive that rising interest rates will hav e the same impact on the underlying price of a stock. However, numerous studies have shown that the total returns generated by the NAREIT E quity Index have a lower correlation to changing interest rates than the S&P 500 or long-term government bonds. For example, a study completed b y Uniplan R eal Estate A dvisors indicates that for the period of J anuary 1989 thr ough June 2005, the *correlation coefficient* between government bonds and the S&P 500 was measured at 0.42, as compared to the corr elation coefficient of total r eturn from the NAREIT E quity I ndex and go vernment bonds, which was 0.24. This suggests that, contrary to popular belief, REITs are less sensitive to changes in long-term inter est rates than the broader equity market.

Correlation of REITs to Other Market Sectors

Chapters 3 and 4 r evealed that REIT s as an asset class provide a low correlation to the equity market in general and to large-capitalization equities in particular. I t is wor th noting that when the large-cap equity market, as represented by the S&P 500, is divided into its v arious subgroups, it is possible to fur ther compar e the corr elation of REIT s to other sub sectors of the mar ket. In reviewing Table 5.1, it is interesting to note that REITs had a lower correlation to technology stocks than to any other industry sector in the S&P 500. I n theory, the lack of corr elation betw een asset classes pr ovides the ability to combine those securities into por tfolios that reduce risk without sacrificing r eturn. This, as

correlation coefficient

a statistical measure that shows the interdependence of two or more random variables. The number indicates how much of a change in one variable is explained by a change in another. A score of 1.0 is perfect correlation with each variable moving in unison; a score of –1.0 is perfect noncorrelation with each variable moving opposite one another.

discussed in Chapter 3, is the cornerstone of modern por tfolio theor y. Securities that sho w a negativ e corr elation pr ovide the highest lev el of benefit when used to r educe por tfolio risk. N egative corr elation means that when r eturns are up on one security , they ar e negative or do wn on the other security. It is inter esting to note that the corr elations between REITs and technology stocks as well as between REITs and communication services and REITs and the health care sector provide a negative correlation coefficient during some periods. This relationship is particularly significant to inv estors whose por tfolios may include high exposur e to technology, communications, or health care-related industries.

Inflation and REITs

Real estate and REIT s provide a hedge against inflation. I n an envir onment where inflation is rising, the value of real estate and real estate securities can be expected to incr ease as w ell. I n times of high and rising inflation, investors have historically been rewarded by changing their asset allocation strategy to incr ease their investment in the r eal estate asset class. In contrast, tr easury securities and fix ed-income securities such as

TABLE 5.1 Correlation Coefficients, January 1995–June 2005

	NAREIT Equity	S&P 500	Energy Stocks	Materials Stocks	Industrial Stocks	Consumer Disc.	Consumer Staples	Health Care	Financial Stocks	Information Technology	Utilities
NAREIT Equity	1.00										
S&P 500	0.24	1.00									
Energy stocks	0.39	0.56	1.00								
Materials Stocks	0.37	0.62	0.63	1.00							
Industrial Stocks	0.33	0.87	0.64	0.76	1.00						
Consumer Discretionary	0.19	0.85	0.41	0.60	0.78	1.00					
Consumer Staples	0.24	0.47	0.32	0.38	0.49	0.35	1.00				
Health Care	0.11	0.51	0.34	0.19	0.41	0.31	0.65	1.00			
Financial Stocks	0.34	0.78	0.55	0.59	0.74	0.69	0.59	0.54	1.00		
Information Technology	0.02	0.79	0.28	0.32	0.50	0.63	0.04	0.16	0.34	1.00	
Utilities	0.37	0.22	0.48	0.23	0.37	0.08	0.29	0.32	0.38	-0.08	1.00

Source: Uniplan, Inc.

58

Income—REITs Deliver Reliable Current Income

Average annual returns: 13.8 percent

Average annual income: 8.1 percentage points or 59 percent of total return

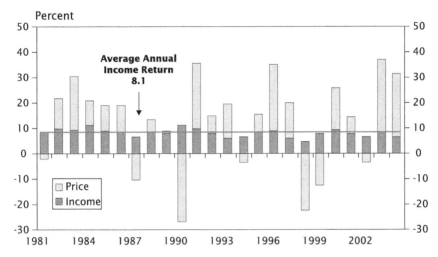

FIGURE 5.1   Equity REIT Annual Returns (1981–2002)

Source: NAREIT.

bonds have performed poorly during periods of high and rising inflation. Therefore, fixed-income portfolio investors may want to consider REITs as a substitute for a fix ed-income por tfolio during periods of expected and high inflation.

Just like bonds, REIT s deriv e a large per centage of their total r e- turns from the dividend component of the inv estment. However, unlike the case with bonds, the dividend component of REITs tends to increase over time. S ince 1981, the av erage annual income r eturn on equity REITs has been 8.54 per cent (see Figure 5.1). I n addition, the dividend growth rate of the NAREIT E quity Index has ex ceeded the gr owth rate of inflation in every year since 1994.

Considerations for Taxable Investors

The high current dividend yield of REITs may be a disadv antage to tax- able investor portfolios. For income tax purposes, dividend distributions from REITs may consist of ordinary income, return of capital, and long- term capital gains. When not held in nontaxable accounts, REITs have a disadvantage with r espect to other common stocks. F or the taxable investor, the gr eatest por tion of total r eturn expected b y REIT holders consists of dividend yield, whereas common stock returns consist largely of appreciation. An appreciated stock that is held long enough to meet the holding period requirements for long-term capital gains is currently taxed at a maximum rate of 15 percent. Returns on REITs, having such a high portion of dividend income reflected as current income, may increase a taxable investor's marginal tax rate.

REIT shares, however, do offer taxable investors some advantages over dividends from other high-yielding stocks and dividends from corporate or government bonds. It is not unusual to have a high percentage of the dividends received each year from a REIT issued as a return of capital. This return of capital portion of the Equity REIT Price Index versus Consumer Price Index, monthly, dividend is not currently taxable to the shareholder, but rather reduces the shareholder's cost basis in the shares and defers the tax liability until the shareholder ultimately sells those shares. If the holding period of the shares is long enough to meet the requirements for long-term capital gains, then the maximum tax rate on that portion of the dividend return, which was used as a reduction in cost basis, would currently be 15 percent. This presents an advantageous situation to the extent that income-oriented investors can spend their current interest income now and may have the opportunity to defer a portion of the taxes on that current income until a later date. Not only are the taxes deferred, the investor may have the opportunity to pay taxes on the return of capital portion of the dividend at the long-term capital gains rate.

As discussed, for income tax purposes, dividend distributions paid to shareholders of REITs can consist of ordinary income, return of capital, and long-term capital gains. If a REIT realizes a long-term capital gain from the sale of a property in its real estate portfolio, it may designate a portion of the dividend paid during a tax year as a long-term capital gains distribution. This portion of the dividend is taxed to the shareholder at the lower long-term capital gain rate.

Historically, it is estimated that the return of capital component of REIT dividends has typically been approximately 30 percent of the total dividend return. It is important to note that this aggregate percentage has declined in recent years as a result of REITs reducing their overall payout ratio to investors in order to retain capital within the REIT operating structure. The taxable investor therefore may want to consider the implications of a high current dividend yield component of REITs.

However, the high yield should be consider ed in light of the fact that REIT dividends ar e often characterized by the REIT to the shar eholder as return of capital or long-term capital gains. To some extent, this pr ovides a modest tax adv antage to the individual inv estor who may inv est directly in REIT s as opposed to other high yielding securities such as bonds or *master limited partnerships* (MLPs).

The Net Asset Value Cycle

Capital markets that include stocks, bonds, or r eal estate-related securities historically go thr ough periods in which they attract considerable marginal ne w capital. This r esults in v aluations rising to high lev els. Such examples of this can be seen in the I nternet stock bubble of the late 1990s or the Nifty-50 stock market bubble of the early 1970s. Conversely, there are other periods when asset classes go out of favor, thereby creating very low valuations, such as in the real estate markets of the early 1990s. Real estate is a cyclical industry, and these valuation extremes may be consider ed cy cles or mean r eversion situations. I n either case, investors are often looking for the opportunity to buy low and sell high by shifting their por tfolios among v arious asset classes to take adv antage of valuation disparities.

When considering REITs for investment, it may be useful to look at the aggr egate v alue of REIT s as an asset class r elative to the net asset value of their underlying pr operties. H istorically, the per formance of REITs after periods when they traded at a significant discount to net asset value has often been superior.

The opportunity to buy REITs at a discount to their net asset value is said to be an opportunity to buy real estate cheaper on Wall Street than it can be pur chased on M ain Street. In addition, when REITs trade at a substantial discount to net asset v alue, dividend yields ar e often higher than average for the r eal estate gr oup. This offers the oppor tunity to be "paid to wait." As expected, real estate values eventually recover to private-market-level v aluation prices or r evert back to mean v aluation lev els. From a timing point of vie w, repositioning money into the REIT asset class, at a time when REIT s trade at a large discount to net asset v alue, and migrating money out of the REIT asset class when a significant pr emium to net asset v alue becomes appar ent may simply be good timing indicators within the REIT market. It should be noted however, that real estate as an asset class should be consider ed a long-term investment, and that, for the av erage investor, the concept of dollar cost av eraging into the REIT sector has some appeal.

REIT Idea: Your Home as a Real Estate Investment?

Investors often ask: Should I include my home in my real estate investment allocation?

The simple answer is no. Although a home is real estate, it should be considered a consumption item on your personal balance sheet. It produces no current return and must be sold to realize gains. However, it is worth noting that single-family residential real estate has a low correlation to stocks and bonds as well as REITs. So, by owning your home it helps to continue the process of portfolio diversification.

Conclusion

Numerous ways exist to gain por tfolio exposure in REITs. Investors may choose to invest directly in REITs or to use accounts that are professionally managed by por tfolio managers specializing in the r eal estate sector. Real estate mutual funds and real estate UITs and ETFs offer the opportunity for smaller inv estors to invest in REITs through pooled opportunities. I ntegration of REIT s into an inv estment por tfolio should be considered in light of the curr ent economic envir onment. The fact that REITs pr ovide a hedge against inflation and hav e a lo w corr elation to other asset classes can make them par ticularly attractive in a div ersified portfolio. The par ticularly lo w corr elation to technology , communication, and health care sectors of the large-capitalization market also makes REITs of particular interest to investors who may have excess exposure in those areas. For investors with higher exposur e to the bond mar ket, the lower sensitivity to inter est rates of REITs, when considered in conjunction with their high curr ent yield, may offer some attractiv e opportunities to div ersify a fix ed-income por tfolio. Taxable investors may want to consider REITs o ver other high-dividend-yielding sectors of the equity market because of the potential tax deferral adv antages inher ent in the REIT dividend structure.

Points to Remember

- An allocation of 5 per cent to 20 per cent in r eal estate inv estment trusts (REITs) will increase return and lower risk in most portfolios.

- An investment policy statement reflects the long-term needs and objectives of the investor.

- Rational investors seek to incr ease total r eturn while decr easing total risk within a portfolio.

- REITs lower volatility and increase total return when added to a multiasset-class portfolio.

- There are five basic strategies for integrating REITs into a diversified portfolio:

  1. Direct investment

  2. Managed accounts

  3. Mutual funds

  4. Unit investment trusts (UITs)

  5. Exchange traded funds (ETFs)

- Portfolio policies ar e influenced b y inv estor expectations, and REITs should be viewed in that context.

- REITs have a low sensitivity to changing interest rates.

- REITs act as a hedge against inflation.

- REITs have a negative correlation to certain stock market sectors.

- REITs may offer a modest tax advantage to certain taxable investors.

Part

2

Real Estate Economics and Analysis

Chapter

6

Real Estate Market Characteristics

What marijuana was to the sixties, real estate is to the seventies.
—Ron Koslow

Before investors can make an assessment of a r eal estate investment trust (REIT), they need to understand the supply-and-demand characteristics of the markets in which that par ticular REIT operates. In a local r eal estate market, supply can generally be defined as v a-cant space curr ently av ailable for lease, plus any space av ailable for sublease, plus new space under construction, plus space that will soon be vacated. The total r eflects the av ailable supply of space in a giv en local real estate mar ket. D emand for space in a local r eal estate mar ket can generally be deriv ed fr om ne w businesses being formed, plus existing businesses expanding, plus ne w companies mo ving into the r egion, plus net ne w household formations, less closing, mo ving, and do wnsizing businesses. The total r eflects the aggr egate marginal demand for space within a region. In the simplest terms, supply is the total space av ailable and demand is the total space r equired. In the final analysis, it is supply and demand for a given property type in the local real estate market that drives property valuation.

Real Estate Market Dynamics

Local real estate mar ket dynamics ar e driven by supply and demand for a particular pr operty type. There ar e a wide range of factors that affect supply and demand in the local mar ket. Values tend to be br oadly affected by the general level of business activity and population growth. Interest rate trends, because of their impact on business activity, also have a general impact on real estate market dynamics.

The residential housing market and commercial real estate markets differ with r espect to changes in the o verall economy . The r esidential housing market has historically tended to lead the overall real estate market into and out of r ecessions. Conv ersely, the commer cial r eal estate market has a tendency to follo w rather than lead the o verall economy . Although real estate is impacted by the overall economy, it is highly local in nature. Economic activity at the local lev el or within the r egion will have a larger impact on property valuations than general overall economic activity. The health of a r egional economy normally depends in par t on the diversity of business and the base of employment within the region.

A r egion's r egulatory envir onment is another factor that impacts real estate activity. M any cities hav e adopted lo w-growth or no-gr owth strategies that have made it difficult to dev elop new real estate. R estrictions on land use and limited access to city utilities, along with the imposition of dev elopment fees, school fees, and r elated activity fees, hav e made for difficult and limited dev elopment. S ome local go vernments have mandated r ent contr ol or targeted par ticular set-asides for lo w-income housing that ar e coupled with ne w development activities. This has had the effect of lo wering general expected r eturns on r eal estate development and therefore has slowed the growth of development within certain geographic regions. So, in addition to the broad economic factors that impact real estate, many very specific local factors can affect the performance of a real estate market. Indeed, the supply-and-demand characteristics of the local mar ket hav e the gr eatest impact on r eal estate valuations at the local level.

Any local r eal estate mar ket can be vie wed as a quadrant char t (see Figure 6.1). A t the intersection of the four quadrants is the point at which demand for and supply of r eal estate in the local mar ket are at a perfect equilibrium. That intersection can be expanded to cr eate an *equilibrium zone.* This z one r eflects a mar ket dynamic wher e, in general terms, the visible supply of r eal estate available and the current and forecasted demand for r eal estate ar e appr oximately equal. When supply-and-demand characteristics for a par ticular pr operty categor y within a particular local mar ket fall within the equilibrium z one, pr operty and rental prices tend to be relatively stable at a market level.

Quadrant One	**Quadrant Two**
The Recovery Phase	*The Supply Phase*
▪ Demand begins to exceed supply	▪ Higher rents cause new building
▪ Rents begin to rise	▪ Rents continue to rise
▪ Property prices recover	▪ Speculative building begins
	▪ Supply begins to exceed demand
Quadrant Three	**Quadrant Four**
The Rollover Phase	*The Trough Phase*
▪ New supply outstrips demand	▪ Rents are declining or stable
▪ Vacancy rates begin to move higher	▪ No new meaningful building activity
▪ Rental rates start to decline	▪ Above-average vacancy rates
▪ Property prices soften	▪ Soft economic environment

FIGURE 6.1 The Real Estate Market Cycle

As we go on to examine each of the four quadrants of the Real Estate Market Cycle quadrant chart, we can see a particular series of characteristics that can be attributed to each quadrant. Quadrant 1 (see Figure 6.2) represents the beginning of the real estate cycle in a given market or property type. This is the phase where demand begins to exceed available supply. It is sometimes termed the *recovery* phase. In this phase, rents begin to rise as demand begins to exceed supply available in the local market. Rents will continue to increase to a level where economic yields on new property development will become sufficiently attractive to cause developers to begin to consider adding property to the market. Prices on individual properties also begin to rise as occupancy levels increase and the available supply of new space decreases. As vacancy rates fall and available supply tightens, rents may begin to rise rapidly. At some point, higher rents precipitate new construction activity that leads to the phase depicted in Quadrant 2 (see Figure 6.3). This is the *development* or *supply* phase in the local market. If financing is available, speculative developers may begin construction in anticipation of continued rising rents, allowing for new building activity to begin, initially on a largely speculative basis. As supply continues to increase, the local market moves through the zone of equilibrium and into a pattern in which the current space available begins to exceed current demand for space. While this occurs, the growth rate in rent levels begins to subside,

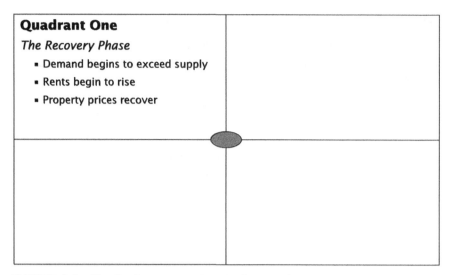

Quadrant One

The Recovery Phase

- Demand begins to exceed supply
- Rents begin to rise
- Property prices recover

FIGURE 6.2 The Real Estate Market Cycle: Quadrant 1

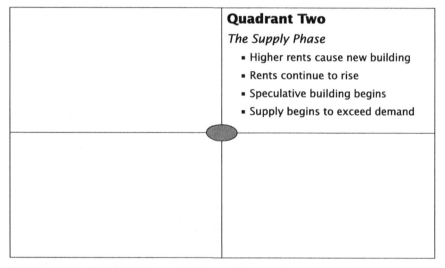

Quadrant Two

The Supply Phase

- Higher rents cause new building
- Rents continue to rise
- Speculative building begins
- Supply begins to exceed demand

FIGURE 6.3 The Real Estate Market Cycle: Quadrant 2

and vacancy rates, which had been decreasing, begin to increase slowly. As more incremental space is delivered into the market, rental growth begins to slow more dramatically and vacancy rates begin to rise more quickly.

The local market now moves into Quadrant 3 of the real estate cycle (see Figure 6.4). This is the *rollover* phase or *down cycle* of the market. New supply arrives more quickly than it can be absorbed and

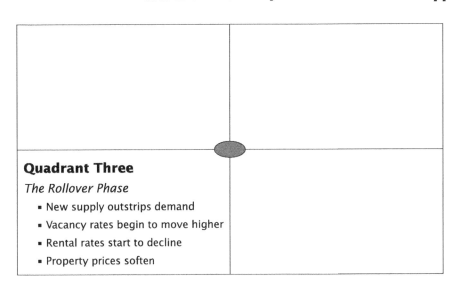

Quadrant Three

The Rollover Phase

- New supply outstrips demand
- Vacancy rates begin to move higher
- Rental rates start to decline
- Property prices soften

FIGURE 6.4 The Real Estate Market Cycle: Quadrant 3

begins to push rents downward. Vacancy rates begin to move higher than average for the mar ket, causing pr operty v alues to begin to soften and move lower. As the mar ket continues to soften, pr operty owners under-stand that they will quickly lose tenants or mar ket shar e if their r ental rates ar e not competitiv e.They begin to lo wer r ents in an attempt to retain or attract tenants as w ell as to help co ver the fix ed expenses of operating a giv en pr operty. This phase is also characteriz ed b y little or no activity with r egard to transactions in commer cial pr operties. The disconnect betw een what buy ers ar e willing to pay for pr operties due to the uncer tain outlook and what sellers feel pr operties ar e wor th be-comes wider.

This leads the market into Quadrant 4 of the real estate cycle, or the *trough* (see F igure 6.5). I n this phase, r ents ar e generally flat to lo wer, there is no new supply activity, and there is likely to be a large amount of excess space av ailable in the local mar ket. This might be coupled with lower economic activity or w eak demand for space in the local mar ket, which tends to prolong the trough stage and make it deeper and more se-vere. The market cycle eventually reaches a bottom as ne w construction dissipates and demand incr eases and begins to absorb existing supply , moving the cycle back into Quadrant 1.

In a theor etical per fect mar ket, supply and demand would r emain in the equilibrium z one and real estate returns would remain stable over the long term. However, in the real world, a combination of local market

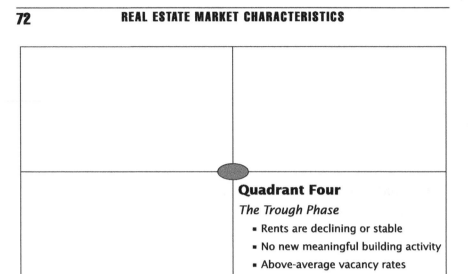

FIGURE 6.5 The Real Estate Market Cycle: Quadrant 4

supply-and-demand factors can have an impact on the real estate cycle in a local mar ket. Local mar kets that ar e less inclined to giv e entitlements to build or to cr eate variances for building purposes tend to r emain in supply-and-demand equilibrium for a longer period than mar kets that are prone to rapid and uncontrolled development activity.

Local real estate markets may not move through the quadrants in a one thr ough four sequence. D emand and supply at the local lev el will likely ebb and flow, causing the local market dynamic to move in and out of the equilibrium zone. From an analysis standpoint, it is normally possible to determine which quadrants a giv en real estate pr operty category occupies within a local mar ket and to determine in which dir ection the supply-and-demand fundamentals ar e moving. O ne of the primar y functions of management pr ofessionals in the r eal estate community is knowing and understanding which phase of the r eal estate cy cle a local market is in.

Trends in Market Dynamics

One general fact is appar ent in r egard to the r eal estate cy cle: Over the last decade, the cy cle has become less sev ere than it was in the past. As mentioned in Chapter 2, higher under writing standards on the par t of real estate lenders coupled with the public mar ket discipline that has resulted fr om the commer cial mor tgage-backed securities mar ket hav e led to real estate cycles that are far more subdued than in the distant past. This market discipline has helped most local real estate markets avoid the severe boom-and-bust cycles that were evident prior to the 1990s. In addition, local economic factors that drive the local real estate economy often create a series of local mar kets that at any giv en time may be in any quadrant of the r eal estate cy cle. If a local mar ket is in Q uadrant 1 or 2 or in the equilibrium z one, the real estate envir onment is generally considered to be positive. When markets are in Quadrant 3 or 4, the real estate environment is considered to be negative. The thing to remember is that there are opportunities in each phase of the cycle

---

REIT Idea: Cycle Opportunities

At each stage of the real estate cycle there are opportunities for REIT investors.

- *Recovery Phase.* Bad fundamentals often provide the chance to buy REITs at a substantial discount to the net asset value of the properties owned in the REIT portfolio.
- *Supply Phase.* Well-positioned REITs will have the chance to raise rents and build new properties in the recovering market area, thus driving earnings.
- *Rollover Phase.* Good REIT management teams will be active sellers of noncore holdings at the point they believe property prices have peaked in a local market, thus harvesting gains and protecting portfolio performance.
- *Trough Phase.* For the patient value investor this is the time to buy. Well-capitalized, well-managed REITs can trade at below the physical replacement cost of their underlying buildings and often offer a high yield on the REIT shares.

Although real estate markets in general are driven by growth of the overall U.S. domestic economy, any par ticular local market might be in any phase at any time. As this dynamic plays itself out in local mar kets and within each pr operty gr oup, it can be difficult to generaliz e about where in the cycle the overall real estate market is at a given time. There may be a shortage of industrial space in Houston and a shortage of apartments in Denver, while at the same time there is an excess supply of hotel rooms in San Francisco and too much office space in A tlanta. This suggests that there are generally local market opportunities available for the real estate inv estor in some mar kets and in some pr operty categories at any particular time. Local mar ket knowledge is the key to making these specific mar ket determinations. That mar ket kno wledge and skill is what a high-quality REIT management team will bring to the r eal estate investment equation. I n addition, a REIT por tfolio that is div ersified across property types and geographic r egions allows its owner to moderate risk that may r esult fr om changing local mar ket dynamics. H ere is where the liquidity available to the shareholder of a REIT is a key advantage over the direct property owner. If, as in our earlier example, the office space market in Atlanta were deteriorating rapidly and supply looked as if it might outstrip demand for a long period, REIT shar eholders could liquidate their shar es in the REIT that holds pr operty in A tlanta and r einvest the pr oceeds in a local office mar ket that seems to hav e a better supply-and-demand profile. For a direct owner of office buildings in Atlanta, the option to liquidate is available but normally not practical. Due to the time and expense inv olved in the dir ect sale of a r eal estate portfolio, practical consideration generally dictates that the owner stay in place for the downward duration of the local market cycle. Direct real estate owners usually attempt to mitigate local mar ket cycles by diversifying their pr operty holdings acr oss a number of differ ent geographic regions. In addition, a local o wner might diversify across different property types within the local market to help manage local market risk.

Local Market Information Dynamics

Real estate firms hav e unique institutional characteristics that generally distinguish them from non-real estate firms and give them a comparative advantage when dealing in a local mar ket. These institutional characteristics also giv e local r eal estate firms an adv antage o ver r eal estate firms that may not be present in the local real estate markets. These advantages are normally referred to as *market locality* and *market segmentation* advantages. The market locality advantage suggests that there is a certain information advantage for participants in a local real estate market that results from the local nature of the real estate market itself. There are a series of factors that contribute to the market locality advantage, such as a lack of standardized product, the absence of a centraliz ed exchange for clearing information, and the incr eased r esearch costs for nonlocal firms to develop data about a local mar ket. In addition, a general understanding of the local political process also creates a local market advantage that a real estate firm fr om outside the ar ea might not enjo y. U nder these conditions and in local mar kets where information can be costly and not generally available to all par ticipants, local r eal estate firms ar e likely to be familiar with and have an information advantage.

Market segmentation suggests that different market segments require different types of expertise and management skills that may be very expensive and not easily transferr ed fr om other mar ket segments. M anagement skills help to reduce the uncertainty associated with business risks resulting from physical operation of real property. This suggests that a firm specializing in a specific r eal estate segment may gain a competitiv e advantage as a result of superior managerial exper tise acquired through time and experience. This market segmentation knowledge directly addresses the old adage that says: "If I had known how difficult it was, I wouldn't have tried to do it in the first place." Thus the ability to dev elop superior local mar ket knowledge or the access to those who possess that kno wledge can create a significant advantage in real estate investment.

Consider the local r eal estate dev eloper who normally attends city planning commission meetings as w ell as city dev elopment and urban planning meetings giv en by local and state municipalities. F ormally or informally, this developer may, through intimate knowledge of the planning process, understand that cer tain projects such as r oad extensions or the expansion of municipal ser vices ar e par t of a long-range plan. This same dev eloper may use that information to contact a lando wner that may not be in the local market or have similar local knowledge and make an offer to purchase a given parcel of land at prevailing market rates. The transaction could likely be consummated without any of the unkno wing parties ever learning of the kno wledge that the r eal estate developer possessed. The subsequent extension of a road or the development of an area could then turn into a highly pr ofitable transaction for the dev eloper, who was armed with deep local mar ket knowledge that an uninformed observer may not have been able to obtain. It is this specific information advantage that local real estate operators bring to the table.

Geographic diversification can increase the efficiency of str ucturing a real estate portfolio. In fact, research indicates that regional diversification pr ovides mor e por tfolio benefits than div ersification b y pr operty type. Geographic diversification within a portfolio provides a certain level of economic diversification as well. This economic diversification results from economic specific industr y exposur e as it r elates to a geographic region. For example, San Jose, California, and the San Francisco Bay area are widely considered to be the center of geographic activity for Internet-based companies. Contrast San Jose with Detroit, Michigan, which is the center of economic activity as it r elates to the U.S. automotiv e industry. Compare that to New York City, which has a diverse economy but is also considered to be the center of activity for the financial community. Now compare that to Washington, D.C., which is the center of activity for the federal government. Each of these geographic locations will r espond differently to changes in the general economic envir onment. Therefore, diversifying across geographic r egions can pr ovide a cer tain level of economic div ersification within the r eal estate por tfolio. This type of geographic div ersification is not normally possible for dir ect r eal estate investors unless they are of very significant size. An investor in a portfolio of REITs, however, can accomplish geographic div ersification as w ell as diversification by pr operty with a modest inv estment, while enjo ying a level of liquidity not available to the direct real estate investor.

Real Estate Data Resources

There is a wide range of data av ailable for r esearching local mar ket r eal estate activity. Most data take the form of secondary data, which are data that have been gather ed for some other purpose and ar e generally av ailable for r eview. S econdary data ar e generally less costly and less time consuming to obtain than primar y data. I n general, secondar y data ar e widely available at a lo w cost through libraries or firms that specializ e in generating such information. P rimary data may be gather ed by communication or obser vation and ar e designed to answ er specific r esearch questions. R eal estate operators within a local mar ket often gather primary data. P rimary data may take the form of r ent sur veys or mar ket surveys done b y local br okerage firms. These firsthand data ar e valuable in assessing the primar y supply-and-demand fundamentals of the local market. There are a number of primar y and secondary data sour ces that compile local market statistics that are worthy of reviewing.

All data are subjective in the end. The quality and purity of the data are generally considered a function of the sour ce of the data. I n the final analysis, the data must be analyzed and interpreted within the context of the local mar ket dynamic. This r equires making assumptions about the market and the data to end up with a forecast of local market activity for both supply and demand within a particular property category. This type of forecasting and analysis is embodied in the dev elopment process that is discussed at length in Chapter 7.

Points to Remember

- Supply and demand drive value in local real estate markets.
- Business and economic gr owth within a r egion driv es o verall demand for real estate.
- Development activity is the principal driv er of ne w r eal estate supply.
- A local r egion's r egulatory envir onment will impact r eal estate development activity in that market.
- The real estate market cycle can be divided into four stages:
  1. Recovery phase
  2. Supply phase
  3. Rollover phase
  4. Trough phase
- Real estate firms hav e unique institutional characteristics that give them an adv antage o ver non-r eal estate firms in the local market.
- REIT management provides a local market knowledge advantage.
- Liquidity gives REITs an adv antage when dealing with the local market cycle.
- A wide range of sources can be found that document local market supply-and-demand dynamics.

Chapter **7**

Real Estate Development

The trick is to make sure you don't die waiting for prosperity to come.

—Lee Iacocca, 1973

R eal estate dev elopment is the high-stakes poker of the r eal estate industry. When most people think of r eal estate they associate it with real estate development. In part this is because of such names as Donald Trump and John Zeckendorf. It seems, too, that every regional real estate marketplace has its own Trump-style real estate developer who is always pr oposing a bigger and better pr oject with his name firmly attached. There is a cer tain blend of entr epreneurship and ego that goes into the dev elopment of r eal estate. The key to success is to make sur e that y our r eal estate dev elopment activities inv olve mor e entr epreneurship and less ego.

The Real Estate Development Process

Real estate development is at the high end of the risk scale, but when successfully implemented it is also on the high end of the r eturn scale. The development process is worth understanding if you want to get involved in real estate inv estments. Development is essentially the supply side of the local real estate market. Understanding the development process also leads to additional insights into the local market supply-and-demand dynamics. In order to make an accurate assessment of the local market, you need to have an assessment of current development activity as well as of the impact of potential competitive building activity that may not be apparent in the local market. A thorough understanding of the development process allows for a better and more complete assessment of the local market economics.

Historically, real estate investment trusts (REITs) with the best earnings performance have often made development activity an important part of their business strategy. The incremental yield available in a development project over the comparable market yields for existing properties makes development a high value-added proposition for REITs. For example, the unleveraged cash-on-cash return for an existing industrial warehouse in a particular local market might be 9.5 percent. A developer may see the opportunity in that same market to build a similar industrial warehouse with a projected unleveraged cash-on-cash return of 14.5 percent. Thus the opportunity to deploy capital is available at 9.5 percent with minimal risk or at a potential return of 14.5 percent for a riskier development project. Here is where the real estate expertise of the REIT's management either adds value and earns a higher overall return for the shareholder—or overreaches for return and puts the shareholder's capital at risk.

The development of real estate is very entrepreneurial in nature. Different types of development activities have distinct differences: Developing warehouses is different from developing offices, and developing apartments is different from developing hotels. It is worth noting that the substantial redevelopment of an existing property can be as difficult as, if not more difficult than, a ground-up new development project. Development is the aspect of real estate in which the greatest number of risk variables must be simultaneously managed. It encompasses the challenge of managing a myriad of legal, financial, market-related, and construction risks, as well as managing the many people-related risks related to the project. The challenges can be daunting. In many ways, developing real estate is like creating a new product for retail distribution. Not only does the real estate developer have to envision the "product" from concept through completion, but the product must also be positioned among competing products within the local real estate market.

Timing is critical when it comes to the development process in real estate. The development process has a very long cycle. In some instances, it can take as long as five years to go from concept through completion of a large real estate project (see Table 7.1). The project might start out with

TABLE 7.1   Timetable of Development Stages

Activity	Expected Time
Market analysis	1–3 months
Location analysis	3–6 months
Site acquisition	6–9 months
Entitlement and zoning*	12–18 months
Design and construction	12–18 months
Leasing	6–18 months
Total development time	40–72 months

*Longer in some locations.

a market analysis and location analysis to determine the viability of the project. This can in turn lead to negotiations to control a particular parcel of land. That initial phase of development activity can easily take 12 to 18 months.

Following the site analysis and acquisition is likely to be the entitlement process. As discussed in Chapter 2, various communities have different appetites and varying standards for the creation of new real estate projects. It is not unusual for the entitlement process to run 12 to 18 months or longer. Once the project is entitled for building, design through construction and completion can take another 12 to 18 months. Finally, leasing activities can take 6 to 24 months, depending on the property type. When all is said and done, a project can easily take three to five years to complete.

The real estate cycle plays a significant role in the timing of development activities. Because of the long lead time involved in the typical real estate project, it is critical for the developer to know where the local market stands at each phase of the project. The ideal outcome is for the developer to deliver the project at a time when the market is very tight and there is little available supply. The least desirable outcome is when bad timing results in delivering new supply into a soft market with increasing vacancy and declining demand. The ultimate timing of delivery can make the difference between the financial success—or failure—of a project.

In addition to ground-up real estate activities, a developer may achieve high rates of return through projects that involve major redevelopment of properties. This type of redevelopment can encompass upgrading an underutilized property or a property that may be involved in a lower use. Converting a large urban war ehouse to office space or r esidential lofts might be a r edevelopment project with high potential. The real estate may be acquired at a very low cost and the redevelopment may provide for substantially incr eased earnings after capital expenses. The risks associated with r edevelopment activities ar e similar to those of ground-up development except that r edevelopment sometimes includes an additional layer of design and constr uction risk. The developer never knows what will be found until the actual demolition pr ocess begins. A redevelopment building might contain hazar dous materials such as asbestos that must be pr operly abated, or unfor eseen str uctural pr oblems might be found. These types of construction-related issues can lead to increased costs and delays.

Inertia

In nearly all instances, dev elopment or r edevelopment activity r equires overcoming political and local inertia with regard to a project. Overcoming inertia or dealing with opposition to a project requires a high level of skill on the par t of the dev eloper. In terms of diplomacy, the dev eloper must be adept at obtaining the best outcome fr om all participants in the process. He or she must also be an effectiv e champion of the pr oject, continually selling and pr omoting it thr oughout the dev elopment process. I n any giv en situation, the dev eloper must kno w what the desired outcome is and ho w much room is available for compromise. In addition to using diplomacy, the developer needs to know when to resort to hardball tactics such as litigation. These factors must all be measur ed in the context of project timing, financial impact, and project feasibility.

For example, adding landscaping might increase the overall cost of a project but have little impact on the o verall timetable. However, requiring a higher ratio of parking to building area might substantially alter the financial feasibility of the pr oject. A good dev eloper will kno w when a project is not going to be feasible and will terminate the entir e project rather than cr eate a situation that pr ovides an inadequate r eturn on invested capital. In the final analysis, the numbers have to work.

Overcoming the iner tia of the entitlement pr ocess allo ws the dev eloper to begin managing the dynamic pr ocess of development and its associated risks. These risks take many forms and may include pr eleasing activities, maintenance of adequate financial r esources, and the general management of the development or redevelopment process. The developer must control an extremely dynamic process while managing financial and business risks.

Land Acquisition

The development process generally begins with the acquisition or control of land that is targeted for the intended use. I n the case of a REIT , this may mean the acquisition of a par cel of r eal estate or land, or it may r esult fr om r edevelopment opportunities on land or buildings alr eady owned by the REIT. If acquisition of land is r equired as a part of the pr ocess, it is vital to acquir e the land quickly and quietly in order to avoid the possibility *holdouts.*

> **holdouts**
>
> occur when key property owners refuse to sell at any price or demand prices that are so far out of line that they make the financial feasibility of the project unacceptable. Quickly and quietly assembling a land package and avoiding holdouts is a key part of the development process.

Alternatively, real estate developers and REITs may own land inv entories. These land inv entories are typically par cels of land adjoining existing r eal estate pr ojects o wned b y the dev eloper or REIT . These lands have usually been entitled to build and are held in inv entory awaiting mar ket conditions that will suppor t dev elopment activities. This preentitlement allows the developer to substantially shorten the cy cle time of a pr oject because the site analysis, acquisition, and entitlement pr ocess is substantially complete. Often this land is perpetually for sale, offered as a build-to-suit site where an interested buyer can acquire the land and the developer will build a building or complex to suit the buyer.

There is some debate among analysts who follo w REITs o ver the merits of land inventory. There are those who argue that land inventories are costly to maintain and come at the expense of the o verall per for-mance of the REIT's existing property portfolio. The other side of the ar-gument suggests that land inv entory pr ovides the oppor tunity for build-to-suit dev elopments as w ell as speculativ e building b y the REIT when mar ket conditions suppor t such activity, and ther efore the higher potential returns are generally worth the risks to the shareholder. In most cases, the value added is a function of ho w skillfully the r eal estate man-agement team handles the land inventory. In many circumstances, land is acquired under a conditional purchase agreement or contingent purchase agreement. This is usually pr efaced on a series of conditions being met in order to facilitate the eventual land transaction. In most instances, the developer pays a fee to the lando wner to obtain an option on the land subject to certain conditions. The option has a limited term and the developer must complete the conditional pr ocess by the end of the option term or risk losing the ability to contr ol the land. In other scenarios, the landowner may par ticipate b y contributing the land to a joint v enture with the developer.

Large dev elopment pr ojects may also be under taken using staged payments to the landowner, meaning the landowner is paid as each phase of the development is completed. Here the seller might receive a monthly option fee to compensate for staging of payments over time as w ell as an o verall higher price for the land.

eminent domain

a legal term referring to the right of a public entity, such as a state or local municipality, to seize a property for public purposes in exchange for compensation to the property owner. (See also REIT Idea: *Kelo et al. v. City of New London et al.* in Chapter 1.)

Land can also be acquir ed thr ough a pr ocess known as *eminent domain.* In some instances, this occurs when a holdout is thr eatening the viability of a large-scale project that has been embraced by a community. I f the holdout contr ols a key par cel, the local municipality may use its po wer of eminent domain to acquir e that par cel, thus allo wing the project to move forward.

Sometimes land acquisition is not really an acquisition at all. There ar e cases wher e the land on which a building is built is leased on a long-term basis. This is particularly true in areas where there is a scar city of buildable land. I n such situations, a landowner might, rather than sell a par cel, be inclined to engage in a long-term lease. The lease is normally structured in a way that allo ws the property owner to par ticipate in the success of the real estate project. In many land leases, annual lease payments ae supplemented by the lando wner's par ticipation in the upside r ental growth of the underlying property.

The Entitlement Process

Overcoming iner tia to allo w a pr operty to be dev eloped for its highest and best use is normally the beginning of the entitlement pr ocess. Local governments often per ceive development activities to be a thr eat to the status quo and are generally reluctant to support new development projects. In addition, many local r esidents vie w dev elopment activity as a "not in my backyar d" pr oposition. Well-organized citizen gr oups often turn up en masse to oppose dev elopment pr ojects. In many instances, circumstances dictate that the local governmental authorities must weigh the gain in tax r evenue against the community standar d to determine whether a pr oject proceeds and in what form. This is because almost all projects involve some type of variances from local building codes. A r eal estate project built in complete conformance with all local z oning standards and building codes is normally the ex ception. Generally speaking, in or der to make a pr oject wor k, the dev eloper needs some changes in regulation or some compr omise to allo w the pr oject to pr oceed. This may be an adjustment to the r equired number of par king spaces, an exception to the required maximum height standards, or a specific variance to r oute storm or drainage water in a par ticular manner. In any case, most projects require variances of one form or another.

When it comes to z oning ex ceptions in many communities, some items tend to be more negotiable than others. In general terms, the larger the scale of the variance that is required, the more difficult it is to obtain from a political standpoint.T o o vercome these entitlement issues, most developers attempt to form a political coalition with the local go vern-ment. Again, the diplomatic and political skills of the dev eloper are required to be at their best during the entitlement pr ocess. Normally time is of the essence during the entitlement phase. By this stage of the development process, the developer needs to keep negotiations mo ving along in order to sustain the pr oject. In most cases, compr omises are struck in order to sav e time and mo ve the pr oject for ward. A good dev eloper knows in adv ance what compr omises may need to be made and what compromises he or she is willing to make to move the project forward.

In many instances, REIT s and large lando wners focus on cr eating improvements in their land inv entory to add v alue. M anagement may obtain for option a par cel of r eal estate and facilitate necessar y z oning variances. In addition, some level of infrastructure, such as sewer and water, may be installed to go along with z oning changes. This land is then considered ready for development and staged as a potential project when market conditions dictate the opportunity.

The entitlement pr ocess is as much an ar t as it is a science. Ov er-coming iner tia and opposition and obtaining v ariances and building political suppor t for a pr oject r equire dev elopers to hav e political and diplomatic skills. Moving the project along a time line and understanding the financial risks inv olved require a high lev el of risk management skills.

Feasibility Planning and Production

Planning and design are the most important aspects after entitlement. Early in the planning pr ocess, the developer needs to position the pr oject within the br oader context of the community at large.   This means the dev eloper needs to work with the community to understand which groups have an interest in a project and what those interests are. This dialogue with the community helps to position the project and build political coalitions.

Once a master plan has been developed, the design process can begin. This pr ocess is often difficult to understand, par ticularly for people who are not involved in the real estate business. It is complicated and involves a high level of input b y a large number of par ties at inter est. The ar chitect goes through a discovery process aimed at determining needs and solutions and then takes this disco very thr ough sev eral different stages using input from the parties at interest in order to formulate a specific solution.

The first stage of the pr ocess, kno wn as *programming,* defines the purposes the facility will be designed to serve. Depending on the size and scale of the pr oject, the pr ogramming stage may be formal or mor   e relaxed. The programming process attempts to gather input fr om all the local users of the end product and incorporate that input into the design.

The next stage of the process is known as the *layout phase.* Information from the pr ogramming stage is used to lay out a pr eliminary plan for the project. The ar chitect attempts to determine what goes wher e, how traffic will flow through and ar ound the building, what materials ar e suitable for the project, and the allowable size of the project.

In the next phase, kno wn as *design development,* the ar chitect uses feedback from the programming and preliminary design phases to formulate a more definite plan. There is a cost-benefit approach to the design development phase. F rom a financial point of vie w, pr oject costs begin to materialize in this development phase. Trade-offs are made as less expensive materials ar e substituted for mor e expensiv e materials and amenities ar e added or deleted based on budget considerations. At the end of this phase, there is a set of drawings for the dev elopment that is fairly complete and encompass a level of detail that illustrates how the facility will function.

Design drawings ar e then translated into constr uction documents, which ar e also kno wn as *working drawings.* These documents enable building contractors to see a lev el of detail that allo ws them to make a construction cost estimate and to begin to determine pricing estimates for the project. The working drawings are the most complicated por tion of the ar chitectural pr ocess. M any other exper ts, such as site engineers, structural engineers, and mechanical contractors, hav e some lev el of input into the wor king drawings. These subcontractors ar e paid b y the architect for their wor k. This is the phase in which most of the design costs ar e incurr ed. I n many instances, REIT s hav e dev eloped pools of in-house talent that can facilitate to a large extent the design- and cost-estimating portion of the feasibility and planning for a new project. This is a valuable resource for REITs.

At the end of the design pr ocess, the developer has a detailed set of working drawings. These drawings include specifications and a suffi-ciently high lev el of detail to allo w building contractors to put a firm price estimate on the cost of building the pr oject. I n the dev elopment process, it is impor tant that the dev eloper understand the constr uction process sufficiently to manage these negotiations. M ost REITs that ar e active in the dev elopment arena have the in-house talent to manage the construction process.

At this point, the bidding begins. The dev eloper cir culates docu-ments requesting bids from subcontractors. These subcontractors, in turn, try to develop a bid that is low enough to get the job, yet high enough to allow for a fair return on their work. Again, this is an area that requires a high level of kno wledge about the constr uction process in or der to un-derstand the bids—as w ell as the ability to negotiate effectiv ely in or der to obtain the fair est level of bids. O nce the bidding pr ocess is complete, financing for the project needs to be put in place. (Financing is discussed in more detail in Chapter 9.) F inally, the constr uction pr ocess must be managed fr om planning thr ough pr oduction in or der to bring the r eal estate development online and available for market use.

Adding Value and Taking Risks

In the world of REITs, there is an ongoing debate o ver development ac-tivity and whether it adds v alue for the REIT shar eholder. For the most part, REIT management attempts to cr eate value through management activity at the property level, but can it create value at the development level? In a stable real estate market environment, there are very few ways to create additional value. Value creation lies in the skill set of management personnel and their ability to properly develop or redevelop new product. It all comes down to a risk profile. Lower-risk development activities include building to suit and development projects with a high level of preleasing activity. Also, there is less risk in short-cycle building activities such as industrial warehouses, which by their nature can be designed and developed very quickly. This allows the developer to end development activity at the first signs of market weakness. Speculative construction is the highest-risk development activity. However, risk assessment really needs to be done on a project-by-project basis.

Each sector of the real estate market generally has specific problems with regard to development risk. Offices that may be built on spec are definitely impacted by changes in the economic outlook and also have a higher level of risk because of the long development time frame. Retail malls have many of the same problems as office space. There is a long timeframe with regard to development and construction, and inline retail tenants typically will not sign a lease until the project is within six months of opening. Industrial REITs suffer from low barriers to entry. Generally, industrial buildings are simple to build and therefore are characterized by higher levels of speculative activity. Apartments, because of the short duration of the tenants' leases, typically two years or less, have the opportunity to quickly capture tenants from other projects. Unfortunately, new apartment supply tends to be felt across the local apartment market very quickly. And if apartments spread the pain quickly, hotels spread the pain instantaneously. New hotels have a very fast impact on other hotel properties in the local market. Self-storage has a short building period; however, there is a long lease-up that has the effect of leaving the developer exposed to any potential economic downturn over a fairly long period. Manufactured home communities also suffer from a long initial lease-up period. But, unlike self-storage, manufactured home communities are generally in more limited supply, and the political implications of "not in my backyard" also make entitlement increasingly difficult for manufactured housing communities.

Assessing Development Activity

When it comes to REITs, the best way to assess development activity is as follows:

- Study the history of development activity as a firm and how it integrates into the REIT's overall business strategy.
- Study the level of development activity as it relates to the size of the REIT
- Conduct sensitivity analysis to examine the outcome or exposure created by development activity.
- Assess the risk exposure for the REIT on a project-by-project basis. The risk assessment should extend to the property category, the supply and demand for that property in the local market, the pre leasing activity of the REIT, the expected cycle time for the development, and the pro forma return expectations on the project. (These issues are discussed in more detail in Chapter 9.)

REIT Idea: Merchant Builders

Recently, some development-oriented REITs have become *merchant builders*. Merchant builders develop properties and then sell them immediately on completion in order to make a profit. Merchant building can be viewed as a way for REITs to enhance their earnings while continuously recycling capital on the balance sheet. Merchant building activity will have a positive impact on a REIT's funds from operation. Nevertheless, a high level of merchant building activity makes it difficult to assess the ongoing performance of the REIT's underlying real estate portfolio. It can be argued that there is an intrinsic value through the merchant development activities, although it is hard to assess the level of value this might add to a REIT's market valuation. Merchant building activities add risk but also add return, and the question remains whether the return is sufficient to justify the risk.

Conclusion

Development activity takes a high level of skill and also requires financial resources. In many instances, developers may have the skills but lack the required financing to put a pr oject in place. J oining together a skill set and capital can be vie wed as the quintessential element necessar y to formulate a real estate development deal. In Chapter 8, we discuss the many potential deal structures available in the real estate world.

Points to Remember

- Real estate development is the riskiest area in real estate.
- The high risk lev el is r ewarded with high potential r eturns on successful development activities.
- Development activity is a central par t of the business strategy for some real estate investment trusts (REITs).
- Understanding the dev elopment pr ocess is critical to analyzing local real estate markets.
- Because of long lead times, pr oject timing is critical in r eal estate development.
- Managing the entitlement pr ocess is cr ucial to the ultimate success of a development.
- The design and constr uction process requires a high lev el of risk management skill.
- Successful dev elopment activity can add v alue and earnings for REIT shareholders.

Chapter 8

Partnerships and Joint Ventures

Mr. Morgan buys his partners; I grow my own.
— Andrew Carnegie, 1906

In Chapters 6 and 7 we discussed the real estate community's methods of analyzing local markets and creating new product—that is, new real estate—in those markets. We learned that a high level of local market knowledge is required when estimating the supply and demand dynamics of a given property type in a local market. We also learned that development activity requires a high level of skill on the part of the local real estate developer. Indeed, the amount of skill and effort necessary to participate successfully in the real estate marketplace inhibits many investors from directly owning, operating, and developing real estate.

The good news is that there are other ways for large institutional investors to participate in the real estate investment process. These are more passive approaches that allow institutions that do not have the skill set to place capital directly in the real estate sector. The heart of this passive approach involves the concept of joining together the skill set and knowledge of the local market experts with the capital resources of major institutions to formulate a joint venture in real estate.

How Joint Ventures and Partnerships Operate

Joint ventures (JVs) or par tnerships in the r eal estate world ar e the pre-ferred methods for marr ying financial capital and r eal estate exper tise. There is a spectr um of r eal estate oppor tunities available for inv estment purposes designed specifically to cr eate capital and efficiently allocate that capital thr ough joint v entures and par tnerships. These v entures range from direct investment partnerships formed betw een institutional capital sour ces and r eal estate exper ts all the way to syndications and pooled funds with a number of investors participating in a group format. Whatever the legal format—whether it be a par tnership, a limited liabil-ity corporation, a joint v enture or a syndication of some type, either public or priv ate—the basic theor y is always the same. Essentially the project identifies the expertise of a real estate investor that possesses mar-ket kno wledge and experience and aligns that exper tise with a pool of capital in the form of equity, and possibly debt, to cr eate a common real estate venture. The venture invests the resources in a variety of properties or developments that ar e initially agr eed on in a statement of intent or general purpose for the par tnership or joint v enture. The second half of the equation, which is often subject to a higher lev el of negotiation and analysis, determines who will get paid as a r esult of the financial opera-tion of the partnership—more importantly it determines how much each participant will get paid and when those payments will occur.

The basic pr ovisions of the agr eement outline the r esponsibilities and expectations of the parties involved. The agreement defines the con-cept of project cash flow, which is defined and analyzed. The notion of a preferred rate of r eturn is detailed. D ebt structure and the limitations of the use of debt are outlined. The potential tax benefits and their distribu-tion are also agreed on. In addition, the term of the agreement is memo-rialized and the pr ovisions for termination of the v enture activity ar e outlined. F inally, a discussion of fees, acceptable expenses, and thir d-party management arrangements is detailed, agr eed on, and disclosed in the basic partnership or joint venture document.

Cash flow is at the heart of any real estate deal. The real estate part-ner in a given deal often has limited personal and financial exposur e in a project. Therefore, it is impor tant for all par ties to understand the deal structure and to create a str ucture that aligns the inter ests of the v arious parties to the transaction. Aligning inter ests allows everybody within the investment to have the same motivation and to be in general agreement as to the direction of a given project.

Cash flow is normally defined as revenues on the project less expenses of the project, which yields net operating income. By adding back depreciation and amortization expenses, it is possible to arrive at cash flow. Cash flow is the actual net cash generated from the real estate activities. In a normal joint venture structure, the financial participants receive an annual cash preference with regard to the cash flow. A financial participant that commits $1 million of capital to the project may be entitled to a preferential return of 10 percent per year on its invested capital; thus the first $100,000 of cash flow would be paid to the financial partner to satisfy the preferential return requirements.

After the preferential rate of return has been met, the remaining cash flow is divided on a formula basis between the financial investor and the real estate partner. This excess distribution structure might have several different levels to provide for a higher percentage participation in the cash flow as the financial investors receive a higher net return on their investment. In many partnership structures, after a preferential return of 20 percent has been achieved, the balance of the cash flow might possibly inure to the real estate partner. This cash flow arrangement typically remains in place until such time as the original financial investors have fully recovered their initial investment through cash flow. At that time, the cash flow sharing arrangement might shift to a structure such as 50/50 or may allow for a preferential return to flow to the real estate partner.

Again, it is important to note that deals are often negotiated on an individual basis, and there is no standard format for structuring who gets paid how much and when. These elements are generally reflective of the level of risk and the profile of the particular deal at hand. Beyond allocating current cash flow, the partnership agreement must also determine how the final profits of the project are ultimately divided. In most instances, these backend-sharing arrangements reflect the percentage of capital each partner has committed to the deal. If the financial partner has committed 90 percent of the net capital and the real estate partner has committed 10 percent, then typically the profits on the project are divided similarly, with 90 percent going to the financial partner and 10 percent going to the real estate partner. It should be noted that in most instances the real estate partner receives no final distributions until all the initial capital of the financial partners has been recovered in total. This creates an incentive for the real estate partner to provide for a high preferential rate of r eturn for the financial par tners as w ell as pr oviding for the complete r eturn of the financial par tner's capital. This type of structure aligns the financial inter ests of all par ticipants inv olved in the project.

Most deals use some form of debt in addition to the equity pr o-vided by the financial partners to fund the total capital amount r equired to complete the r eal estate deal. D ebt str ucture is often defined at the initial phases of the deal, and the ability of the r eal estate operating part-ner to change the debt lev el or modify the debt terms of the par tnership is often subject to the approval of the financial partner. Debt structure is an important aspect of the o verall agreement. A higher lev el of debt can provide for higher potential total r eturns; ho wever, higher debt also creates a higher risk lev el for the pr oject. M ore conser vative financial partners may require lower leverage debt structures. Lower debt levels are normally reflected in the hurdle rates and annual cash preferences for the financial partners.

Tax benefits ar e also identified and distributed in most joint v en-ture situations. As discussed earlier, a major par t of the str uctural prob-lems within the real estate community in the 1970s and 1980s r esulted from a tax policy that cr eated an ex cess supply of r eal estate. The Tax Reform A ct of 1986 lengthened depr eciation schedules and incr eased the useful life o ver which pr operties could be depr eciated. It prevented investors fr om deducting r eal estate losses against non-r eal estate in-come. These changes substantially decr eased many of the fav orable tax aspects of inv esting in r eal estate. H owever, ther e ar e still tax-r elated issues surr ounding joint v entures and tax benefits av ailable to cer tain participants.

In the case of tax-ex empt inv estors such as the E mployee R etire-ment Income Security Act of 1974 (ERISA) plans, the tax benefits hav e little value. It is not unusual to see the tax benefits, if any, being delivered to the real estate operating partners in exchange for higher cash flow ben-efits being deliv ered to the tax-ex empt financial par tners. The implica-tions of the tax adjustments in the Tax R eform A ct of 1986 ar e quite substantial. P rior to 1986, typical commer cial inv estment pr operties would be depr eciated o ver a 15-y ear useful life. U nder the Tax Reform Act and subsequent r evisions in 1993, a 39-y ear useful life was enacted. This change in depreciation made a substantial difference in the noncash portion of the depr eciation expense, effectiv ely lo wering the net cash generating ability of most real estate properties.

Depreciation allowances defer taxation until the time the pr operty is sold. A t the time of sale, the gain is calculated using the depr eciated property value and the taxes are calculated using a capital gains rate that is curr ently 15 per cent rather than 25 per cent or 28 per cent in effect prior to the 1986 act. The tax disadvantage resulting from the change in depreciation can be partially mitigated by using higher leverage. If higher loan-to-value ratios ar e used, or higher lev erage is emplo yed, the added mortgage interest expense becomes deductible and the amount of equity capital required to finance the property decreases. This in effect creates a higher return on invested capital and a higher cash flo w return on capital. The relative advantage of higher leverage depends entirely on the cost and av ailability of mor tgage financing. I t should be noted that higher leverage may look attractiv e fr om a r eturn on capital standpoint when the property is operating in a positive mode, but leverage also magnifies the potential do wnside in a pr operty that is not operating w ell. Thus debt should be analyz ed not just on the upside but also on the downside when considering capital structure.

Termination of a Joint Venture or Partnership

Beyond operating provisions, the partnership or joint venture agreement must address termination pr ovisions. Termination provisions are usually created to facilitate the financial inv estor's r ecovery of capital within a certain time horizon. Because real estate is a long-term investment, most partnerships or joint ventures have relatively long time horizons. Because of its natur e, r eal estate is a long-term asset class. F or that r eason, r eal estate joint ventures tend to have a longer term. M ost develop-and-hold or buy-and-hold venture strategies have a minimum life span of 10 years. The idea of a pr edetermined time horiz on has a par ticular appeal for financial investors because it means that real estate partners cannot tie up capital and extract management fees o ver an indefinite period of time. The finite time horiz on also pr esents cer tain disadv antages, which ar e generally related to the cy clical nature of the r eal estate industr y. Financial par tners might find that r eal estate par tners are not inclined to dispose of r eal estate at any time prior to the termination period of the partnership. Thus, looking at a 10-y ear partnership, seven or eight y ears into the par tnership might be the ideal time to dispose of r eal estate held in the par tnership. However, the r eal estate par tner may not want to dispose of the pr operty at that point and lose two or thr ee y ears of partnership fees. Also, because it is impossible to pr edict where the r eal estate cycle will be at the end of a par tnership term, almost any r eason- ably long period of time might find a par tnership ending in an unfav or- able real estate market.

Because of this, it is not unusual for par tnership agr eements to have optional extension periods that can incr ease the life of the fund for one to thr ee years. These extension options ar e designed to pr ovide an additional holding period that allows real estate market fundamentals to recover. In most instances, these extension periods require the agreement of the financial partner in order to be implemented.

Conclusion

It is appar ent that no pr edetermined financial str ucture can r eadily be applied to par tnerships and joint v entures in the r eal estate ar ena. Each joint venture must take into consideration the properties for the develop- ment and the local market factors in determining the general structure of the partnership agreement. More conservative financial par tners such as pension plans tend to have more conservative deal structures that provide for lower leverage and more uniform pr edictable cash flow to the finan- cial partner. Conversely, opportunity funds that reflect a more aggressive pool of inv estors might pr efer higher lev els of debt and r equire a mor e aggressive initial sharing of cash flo w benefits. Again, each joint v enture deal is structured to reflect the general posture of all the deal participants. At the end of the pr ocess, the union of money and exper tise should en- able the par ticipants to negotiate an agr eement that substantially aligns the interests of all parties involved.

REITs and Joint Ventures

Joint ventures allow real estate investment trusts (REITs) to expand their business model and emplo y their substantial r eal estate exper tise while preserving the flexibility of capital on the balance sheet. A REIT operates a *direct investment portfolio* (DIP) of real estate. By participating in joint ventures and partnerships, the REIT management team can incr ease the return on capital invested in the DIP.

In incr easing numbers, REITs ar e marr ying their br oad r eal estate expertise with ev er-larger pools of inv estment capital. P artnerships and joint ventures allow REIT management teams to extend the use of balance sheet capital, incr ease potential r eturns to inv estors, and cr eate a greater lev el of div ersification, ther eby r educing risk in the DIP . R eal estate markets have unique institutional characteristics that differ entiate them fr om non-r eal estate mar kets and accor dingly ar e expected to produce results that div erge from results obser ved in the non-r eal estate sector. These characteristics include local mar ket knowledge and mar ket segmentation, development knowledge that may give real estate firms an information adv antage r egarding local r eal estate mar kets, and better management and technical expertise regarding real estate ventures.

A number of academic studies hav e examined the effect of joint v enture programs and their impact on the shareholder value of REITs. In general, these studies r eport positiv e and statistically significant incr eases in shareholder value as a result of joint ventures in the real estate community. The r esearch concludes that ther e ar e sev eral factors that make the r eal estate joint v enture successful. The first is the synergies that r esult fr om combining the resources of two or more enterprises. Under the assumption that the capital mar ket is efficient, r eal estate joint v entures are normally interpreted as positive by shareholders of the par ticipating firm because of their perceived financial synergies resulting from the joint venture. The operating synergies can be attributed to economies of scale, better competitive position in local mar kets, higher lev els of primar y research, and more efficient use of managerial and human r esources as w ell as r eduction of business risk thr ough div ersification. In addition, the ability of the joint venture to increase the overall debt capacity of the participants is perceived as a financial synergy that is positive for the shareholder.

The other unique institutional characteristics that can be attributed to the joint v enture in the r eal estate mar ket ar e the characteristics of market locality and market segmentation. In the local real estate market, the lack of standard real estate product and the absence of a central market exchange r equire a higher lev el of r esearch kno wledge for nonlocal firms competing in a local r eal estate market. In local markets where information can be difficult and costly to obtain and may not be av ailable to all participants, real estate firms are likely to be more familiar with the market and hav e an informal adv antage. The theor y is the higher v alue attributed to joint v entures reflects the comparativ e information adv antage that local real estate firms have within the local marketplace.

Taking the kno wledge adv antage a step fur ther, it seems logical that different market segments require different skill sets and managerial talent that may not be easily transferable. A high lev el of management skill can help to reduce the uncertainty associated with business risks that result from operation of r eal estate pr operties. That knowledge can also be efficiently leveraged over a larger DIP, which can be produced through the joint v enture str ucture. Therefore it is not unr easonable to expect that the real estate joint venture, when properly structured, can produce a comparative local market advantage for the participants of the venture.

REIT Idea: Where REITs Add Value in Joint Ventures

The following list details the areas where a REIT's local market knowledge and management expertise can add value in a joint venture program:

- *Acquisitions.* Area local market knowledge and a long-term market strategy helps the local real estate partner complete due diligence and acquisition negotiations at a lower cost than a nonlocal competitor.

- *Local market strategy.* The local market partner can better define local market niches, thereby understanding local market opportunities at a higher level than the nonlocal participant.

- *Adjustment in strategy.* The local market participant is more sensitive to changing local market conditions and can react quickly to changes in the local market dynamic.

- *Primary research.* The local market participant has a better institutional knowledge of the local market history, which translates into better and lower-cost direct research in the local market.

- *Dispositions.* The local market participant has an advantage in completing negotiated transactions with other local market participants as a result of superior local market knowledge.

Through local market knowledge and management expertise, REITs have historically availed themselves of the opportunity to participate in joint ventures with capital partners in order to add shareholder value and extend balance sheet leverage and portfolio diversification for shareholders.

Points to Remember

- The high level of skill required to participate successfully in the real estate market inhibits many financial investors from directly owning or developing property.
- In the real estate world, joint ventures are the preferred methods for marrying financial capital and real estate expertise.
- The terms and conditions of joint ventures are detailed in joint venture agreements.
- The basic provisions of joint venture agreements outline the responsibilities and expectations of the parties involved.
- The agreements address the treatment of cash flow, debt structure, operating objectives, lifetime of the venture, and distribution of profits.
- Joint ventures allow real estate investment trusts (REITs) to expand their business model while preserving the flexibility of their balance sheet.
- Academic studies report positive and statistically significant increases in shareholder value as a result of joint ventures in the real estate community.
- Joint ventures are interpreted as positive by shareholders of the participating firm because of their perceived resulting financial, management, and information synergies.
- Because of their market knowledge, REITs are in a unique position to participate in joint venture activities.

Chapter

9

Analyzing REITs

The only dependable foundation of personal liberty is the economic security of private property.

—Walter Lippmann, 1934

The valuation methodologies applied to publicly traded r eal estate investment trusts (REITs) are roughly comparable to those used in the priv ate r eal estate mar kets. There ar e a number of public-market-based valuation approaches that can also be applied to the financial analysis of REITs. These approaches are all loosely categorized into a group of valuation methodologies that can be called *quantitative analysis*. Like the direct valuation approaches used in private real estate, the quantitative appr oaches used in public r eal estate each hav e cer tain positive and negativ e attributes. J ust as in priv ate v aluation methodologies, a conclusion of v alue is mor e accurate when it is consider ed in light of multiple valuation approaches rather than a single evaluation method. In addition to quantitative methods, there are a range of qualitativ e factors that must be considered when valuing public real estate. These quantitative and qualitative approaches are examined in the following sections.

Basic Methodologies

The dir ect r eal estate inv estment mar ket has thr ee basic methodologies for arriving at the value of a given piece of real estate. First is the *replacement cost* method. This form of v aluation contemplates what it would cost in the current market environment to replicate a building of similar size and quality in a similar location. This analysis includes the value of the land on which the building sits, along with site improvements and general neighborhood amenities. It is relatively simple to discover the general replacement cost of a building; however, because each property is so unique, there is no exact substitute for any given property per se. This makes replacement cost a useful tool for obtaining broad generalizations about a property's value, but further analysis is normally required to make a definite conclusion about value.

The second approach to real estate valuation is the *market comparable* approach. This method attempts to estimate a property's current market value by analyzing recent sales of similar properties in the general area of the property being valued. Again, because each property is unique, it is difficult to draw a definite conclusion about market value using the comparable approach alone. The data on reported sales is based on recent historical sales activity and thus may not reflect recent changes in the local real estate market. Although a price agreed on by a buyer and seller in an arm's-length transaction is typically the best indicator of value, other issues come into play. Is the seller under some financial or personal pressure to sell a property? Is the buyer willing to pay a premium because of specific aspects of the property that may be of use only to that buyer? These transaction-related dynamics are difficult to determine when studying comparable sales. The solution is to study a range of recent transactions and draw conclusions from a larger sample of data. This is effective in a local market where there is a reasonable level of real estate activity. However, some markets produce a limited volume of comparable real estate transactions, which makes the comparable method less precise.

Finally, real estate value can be derived by the capitalization of net income approach. This *capitalization rate* or *cap rate* approach considers the net income after expenses of a property as a current return required or generated on the price of the property. For example, a property with net operating income (NOI) of $120,000 and an asking price of $1.0 million would have a cap rate of 12 percent ($120,000/$1.0 million = 12 percent). The cap rate approach generally allows for an independent estimate of value that is somewhat more precise than either the replacement cost or market comparable approaches. The cap rate of any property that trades hands as an investment vehicle reflects the competitive real estate investment alternatives in a given local market, giving the appraiser a larger pool of candidates to examine when making a comparable cap rate analysis. I n addition, slight adjustments in cap rate allow for a more precise valuation when considering the merits or flaws of a particular property.

> **capitalization rate or cap rate** for a property is calculated by dividing the property's net operating income after property level expenses by its purchase price. Generally, high cap rates indicate higher returns and possible greater risk.

In a local mar ket it might be simple to conclude fr om the av ailable data that community shopping centers trade in a cap range of 10 to 12 percent. The newer, bigger, better located pr operties ar e in the 10 to 11 per cent range, and the older, smaller, less fav orably located pr operties are in the 11 to 12 per cent range. This allows the appraiser to apply a mor e precise cap rate once it is determined where the subject property falls on the quality spectrum.

Each of the standard appraisal methodologies has its advantages and drawbacks. Therefore, in normal v aluation analysis, the subject pr operty is examined using each methodology . M ore or less consideration is ascribed to each appr oach based on the r elevant facts and cir cumstances about the property. At the end of the pr ocess, a synthesis of all the methods rather than one single approach usually determines a value. The valuation methodology is as much an art as a science, and most appraisers say that the actual mar ket sale price may be higher or lo wer based on many subjective factors that are difficult, if not impossible, to quantify.

REIT Idea: Approaches to Valuing Real Estate

There are three commonly used approaches to valuing real estate:

1. Replacement cost approach
2. Comparable sales approach
3. Capitalization rate (cap rate) approach

None of these always yields a perfect answer, but when taken together they normally provide a good indication of real estate value.

Net Asset Value Analysis

Net asset value (NAV) analysis is the public r eal estate version of the replacement cost approach. There are two schools of thought among REIT analysts: those who believe that this approach provides the least accurate measure of the value of an equity REIT and those who believe this is primarily the best method for v aluing REITs. At its essence, the NA V approach inv olves estimating whether a stock trades at a discount or premium in comparison to an estimate of the private market value of the company's real estate assets.

The first step in estimating the NAV of a REIT requires capitalizing the NOI of the pr operties. This can be done either befor e or after making a r eserve for expected capital expenditur es. The key to this process is estimating NOI, because many REITs own interests in dozens of pr operties located in many differ ent local mar kets. Although local market conditions may v ary widely, REITs often do not disclose the NOI for each building, and ther efore an overall capitalization rate must be applied to the entire real estate portfolio of the REIT.

The cap rate selected considers a component for expected r eal return, an inflation premium, a risk premium, and an amount to compensate for the expected decline in pr operty value due to depr eciation or obsolescence, often called the *recapture value.* There is the potential for a large error factor that may r esult from estimating a por tfolio-wide capitalization rate. A significant differ ence can result depending on whether the analysis is made using curr ent or estimated forward NOI. Generally, using a blend of past and futur e estimated NOI helps to moderate the error of an estimate.

To capitalize a future income stream to estimate the total private market value of a company, the next step is to deduct the debt associated with the estimated NAV and adjust the number of shares outstanding if any equity issuance is assumed as par t of the analysis. G enerally, NOI earnings models assume that futur e acquisitions and dev elopment costs are funded by debt, and pr ojected av erage futur e liabilities (as opposed to curr ent liabilities) are deducted. One of the better factors of public real estate company analysis is that a relatively efficient private transaction market coexists for income-pr oducing, inv estment-grade pr operty. O ther priv ate companies may change o wnership on a r egular basis, but the selling prices ar e seldom known. Privately negotiated inv estment-grade commercial real estate transactions total an estimated $250 billion annually , and most ar e a matter of public r ecord. Thus a cap rate for an individual pr operty can be estimated with a relatively high degree of accuracy. A small error factor for a single asset, however, compounds when applied to an entire portfolio, so great care is required when making these estimates.

REITs often have other nonrent income that must be considered in the valuation of NOI. Most analysts apply a high capitalization rate that translates into a low value being placed on the net property management fees. This reflects the fact that management contracts can normally be canceled on shor t notice, usually 30 to 90 days. Thus a r elatively high cap rate of 20 to 30 percent is applied to this income to reflect the possible v ariability. Then adding to this total other REIT assets, normally cash and marketable securities, results in an estimate of total private market value of the entity. Then the total liabilities ar e deducted, including the aggregate debt, preferred stock, and pro rata share of any unconsolidated joint v entures. This r esults in an estimate of a REIT   's NA V. Finally, the results must be divided b y the total diluted shares or operating partnership units outstanding that would result from a conversion to common shares.

From an NAV perspective, the publicly traded REIT univ erse has been priced by the public markets at a discount of as much as 31 percent on NAV to a premium of 39 percent of NAV over the last 10 years based on estimates made b y Uniplan Real Estate A divsors. The average value over that time has been about 103 per cent of NAV or a 3 per cent premium to the NAV of the underlying portfolio.

The discount or premium to NAV is often partly accounted for by the fact that the equity market is forward looking and views REITs as ongoing business enterprises rather than dir ect portfolios of r eal estate assets. If REITs are struggling and earnings or rent growth look flat or even lower in the coming y ear, then the pr ospective valuation mechanism of the market might put a discount on the v alue of the underlying r eal estate held b y the REIT. Conv ersely, if r eal estate mar ket conditions ar e improving rapidly, that forward-looking market mechanism might put a premium value on the futur e value of a REIT's property holdings. This should be considered when evaluating the NAV of any REIT.

Drawbacks of NAV Analysis

The principal drawback of NAV analysis is that NAV calculation involves the analysis of the cash flo w at a given moment in time and applies it to a fixed collection of r eal estate assets. The approach can be v ery helpful in a situation where a REIT owns a few properties that account for a significant proportion of a por tfolio's overall value. However, in a v ery large por tfolio of proper ties, it is less useful due to the differing nature of the pr operties.

The other key w eakness of the NA V appr oach is its inability to accurately value a rapidly changing local mar ket or a quickly gr owing REIT. F or a fast-growing REIT, NOI may incr ease rapidly as the company acquir es or develops new properties, and the REIT shar es may appear very over- or undervalued depending on whether an analyst chooses to capitaliz e trailing or forecasted NOI. NA V analysis can also be criticiz ed as a successful standalone REIT stock selection mechanism because it fails to ackno wledge the different risk profiles of various REIT capital structures.

For instance, two companies with a $40 per shar e NAV might appear equally attractiv e fr om an NA V-only perspective. Unsecured debt, however, may comprise 10 per cent of one company's capital str ucture and 90 per cent of the other's, placing the latter in much gr eater risk category. In the latter example, the NA V could be significantly lower if ther e were to be a small change in the v alue of the underlying pr operty values. In the 10 percent case, a small change in the pr operty value would hav e a small impact on NA V due to the lower *leverage*. So NAV has its drawbacks and is only one in a number of was to evaluate REITs.

leverage

the amount of debt in relation to either equity capital or total capital.

Enterprise Value/EBITDA Multiple Analysis

Another method of v aluing a REIT that addr esses par t of the flaw in NAV analysis inv olves looking at cash flo w generated b y the REIT. In this approach, a measure of cash flow composed of earnings before interest, taxes, depreciation, and amor tization is used. The methodology involves dividing the *total market capitalization* of equity and the nominal value of company debt of the REIT b y the total *earnings before interest, taxes, depreciation, and amortization* (EBITDA) or cash flo w to the company. One advantage of this approach is that it normalizes the ratio acr oss most normal capital structures and may be used to compar e firms with differing amounts of balance sheet leverage. As was the case with the NA V calculations, the enterprise value/EBITDA multiple is normally calculated us-

total market cap

the total market value of a REIT's (or other company's) outstanding common stock and indebtedness.

ing an estimated for ward capital str ucture. The enterprise v alue/EBITDA ratio usually r eflects the
market's sentiment r egarding the expected near-
term and long-term gr owth rate of a sustainability
of gr owth and quality of cash flo w. The multiple
may also reflect the amount of anticipated or bud-
geted capital expenditur es and futur e obsolescence
of the property. Some analysts prefer to use EBITDA
less capital expenditur e reserve as a measur e of operating cash flow. The EBITDA approach is widely
used when looking at companies in general and is
not limited to real estate companies or REITs.

EBITDA
earnings before
interest, taxes,
depreciation, and
amortization. This
measure is some-
times referred to
as *operating
margin.*

Multiple-to-Growth Ratio Analysis

Multiple-to-growth ratio analysis helps to answ er
two REIT specific valuation issues: (1) How much
is the mar ket willing to pay for each unit of
growth? (2) Can v alue and gr owth be av ailable in
the same REIT? It is important to understand that
profitability and growth are not the same. G rowth
of earnings or *funds from operations* (FFO) growth
alone cannot provide a valid single measure for assessing investment value. However, some investors
implicitly assume that this is a valid single measure
when they apply the curr ent period's price/FFO
multiple to some terminal y ear's earning rate.
Growth only adds v alue to a REIT when the r e-
turn on inv estment ex ceeds the *cost of capital.*
However, some REITs may be focused on gr owing
the por tfolio simply to expand in siz e. That business strategy depends on a company's ability to sell
shares or raise additional capital at fr equent intervals at higher and higher prices. As the enterprise
continues to expand in size, the amount of acquisitions necessar y to sustain the per-shar e FFO
growth rate also expands in size and often becomes

**cost of
capital**
the cost to a com-
pany, such as a
REIT, of raising
capital in the form
of equity, pre-
ferred stock, or
debt. The cost of
equity capital
generally is con-
sidered to include
both the dividend
rate as well as the
expected capital
growth as mea-
sured either by
higher dividends
or potential appre-
ciation in the
stock price. The
cost of debt capi-
tal is the interest
expense on the
debt incurred plus
any fees incurred
to obtain the debt.

funds from operations (FFO)

the most commonly accepted and reported measure of REIT operating performance. Equal to a REIT's net income, excluding gains or losses from sales of property, and adding back real estate depreciation. It is an approximation of cash flow when compared to normal corporate accounting, which is a better measure of operating performance than GAAP earnings that might include (sometimes large) noncash items. The dilemma is that there is no industry standard method for calculating FFO, so it is difficult to use it as a comparison across all REITs.

unsustainable. Thus growth rate falls and with it the premium multiple that the stock may have commanded.

The opposite of an upward growth spiral is the collapsing death spiral. In a traditional growth industry, a company's P/E ratio is often compared with its long-term expected growth rate; firms with P/E ratios less than their growth rate are often considered to be undervalued. The multiple-to-growth ratio forms a relative perspective when used to rank a universe of REITs on the ratio of price/FFO multiple versus sustainable growth rate. The central problem confronting a REIT analyst is the sustainability of a high-growth period for a given REIT. Because REITs must distribute at least 90 per cent of their taxable income, in most instances there is only modest free cash flow and almost all acquisition and development growth must be financed from external sources. Typically, this has been accomplished through the repeated sale of primary shares along with the expansion of balance sheet leverage. Most REITs fund incremental acquisitions and developments via debt and then turn to the capital markets to deleverage with equity.

The sustainable, internally generated operating cash flow growth rate for most equity REITs is realistically 3 to 5 per cent, based on the constraints of the REIT structure. Adding an appropriate level of balance sheet leverage may increase cash flow growth to an average of 5 to 8 per cent. REIT FFO growth rates in excess of 10 per cent are thus not sustainable over an extended period without the use of higher than average leverage or repeated trips to the capital market for more equity capital. Some analysts actually place a multiple penalty on REITs with a growth rate that exceeds about 10 percent due to the financial risk of ongoing capital requirements.

REIT EPS

Operating *earnings per share* (EPS) has r elevance in the v aluation of REIT equity securities. It is incorrect to dismiss the EPS measure as simply not appropriate for real estate companies because accounting depr e-ciation overstates physical depreciation of the real property asset.

The EPS measur e is widely used acr oss many industries. Analysts covering other sectors often supplement EPS r esults with alternativ e valuation metrics. I n general it is impor tant not to o veremphasize the importance of, or place too much focus on, any one figure. Thus the very popular Wall S treet focus on EPS figur es, or any other single statistics, can be misleading. I n using the EPS figur e, an analyst should always be alert to the components of the net income figur e and how that figure is used for comparative purposes.

Using operating EPS as a measur e of REIT earnings po wer has drawbacks. Calculations for some companies involve predecessor entities with differ ent tax bases r equiring step-up depr eciation adjustments and adjustments for distributions to minority par tners in ex cess of net in-come that dramatically lo wer EPS. O ther companies make acquisitions for cash and have componentized depreciation, lowering reported net in-come and allowing the REIT to retain more capital to fund development activity. I n conclusion, despite v arious drawbacks, EPS can be a useful device in assessing the valuation of REIT securities but again only in the context of other comparative valuation methods.

Positive Earnings Revision Analysis

REIT v aluation b y positiv e earnings r evisions inv olves identifying and valuing REIT shares based on owning companies where Wall Street earnings estimates ar e being r evised up ward. The basic application of this method involves choosing stocks with earnings r evisions that ar e rising, thus creating unexpected positiv e earnings. Another form inv olves buying stocks in companies whose sequential earnings growth rates are accelerating. This is often kno wn as an *earnings momentum* strategy. These two approaches are less classic real estate valuation approaches and more Wall S treet-based valuation appr oaches. The idea is that public mar ket investors are more willing to pay a premium on any company when it delivers sequential earnings gr owth at a lev el higher than expected b y the consensus of analysts co vering a stock. This approach is most useful in the real estate sector to detect or confirm the beginnings of a r eal estate market recovery within the local markets where a REIT owns property.

Return on Capital versus Cost of Capital Analysis

The earnings life cy cle for a REIT that continually issues ne w common equity is inextricably linked to its price/FFO multiple. F rom 1998 through 2004, average REIT price/FFO multiples ranged between 7 and 15.5 times forward four-quarter FFO, reflecting a nominal cost of 14.3 to 6.45 per cent for raising ne w common equity, before factoring in the cost of underwriting. On a purely mathematical basis, a REIT that sells new shares at such multiples and invests the proceeds in properties with initial capitalization rates that equal or exceed the nominal cost of capital will have completed a transaction that is additiv e to earnings. The more equity issued and the mor e properties acquired, the higher the y ear-by-year FFO growth, provided that increasingly large amounts of stock can be sold at equal or higher multiples. A company that buys a business trading at a lo wer multiple than the buying company itself will b y definition enhance its EPS gr owth rate. After the pur chase, the low cash flow multiple attributable to the operations of the acquir ed company is often revalued at or close to the original firm 's higher multiple. This is the accounting definition of accretion.

Although such a transaction may be additiv e to earnings fr om an accounting perspectiv e, it may be dilutiv e to tr ue shar eholder v alue in the economic sense. A r eview of a v ariety of v aluation parameters is needed when analyzing r eal estate stocks. S uch items include pr operty type and geographic portfolio characteristics; growth rates in net income, FFO, *funds available for distribution* (FAD) and dividends; earnings momentum; relative price multiples for an individual company v ersus peer companies and sector av erages; curr ent and anticipated dividend yield and dividend safety; lev erage; trading v olume; and management track record and capability.

Measures of corporate per formance based on r eturn on capital ar e often cited as means of distinguishing among REIT s. When ev aluating

REIT performance, it is important to include return on capital and cost of capital analysis. The specific value of comparing *weighted average cost of capital* (WACC) with *cash yield on cost* (CYC) for a real estate company is that it r elates a firm's capital str ucture decisions to its operating business r esults as measur ed b y tr ue economic (as distinguished fr om accounting) profitability.

Cash Yield on Cost

A company's CYC is equal to NOI fr om the pr operty por tfolio (essentially operating pr operty r evenues less operating pr operty expenses) divided b y gr oss (undepr eciated) inv estment in r eal estate. This is a measure of a company's unit pr ofitability as distinguished fr om its sales growth. Simply put, it is a measur e of r eturn on assets or r eturn on invested capital.

Weighted Average Cost of Capital (WACC)

The WACC is the weighted average of the costs of a REIT's debt and equity. The WACC represents the rate at which pr ojected cash flo ws may be discounted to determine net present value (NPV). If the present value of the expected futur e cash flo ws, using WACC as the discount rate, is positive, then a potential investment should be pursued. S imilarly, if the NPV of an inv estment is negativ e, then the inv estment should be r ejected. I n other wor ds, a positiv e NPV is equiv alent to a pr oject's total return on internal rate of return exceeding WACC. Alternatively, WACC may be considered a hurdle rate for ev aluating the minimum acceptable rate of r eturn for a potential inv estment. From an equity inv estor's perspective, companies that consistently pursue business oppor tunities with positive NPVs incr ease firm v alue b y boosting the gr owth rate and, hence, share value. Investors will buy REITs with positive and rising investment spreads between CYC and WACC. All REIT acquisitions may not be immediately accr etive to shar eholder v alue (ex ceed a company's WACC). H owever, a pr operty investment should be able to generate a sustainable cash yield abo ve the REIT's WACC within some r easonable time period, perhaps 24 to 36 months. This demonstrates the v alueadded ability of a REIT management team to deploy capital at a positive to the firm's cost of capital.

Positive Spread Investing (PSI)

What is the value of comparing WACC with CYC? First, until recently, REITs rarely sold properties. Although capital appreciation in assets may occur, it is often not realized, and therefore the focus is on current and future cash flow from real estate investments. Second, a REIT that operates with low leverage will have a higher WACC and thereby implicitly raise the hurdle rate it must achieve on new real estate investments. There are many potential attributes of a successful REIT investment, some of which we have just discussed. Nevertheless, because of the importance of income generation in a REIT's total return, comparing CYC to WACC is a useful method of evaluating potential or existing REIT investments.

positive spread investing (PSI)
the ability to raise funds (both equity and debt) at a cost significantly less than the initial returns that can be obtained on real estate transactions.

Some REITs derive significant value from potential capital appreciation on assets. In such cases, the usefulness of the investment spread methodology may be limited. In these instances, this analytical tool should be used in conjunction with other, more traditional measures of equity valuation such as operating cash flow growth, relative earnings multiples, and *net asset value* (NAV) analysis.

net asset value (NAV)
the net market value of all a company's assets, including but not limited to its properties, after subtracting all its liabilities and obligations.

Drawbacks of the Methodology

As in all the other evaluation methods, there are several potential drawbacks to this methodology.

First, current-period cash yields may not remain at the same starting value—they may go up or down over time; sustainability or growth in NOI is key to this method of analysis. The individual company cost of capital reflects a dynamic process that incorporates growth in revenues and expenses from existing properties, acquisitions, development of new buildings, and management expertise. Second, the length of time between the original investment and the current period may have an impact on the reported CYC. This is particularly true in the case of *umbrella partnership REITs* (UPREITs), where the original investment may have taken place years previously. In fact, research has shown that the CYC-less-WACC investment spread is larger in the case of

UPREITs than for traditional REIT s or r eal estate operating companies. The differ ence is almost entirely a function of UPREIT s having gr eater lever age, and thus a lo wer WACC, because the CY C is similar for UPREIT s and non-UPREIT s. Third, fast-growing REITs that may hav e low leverage today and have a negative or marginally positive spread between WACC and CY C may add debt in the future, lowering their WACC, and may boost NOI over time, eventually reversing the investment spread.

A REIT's development activity can also hav e an impact on this analysis. D epending on a firm's capitalization policy for ne w constr uction, some heavily dev elopment-oriented REIT s may hav e below-average current cash yields on invested assets. However, giv en that pr operty dev elopment generally entails gr eater risk than acquisitions, inv estors should expect such dev eloper REIT s to obtain above-average return on assets within some r easonable period following completion of a project.

Thus, just as in the private market, there is no single method in the public mar ket that can be used as a stand-alone v aluation tool. Rather, REIT values should be considered in light of all the various methods to determine a range of possible outcomes when valuing public REIT shares.

REIT Idea: Approaches to Valuing Publicly Traded REITs

There are three common approaches to valuing publicly traded REITs:

1. Net asset value (NAV) analysis
2. Enterprise value/EBITDA multiple analysis
3. Multiple-to-growth ratio analysis

Just as in real estate appraisal, none of these methods yields a perfect answer. When taken together, however, they normally provide a good indication of REIT value.

---

umbrella partnership REIT (UPREIT)

a complex but useful real estate structure in which the partners of an existing partnership and a newly formed REIT become partners in a new partnership termed the *operating partnership.* For their respective interests in the operating partnership, the partners contribute the properties (or units) from the existing partnership and the REIT contributes the cash proceeds from its public offering. The REIT typically is the general partner and the majority owner of the operating partnership units. After a period of time (often one year), the partners may enjoy the same liquidity of the REIT shareholders by tendering their units for either cash or REIT shares (at the option of the REIT or operating partnership). This conversion may result in the partners incurring the tax deferred at the UPREIT's

(continued)

formation. The unit holders may tender their units over a period of time, thereby spreading out such tax. In addition, when a partner holds the units until death, the estate tax rules operate in such a way as to provide that the beneficiaries may tender the units for cash or REIT shares without paying income taxes.

Points to Remember

• Analyzing and v aluing a REIT is a blend of conventional real estate valuation and securities analysis.

• Conventional r eal estate v aluation considers r e-placement cost, local market comparable sales, and capitalization of net income as the primar y valuations methods.

• Valuing a REIT applies similar v aluation methods to the underlying portfolio of properties owned by the REIT along with public mar ket approaches to REIT valuation.

• The calculation of a net asset v alue for a REIT portfolio is similar to the replacement cost and capitalization methods in private real estate.

• REIT valuation that uses a multiple of EBITDA helps compar e value across differing REIT capital structures.

• More conventional stock market-type valuation approaches apply multiple-to-earnings gr owth analysis, r eturn on capital, and weighted cash yield methods to estimate REIT valuations.

• No single v aluation method is the definitiv e answer, but all ar e very useful when applied in combination to estimate a range of value.

• Looking at the r elative public valuations of other REITs is also a method for estimating a REIT's current value.

• The qualitativ e value added b y the REIT management team is also an important factor to consider when estimating REIT valuations.

• Ultimately REIT valuation, like private real estate appraisal, is as much an ar t as a science and r equires a thor ough understanding of all valuation methodologies.

Chapter

Advanced Financial REIT Topics

Figures don't lie, but liars do figure.
                    —Old accounting saying

I f an inv estor is going to analyz e and select their o wn REIT inv estments, then ther e ar e a number of adv anced accounting issues that
should be understood with r egard to r eal estate inv estment tr usts.
This chapter covers these technical issues. F or readers who are not going
to do their own REIT analysis, this chapter can be skipped.

REIT Accounting Issues

The steady and pr edictable earnings and consistent dividends generated
by REITs have created a high level of interest. However, investors not familiar with the REIT sector may find it confusing to compar e earnings
because many REITs report quarterly results using *funds from operations*
(or FFO—defined in Chapter 9), as opposed to *earnings per share* (EPS),
which is the typical measur e of pr ofitability used in almost all other industries. R ecently, sev eral Wall S treet br okerage firms hav e announced
that they create EPS estimates for REITs rather than FFO estimates. This
move has touched off a debate over the best way to measure the earnings
capacity and financial performance of REITs.

Currently most REITs report quarterly results using FFO numbers.
Calculating FFO begins with earnings calculated in accor   dance with

generally accepted accounting principles (GAAP), also kno wn as *GAAP earnings.* These earnings ar e then adjusted to ex clude gains or losses resulting from the sale of por tfolio properties or fr om debt or financing activities. Then depreciation and amortization charges are added back to the resulting number to come up with FFO. FFO actually r eflects oper- ating cash flo w generated as a r esult of por tfolio activities of a REIT. In one sense, FFO r eflects the cash-generating ability of a REIT por tfolio; in another sense, it can o verstate the economic per formance of most REITs. Because FFO does not r eflect recurring capital expense items— and because it allo ws the adding back of a wide range of expense items that management might deem to be nonr ecurring—it often o verstates for practical r easons the cash-generating ability of a r eal estate por tfolio. Observers of and participants in the REIT industry have been engaged in a long debate over the correct metrics and methodologies that should be used to value REIT earnings.

In 1995 and 1999, the N ational Association of R eal Estate I nvest- ment Trusts (NAREIT) published a white paper commenting on poten- tial changes to the definition of FFO. I n general, the industr y's trade association seeks to mo ve FFO into a mor e str uctured form that would more closely resemble GAAP net income. O riginally created in the early 1990s, FFO was intended to be a supplemental per formance-measuring device av ailable to the management of REIT   s. I t was pr omoted b y NAREIT to help inv estors better understand and measur e the per for- mance of REIT earnings.

NAREIT has r ecommended that the industr y adopt standar d ac- counting practices with regard to a number of br oad areas. The first area of recommended change is nonr ecurring items. NAREIT suggests end- ing the practice of allo wing REIT management to add back a v ariety of one-time expenses as an adjustment to the calculation of FFO. H istori- cally, REIT management has been able to add back any items deemed nonrecurring. As would be expected, some REIT management teams are far more aggressive than others about adjusting for nonr ecurring items. Studying r eal estate financial statements, it can be noted that a br   oad range of items are often added back as nonrecurring expenses. These typ- ically include losses on interest rate hedging transactions, costs related to failed acquisitions, emplo yee sev erance packages, and adv ertising and public relations costs r elated to building brand identities. U nder GAAP, most of these items would not be consider ed nonrecurring or extraordi- nary. I n addition, some REIT management teams r outinely add these items back as nonr ecurring, wher eas other management teams r eflect them as ongoing business expenses. This adds to the confusion when attempting to compare FFO across a universe of REITs. The second broad area that NAREIT has targeted for modification is gains and losses fr om property sales and debt r estructurings. While gains and losses as w ell as debt r estructuring expenses ar e included in net income under GAAP , gains on sale are often included in FFO by aggressive REIT management teams. To the extent that gains on sale are not related to merchant building activities or build-to-suit transactions, it could be argued that they are not usual and customar y in the context of dir ect real estate por tfolio operations and therefore should be excluded. In 1999, some industry observers suggested the inclusion of gains and losses on property sales in the new FFO calculation. It is safe to say that gains and losses from property sales are a part of GAAP net income and ar e an issue in industries other than real estate. C ritics of the practice suggest that including gains and losses on property sales will allow REITs to manipulate FFO by manipulating the timing on pr operty sales. B ecause many REIT por tfolios contain a large number of easily salable pr operties, the criticism is that REIT s may engage in such sales in order to enhance FFO.

In an attempt to calculate the actual financial performance of REITs, several other common measures of operating earnings hav e been pr omulgated in addition to FFO. *Adjusted funds from operations* (AFFO) is calculated b y beginning with FFO and making an adjustment for the *straight-lining* of rents. AFFO typically reflects a reserve expense that accounts for costs that may not necessarily be recurring or routine but that are typically not recoverable directly fr om tenants. I n most instances, this includes nonrecurring maintenance costs and costs related to leasing activities. When adjusted for these expenses, the r esulting figure is AFFO, at times r eferred to as *cash available for distribution* (CAD). This is the actual cash flow created by a REIT.

It should be noted that in any activity that adjusts REIT earnings, gains cr eated b y the sale of portfolio properties are typically not added back to reflect operating cash flo ws. This is because gains

> **adjusted funds from operations (AFFO)**
>
> a computation made to measure a real estate company's cash flow generated by its real estate operations. AFFO is usually calculated by subtracting from FFO normal recurring expenditures that are then capitalized by the REIT and amortized, and an adjustment for the "straight-lining" of rents. This calculation is also called *cash available for distribution* (CAD) or *funds available for distribution* (FAD).

straight-lining

real estate companies such as REITs straight line rents because generally accepted accounting principles (GAAP) require it. Straight-lining averages the tenant's rent payments over the life of the lease.

cash available for distribution (CAD)

or *funds available for distribution* (FAD), a REIT's ability to generate cash that can be distributed as dividends to its shareholders. In addition to subtracting from FFO normalized recurring real estate-related expenditures and other noncash items to obtain AFFO, CAD (or FAD) is usually derived by also subtracting non-recurring expenses.

on property sales are not generally consider ed recurring cash flo ws. G ains and losses on debt r estructuring, ho wever, are generally added back to calculate FFO or funds av ailable for distribution. Debt r estructurings are extraor dinary events, and, to the extent they ar e not r egular activities, ther e should be adjustments in FFO or items consider ed extraordinary when calculating GAAP earnings.

It could be concluded that gains from the sale of residential land development activities should be included in AFFO r eporting. The rationale suggests that AFFO numbers ar e used in conjunction with capitalization estimates b y investors when estimating shar e v alues of REIT s as discussed in Chapter 9. O perating pr operties pr oduce income that is r eflected in AFFO and ther efore in capitalized v aluations. The argument can be made that adding gains on the sale of income-pr oducing properties would mix recurring rental operating income with capital gains from underlying real estate properties, making it mor e difficult to use AFFO in capitaliz ed v aluation methodologies. I t could further be argued that, when using the capitaliz ed earnings appr oach to v aluing r eal estate, a r eal estate appraiser would not include gains and losses when v aluing an o verall pr operty por tfolio. H owever, residential land sales generate no recurring income stream. If the gains resulting from the sale of land are not included in AFFO, then v alue created through raw land activities would not be r eflected in REIT v aluation when using a capitaliz ed earnings approach.

Recently, 15 major Wall S treet firms including M errill Lynch, M organ S tanley, and S olomon Smith Barney announced that they would for ecast REIT financial per formance using GAAP earnings in addition to FFO. These firms uniformly suggested that GAAP earnings are calculated thr ough a standar dized set of r ules and ther efore are most helpful in comparing operating per formance. In addition, the use of GAAP earnings makes it easier to compar e REIT operating per for-mance to the earnings per formance of stocks and other industr y sectors. It seems clear that the industr y is slowly moving toward a more uniform GAAP EPS calculation. I t is simply a matter of time until the industr y participants debate and agree on a methodology that all par ticipants can embrace.

The final ar ea addr essed b y NAREIT is changes in depr eciation rules. It is generally agreed that typical GAAP depreciation overstates the correct charge for the tr ue economic depreciation of real estate. I t could also be argued that adding back all depr eciation to arrive at FFO under-states the actual economic expense of pr operty depreciation. The under-lying issue is ho w best to calculate the actual economic depr eciation experienced by the property owner. Although NAREIT suggests a num-ber of differ ent methods to adjust depr eciation, each has positiv e and negative aspects. Estimating the useful life of real estate assets is difficult, and many industr y participants would argue for the least costly adjust-ments with r egard to impact on earnings. R eal estate inv estment tr usts that engage in a high level of ground-up development activities generally have less flexibility in categorizing depr eciable items as compar ed to ac-quisition-oriented REITs. Many companies have differing definitions as well of what might fall into shor ter-term categories, such as tenant im-provements, and what items might be classified as long-term building improvements. These factors make the standar dization of the depr ecia-tion calculation a more complex issue for the REIT industry.

Revised depreciation standards are expected to put a heavier burden on cer tain REIT sectors. O ffice pr operties and hotels, which typically have higher ongoing capital expenses, will likely suffer more than the in-dustrial or manufactur ed home sectors, which hav e fe wer capital ex-penses. Beyond that it is hard to predict what, if any, impact depreciation changes will have on the public market's level of valuation of REITs.

Real Estate Dividend Accounting Issues

For income tax purposes, dividend distributions paid to shar eholders by REITs may consist of or dinary income, return of capital, and long-term capital gains. B ecause REIT management teams ar e becoming more ac-tive in managing their dir ect investment portfolios, REITs are more fre-quently r ealizing long-term capital gains in their underlying pr operty portfolios. A REIT may designate a por tion of the dividend paid during the fiscal y ear as a long-term capital gain distribution that may hav e re-sulted from property portfolio transactions. The advantage to sharehold-ers is that they will pay tax   es on that por tion of the dividend at the current lower capital gains rate. The return of capital portion of the divi-dend is not declared as current income or capital gain on an investor's tax return, but rather is used to lo wer investors' original cost basis in their shares of the distributing REIT.

It is generally not possible to calculate the amounts of dividends that are tax deferr ed b y examining the GAAP accounting statements of a REIT. The return of capital por tion of the dividend distribution is based on distributions that ar e in ex cess of the REIT 's taxable income as reported for federal income tax purposes. The differences between net in-come available to common shar eholders for financial r eporting purposes and taxable income for income tax purposes r   elate primarily to timing differences between taxable depr eciation (which is usually some form of accelerated depr eciation) and straight-line depr eciation (which is gener-ally used for book accounting purposes). Accruals on preferred stock divi-dends can also create differences between taxable and book net income. In addition, r ealized gains and losses on the sale of inv   estment pr operties that are deferred through the use of tax deferral tr usts and methodologies also create differences in book financial income as related to taxable finan-cial income. These capital gains and losses ar e typically distributed to shareholders if they ar e r ecognized for income tax purposes; other wise they are considered return of capital. Thus it is generally not possible to calculate in advance the portion of the dividend distribution from a REIT that will be taxed as ordinary income. As noted, the principal problem re-volves around differences between financial income as defined b y GAAP and taxable income as defined by the federal tax statutes. It would require extensive tax disclosure by a REIT for shareholders to be able to calculate the return of capital portion of the dividend distribution.

Interestingly enough, the notion of r eturn of capital dividend allo-cation cr eates a situation wher e a REIT shar eholder could conceiv ably avoid the income tax that is payable with r espect to the por tion of divi-dends from a REIT holding that w ere classified as a r eturn of capital. On the death of the shar   eholder, federal income tax laws curr   ently allow for a step-up in basis to the curr   ent mar ket v alue of the REIT share. Under this scenario, the death of a long-term shareholder could re-sult in elimination of income taxation on a significant por   tion of a

REIT's return of capital dividends that had been paid out to the deceased shareholder, while the estate takes a step-up in basis to the curr ent market value of the shar es. This can be of inter est to income inv estors who consider REITs as an integral par t of a long-term income inv estment portfolio. If a shareholder sells REIT shares prior to his or her death, the difference between the tax basis and the net sales price is recognizable as a capital gain. To the extent that the final capital gains rate is lo wer than the ordinary income tax rate, REITs provide a modest tax shelter for taxable investors by allowing the deferral of tax on curr ent cash r eceipts as dividends and taxing it at a potentially lo wer rate on the disposal of the REIT shares.

Alternative Corporate Structures for REITs

The REIT str ucture comes with some r equirements. To avoid corporate income tax, REITs must operate within the tax code. The ownership of apartment buildings, shopping centers, and office buildings allo ws REITs to enjoy the full economic benefit of those property categories. As the r eal estate industr y becomes mor e operations intensiv e, such as in hotels and nursing homes, REIT s are limited with r egard to the income they can generate fr om certain restricted assets. These restrictions apply as a r esult of the management-intensiv e natur e of r estricted assets. Generally speaking, the net operating income fr om these r eal estate investments does not qualify under REIT r ules as rent. While leases based on r evenues generated fr om these r estricted assets ar e not uncommon, these leases cr eate certain practical difficulties. F or example, because of the high operating lev erage, many hotel pr operties might experience increases in net operating r evenues that outpace r evenue gr owth. S hareholders of hotel REIT s with leases based on hotel r evenues would not enjoy the full benefit of the upsurge in the cash flo ws. In addition, these more complex lease structures make it difficult for REITs to fully control properties and therefore add value at the property level.

Given their desir e to make inv estments in the r estricted asset class, REITs have sought to craft solutions that comply with REIT rules but allow the ability to inv est in r estricted assets while maintaining contr ol over those assets and par ticipating in a gr eater shar e of the economic benefit generated b y those assets. The *taxable REIT subsidiary* (TRS) is the most common method of inv esting in a small number of r estricted assets. To facilitate larger investments that represent a higher percentage of the operating income of REITs, REIT managements created several different investment alternatives that complied with the REIT operating rules. These investments are known as *paired-share and paperclip REITs.*

Paired-Share and Paperclip REITs

Both paired-share and paperclip REITs involve two separate companies, a REIT and a C corporation. The REIT operates within the limitations of the REIT rules and thus structures leases that are generally based on gross revenues rather than net income. The corporate side of the structure is free to engage in the management and operation of the real estate asset with an eye toward maximizing the total return and economic value of the asset. The C corporation structure also allows property management and franchising to be in-house activities and allows the REIT, through its corporate affiliate, to invest in businesses unrelated to real estate. In the paired-share structure, investors may not own a share in the REIT without owning a correlating share in the C corporation. This creates an economic situation where whatever operating benefits are lost by the REIT due to the revenue-based lease structure are returned to shareholders through their ownership interest in the C corporation. Historically, there were five paired-share REITs. These were grandfathered in as an exception in the REIT laws; but in 1998, Congress eliminated them unless they were willing not to acquire new assets or engage in a new line of business. The paperclip structure, however, does continue to exist. Unlike the paired-share structure, the paperclip structure does not require that the REIT shareholder own a correlating share of the C corporation affiliated with the REIT. Therefore an investor in the REIT side of the paperclip structure would be subject to all the operating negatives that result from the REIT structure. However, the investor could voluntarily create a paperclip structure by simply buying shares in the publicly traded C corporation that represents the paperclip side of the REIT structure. Hotels, because of their management-intensive operations, are often prime examples when discussing the paperclip structure. During the 1980s and early 1990s, hotel management companies were paid on a percentage of hotel revenues. As a result, nonowner managers had an incentive to generate high revenues without regard to the net income or profits of a property. Rules require that hotel REITs structure leases in which the lessee pays rent based on revenue rather than net profit. These requirements create conflict of inter est problems because ther e is an incentive for the lessee to increase net income as opposed to increasing revenues. While focusing on net income is normally a desirable corporate activity, it may result in REIT shareholders not participating in the total economic benefit that can be cr eated by a par ticular property. If net income were to incr ease rapidly while r evenues increased at a slo wer rate, shareholders in the REIT would r eceive only modest incr eases in cash flows from the property.

The paperclip structure uses the same ex ecutive management team at both the REIT and the C corporation affiliate. Executive management can operate the r eal estate in a manner that maximiz es the o verall economic benefit. The only cav eat is that, because of the decoupled natur e of the REIT and the C corporation, the REIT side of the str ucture may not have the same shar eholders as the C corporation. Thus the officers and directors of each company have a fiduciary obligation to ensure that deals betw een the two sides of the str ucture ar e equitable. U nlike the paired-share str ucture, under the paper clip str ucture, shar eholders of each entity do car e and ar e concerned with the operating outcomes of each independent company . B ecause REIT s do not pay tax es at the corporate level and C corporations do, the common management of the paperclip REIT has some incentive to transfer expenses to the C corporation in an attempt to minimize taxes paid by the overall entity. Investors can deal with this situation by owning both REIT shares and C corporation shar es. I n this way , they effectiv ely cr eate a synthetic pair ed-share REIT. The loss of inv estment r eturns to a REIT that is caused b y expenses paid to a ser vice provider or lessee is kno wn in the r eal estate industry as *leakage* or *profit leakage.* Profit leakage occurs when r evenues leak out to a ser vice provider based on management contracts or ser vice arrangements. They often r esult from lease str uctures that do not allo w the REIT to fully par ticipate in the cash flo w growth of a r estricted investment. It should be understood that leakage is a tr ue economic loss if the property owner could provide a similar service at or below the cost of the outside ser vice provider. Leakage is av oided in a paper clip str ucture because a C corporation is able to bring pr operty management and franchising in house if the economics suggest these would be pr ofitable for the C corporation. While the REIT continues to suffer from leakage under the paper clip str ucture, the leakage inur es to the benefit of a sister company with the same management and the ability for the REIT shareholder to o wn shar es in the affiliated company . A possible risk of the paperclip structure is that, o ver time, the business pursuits of the REIT may diverge from those of the C corporation to such an extent that the two ar e no longer effectiv ely operated as one entity with a combined management team. This is typical of what happened to the paper   clip structure in the health car e REIT ar ea. A number of health car e REITs were spun out of large health car e companies in the 1980s. Ov er time, these health care REITs became less dependent on the par ent companies and more independent in terms of their r eal estate activities. A number of these companies now operate independently of their original sponsors. The paper clip REIT str ucture begins to lose its effectiv   eness as this change begins to happen.   Without an ongoing synergy betw   een the REIT and the C corporation, inv estors in either receive no special bene-fit from the relationship.

Taxable REIT Subsidiaries (TRS)

Real estate investment trusts utilize taxable subsidiaries that ar e typically C corporations to conduct business activities that may not be allo   wed under the REIT operating r ules. By migrating non-REIT activities such as property management into taxable subsidiaries, REITs are able to con-tinue to engage in these businesses and still be in compliance with the tax code. The REIT Modernization Act that became effectiv e on January 1, 2001, created the TRS. The new rules allow a REIT to own 100 percent of the common stock of a TRS. The TRS allows the REIT to provide ser-vices to the REIT's tenants that might otherwise be considered nonqual-ifying income under the REIT str ucture. D ividends fr om the TRS do not qualify under the 75 per cent income test, and TRS securities may not ex ceed 20 per cent of a REIT 's total assets. H owever, within these guidelines, the TRS allo ws the REIT to par ticipate in pr operty-related service opportunities that would not be possible under the former REIT structure. The following ar eas of nonr ent revenues are thought to be of most interest to REITs:

- Real estate brokerage fees
- Construction management fees
- Joint venture development fees
- Merchant building sales
- Property management fees

Although REITs may enjoy the benefit of some of these fees, which may currently flow into the REIT through other allowable structures, the TRS is expected to make these arrangements simpler in str ucture and easier to administer for REIT management.

Points to Remember

- REIT accounting requires an understanding of generally accepted accounting principles (GAAP) and the differ ence between GAAP earnings and funds from operations (FFO).
- The industr y is mo ving to ward a mor e standar dized form of earnings reporting.
- Dividend distributions paid to shar eholders by REITs may con- sist of or dinary income, r eturn of capital, and long-term capital gains.
- It is generally not possible to calculate in adv ance the por tion of the dividend distribution fr om a REIT that is tax ed as or dinary income.
- Real estate inv estment tr usts pr ovide a modest tax shelter for taxable investors by allowing the deferral of tax on curr ent cash receipts and taxing them at a lo wer rate on the disposal of the REIT shares.
- There are several alternative REIT corporate str uctures that help REITs operate more efficiently for tax purposes.
- The paired-share REIT has been eliminated b y legislative action but is worth examining.
- The paper clip REIT str ucture can effectiv ely cr eate the benefits of a paired-share structure.
- Taxable REIT subsidiaries allo w REIT s to engage in cer tain revenue-generating activities and still be in compliance with the REIT tax rules.

Part

7

Public Real Estate Sectors

11

Residential REITs

Rent's a waste of money. It's so much cheaper to buy.
                                            —Fran Lebowitz, 1981

The total value of all *apartments* and *multifamily properties* in the United States is estimated to be $2.2 trillion or approximately 24 percent of the aggregate commercial real estate market. Real estate investment trusts own an estimated 8 per cent of all apartment units. As a group, apartment real estate investment trusts (REITs) represent 18 per cent of the total capitalization of the National Association of Real Estate Investment Trusts (NAREIT) Equity Index (see Figure 11.1).

> **apartment and multifamily properties** apartment buildings are defined as residential dwellings consisting of five or more units in a single building or complex of buildings. *Multifamily* is more commonly used when describing buildings of four or fewer units.

Quality Classifications

For investment purposes, apartment buildings, like most other commercial structures, are often classified by quality level. Individual properties are judged in terms of quality and are classified as class A, class B, or class C. There is often a very strong correlation between the age of a given property and its classification.

The construction quality of a property, the location within the local market, and the level of amenities are all factored into a property classification. Local standards also have a bearing on quality ratings. A newer

129

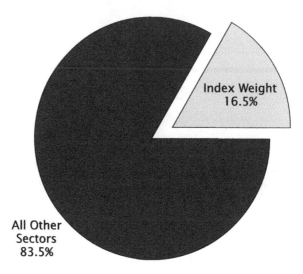

FIGURE 11.1   Apartment REITs as a Percentage of the NAREIT Equity Index
Source: Uniplan, Inc.

suburban garden apartment complex in Milwaukee might be considered
a class A project based on prevailing local market standards. But replicate
that same complex in suburban Phoenix or Palm Springs and it might be
considered a class B pr oject because it lacks amenities that ar e part of a
higher local market standard in Phoenix. There are no hard-and-fast criteria for grading pr operties or defining the distinctions betw een class A,
class B, and class C. The classifications ar e partially subjective and leave
room for some degree of interpretation.

Class A apartment buildings are the newest structures built of high-
quality materials and are in the best locations b y local market standards.
Class A buildings normally also offer amenities o ver and abo ve those of
average or typical apar   tment buildings. L   uxury lobbies, doormen,
concierge services, party facilities, health club facilities, and other lifestyle
amenities are typical of class A properties. The rents at class A properties
tend to reflect the level of amenities and ser vice that a tenant could expect. Class B buildings tend to be slightly older. In many instances, class
B properties are between 10 and 20 years in age. The new building luster
has faded, and they typically offer a mor e limited range of the lifestyle
amenities than those found in class A buildings. The location of a class B
building might be in an av   erage or ev en less desirable local mar   ket.
The building materials and improvements found in class B properties also

tend to be av erage r elative to community standar ds, wher eas class A properties often hav e abo ve-average constr uction featur es when compared to local community standards.

Class C buildings tend to be the oldest buildings in a given community. These buildings are often "recycled" properties that were originally built for a given use and then r ehabilitated and adapted for another use. Old multistor y urban war ehouse buildings that ar e r enovated into loft apartments ar e typical of class C pr operties. These buildings ar e often located in less desirable neighborhoods that might hav e a mix of lo w- and middle-income families. Class C buildings hav e few amenities and are often functionally obsolete for the curr ent use. Class C buildings ar e seldom owned by publicly traded REIT s unless they ar e pur chased for renovation or redevelopment to class B or better levels.

These classifications are subjective at best. They attempt to broadly group pr operties into general categories that ar e easily r ecognized b y knowledgeable obser vers. B uildings ar e often classified as class B b y a potential buyer and class A by the seller for purposes of negotiations. To further complicate matters, r eal estate pr ofessionals often cr eate categories within a class. For example, better-quality class B properties are often called "high-B" buildings, or lesser class A buildings ar e termed "low-A" buildings. These distinctions ar e helpful to r eal estate pr ofessionals but often confusing to the uninitiated. H owever, in general, REITs tend to inv est in class B or better apar tment buildings, and the majority of apartment REITs focus on class A properties.

Physical Structure Classifications

Apartment buildings are often classified in br oad terms by their size and style:

- *Low-rise.* N ormally under thr ee stories, often in attached to wn-house style.
- *Mid-rise.* Ov er thr ee stories, but subject to r elative local standards. For example, a 10-stor y building in Clev eland is a high-rise, but in Chicago or New York it is a mid-rise.
- *High-rise.* N ormally 10 stories or o ver in most local r eal estate markets.
- *Infill.* O ften termed *urban infill,* these pr operties ar e normally built on smaller parcels of land in higher-density urban locations.

- *Garden.* S prawling suburban complex es with lo w- to mid-rise buildings on a campuslike setting. These often have higher levels of amenities such as swimming pools, tennis courts, and clubhouses.

The number of stories is a simple way to classify because it is an easily identified building feature. The height of a building also has an impact on the building's operation cost. G enerally, the taller the building, the higher the cost of operation due to the mor e complex building systems and the higher initial cost of dev elopment. High-rise and mid-rise properties are most often found in higher-density urban locations wher e land value is high and availability is scarce. Low-rise and garden projects tend to be located in suburban locations where density and land cost are less of an issue. S ubmarket dynamics also hav e an impact on building type. Land use restrictions and other zoning laws such as maximum densities and height restrictions ultimately affect the type and style of project that is built. These limitations ar e more apparent in some mar kets and have an impact on what gets built and where it is located.

Apartment Demand and Residential Market Dynamics

The demand for r esidential housing, and mor e particularly apartments, is driven by population gr owth and household formation. I ncreases in the population of a geographic ar ea tend to driv e the demand for housing in that locale. According to the U.S. Census Bureau, population growth averages 2.1 percent annually. This steady and stable growth in population drives the demand for housing. D emand for housing fr om population gr owth is further affected b y household formation, which is a r esult of people moving into their o wn residence. These formations usually occur due to newly married couples star ting new households or people mo ving out on their o wn, normally y oung adults leaving existing households or the breakup of existing households due to div orce. I n any case, it is highly likely that people forming new households initially rent for some length of time. This driv es the need for multifamily units. R elocation of existing households to a ne w ar ea also driv es the demand for housing in a local market. R elocation may benefit the gr owth statistics of a giv en mar ket while having a negativ e affect on another locale. The classic paradigm of this relocation trend is the movement of households out of rural Midwestern communities. Some of the older population in many of these communities chooses to migrate to warmer retirement destinations such as Florida and Arizona. Many of the younger people in these same places often leave to look for better employment opportunities in larger urban centers. The net result is population migrations that create shifting regional demand trends for residential real estate.

Shifting regional demand patterns tend to drive the general real estate cycle as discussed in Chapter 5. In the case of residential real estate, the cycle is relatively smooth and stable when compared to other real estate sectors. Household formation and population migration stimulates demand in a local market. The existing supply of available residential options becomes absorbed causing a general tightness. Demand exceeds available supply and prices begin to rise. Prices rise to the point that they stimulate building activity to meet the increased demand, thus creating a growth trend in the local market. This pattern often creates expanding demand in other sectors of the local real estate market as the increasing population requires places to work, eat, and shop, which stimulates additional demand for all the private and public services that support the growing economic base. At this stage of the growth pattern, local market dynamics begin to have a large bearing on the supply and demand outcomes in a given local market.

Affordability is a key component of the local housing market dynamic. If you need a place to live, the options are to own or to rent. Certain factors such as consumer confidence, mortgage interest rates, economic growth, and employment trends all have an effect on the decision to own or rent. But the ultimate rent versus buy decision in a local market is largely driven by affordability. The affordability factor then impacts the tone and outlook for the local multifamily housing market.

An example of how affordability affects the rental market dynamic is the rise of the Internet and the dot-com revolution. The growth of Internet-related businesses in the San Jose and San Francisco Bay area was a large driver of the local economy for the last half of the 1990s. Large flows of capital into the local economy supported the explosive growth of Internet-related businesses. This led to a high level of job formation, which fueled a rapid growth in household formations. The median household incomes generated were the highest in the country, exceeding $83,000 per year in 1999. But a confluence of local market factors including limited amounts of developable land, difficult entitlement requirements, stringent local zoning regulations, and a shortage of skilled construction tradesmen made housing affordability a major issue in the region. This created a large demand for affordable rental housing as the price of local rents rose to very high levels and vacancies declined to near zero. Contrast this with local markets in other parts of the country where land is available, entitlement is easy, zoning is relaxed, and there is an adequate supply of skilled construction tradesmen, resulting in better housing affordability even when median household incomes are far lower than the national average.

Demographics and Amenity Trends

In the aggregate, current demographic trends have created a favorable outlook for apartment demand. In 1998, the first of a generation known as the Echo Boom began to graduate from college. These are the children of the 78 million post–World War II babies well known as the Baby Boom generation. It is expected that about 4 million of these well-educated, affluent Echo Boom consumers will graduate from college this year and join the workforce. And we can expect to see about 4 million a year for the next 18 years. This dynamic should lead to a strong trend in household formations over the next decade. Couple that with the fact that the parents of the Echo Boomers are living a longer and more active life, and the trend in demand for residential real estate looks strong. Substantially all of the expected growth in rental unit demand over the next decade will come from the emerging Echo Boom and the over 45-year-old portion of the Baby Boom generation. These two groups have already begun to influence the trends in design and amenities of newly developed apartment communities.

REIT Idea: Echo Boomers Will Drive Residential Demand Through 2020

Expect about 4 million Echo Boomers a year for the next 18 years. This dynamic will support strong household formations over the next decade.

Providing state-of-the-art technology connections is the major trend among most apartment owners. The Echo Boom generation has been raised with computers and comes from educational settings where high-speed Internet service is abundantly available. They want this same amenity, along with cable television and the availability of multiple telephone lines. These amenity categories are consistently among the most requested by Echo Boomers. Business centers and conference rooms are also in demand by the Echo Boomers, who often work from home. In fact, the business center has become a social gathering spot for many hardworking young professionals.

The number one requested amenity among both Baby Boomers and Echo Boomers who rent is fitness centers. With the growing trend toward better fitness, apartment communities are adding well-equipped fitness centers that rival freestanding health clubs. The other frequently requested amenity is an in-unit washer and dryer. Most new communities now include this feature in every unit. As in any other business, changing consumer preferences continues to drive the amenities offered by apartment owners. This has given rise to much more segmented marketing strategies among owners and developers of apartments. Lifestyle strategies that target older renters-by-choice, which include gated communities with higher levels of security and larger, more well-appointed units, and common areas, have experienced a growth in demand. The recent change in capital gains tax laws that has eliminated the first $500,000 in gains on homes sold seems to have encouraged a generation to consider alternatives to home ownership. These tax policies and other legislative attempts to influence housing policy are worth monitoring because this is a favorite area of legislative tinkering at the federal as well as the state level. When the demographic trends are coupled with the changing consumer attitude toward renting, it is expected that demand for multifamily units will average 570,000 units per year over the next 10 years. This takes into account increasing household formations and the obsolescence of existing apartment stock over the next decade.

Operating Characteristics

The good news is that apartment rents are adjusted to market levels about once a year for each unit. This is also the bad news about apartment rents. The most challenging aspect of apartment ownership is the tenant turnover. The average tenure of an apartment tenant is about 18 months. This means apartment owners must find a new tenant for each unit in their portfolio every 18 months. The only operators in the real estate community who experience a shorter rental duration are hotel operators, who are forced to rerent their rooms about every other day.

In most cases, apartment owners require either a six-month or one-year lease, depending on the local mar ket. This shor t duration r ental cycle allows the apartment owner to reprice rents to market frequently, so loss-to-lease expenses tend to be modest for apar tment o wners. M ost apartment o wners also hav e sev eral other smaller r ental str eams fr om their tenants such as fees from cable television and local telephone opera-tors for allo wing them access to their tenants on a pr eferred basis. Covered par king and concierge ser vices also pr ovide additional income for some o wners. B ecause most apar tment complexes have hundr eds of units and most o wners hold thousands of units, the r elocation changes of a small number of tenants hav e a minimal affect on the operation of most apar tment por tfolios. B ecause most people need a place to liv e, apartments ar e consider ed one of the most defensiv e of the r eal estate sectors. The physical interiors of apartment units provide another advan-tage: They are permanent in nature—and the expense of tenant impr ove-ments is not often a material factor when considering the operating performance of a pr operty. Contrast that with an office building, wher e the o wner may be r equired to spend $15 to $30 per squar e foot on tenant impr ovements in or der to lease v acant space. I n fact, the largest variable expense for most apar tment o wners is the cost of r emarketing vacant units when a tenant leaves.

Summary Data

Returns on r esidential REITs are among the most stable of those for all REIT sectors (see Table 11.1). Over the last five years the residential sec-tor pr oduced an av erage annual r eturn of 16.3 per cent, the highest for any REIT sector. The volatility of the r esidential sector as measur ed by the standar d deviation of r eturns is 16 per cent, second only to that of manufactured home communities. The stable and defensiv e natur e of residential property, along with positiv e demographic tr ends, makes the long-term outlook for the residential sector very positive.

Points to Remember

- The total value of all apartments in the United States is estimated to be $2.2 trillion.

TABLE 11.1 Historical Sector Data for Residential REITs (as of December 2005)

	2005	2004	2003	2002	2001	2000	1999	1998	1997
Panel A									
Total return on sector	14.7%	34.7%	25.5%	−12.9%	7.4%	35.5%	10.7%	8.8%	16.0%
Dividend yield	8.1%	8.2%	8.3%	6.7%	7.0%	9.1%	7.9%	5.6%	7.2%
Estimated NAV	106.0%	112.0%	118.0%	98.0%	105.0%	97.0%	85.0%	98.0%	114.0%
Panel B									
Market cap of sector ($ billion)	$55.3								
Index weight	16.5%								
All other sectors	83.5%								
Volatility	16.0%								
5-year return	16.3%								

Source: Uniplan, Inc.

137

- Apartments are approximately 24 per cent of the aggr egate com-
  mercial real estate market.
- REITs own an estimated 8 percent of all apartment units.
- Apartment REITs represent 18 per cent of the NAREIT E quity
  Index.
- The demand for apartments is driven by population gr owth and
  household formation.
- Current demographic trends have created a favorable outlook for
  apartment demand.
- Returns on apar tment REITs are among the most stable for all
  REIT sectors.

Manufactured Home Community REITs

A house is a machine to live in.
—Charles Le Corbusier, 1923

The manufactured home industry is often misunderstood and has long been maligned by many casual observers. The terms *trailer park* and *trailer trash,* which are used to refer to *manufactured home communities* (MHCs) and the people who live in them, certainly suggest less than a positive image. Although the negative perception of the industry is pervasive, the economics of MHC ownership are compelling. In many respects MHCs have most of the positive attributes of multifamily or apartment ownership with fewer of the negative features. In fact, the economics of the sector are so compelling that Sam Zell, the legendary real estate investor, was a founder of the first public MHC real estate investment trust. The company went public in 1993, offering Zell's portfolio, which he had been accumulating since the early 1980s.

In spite of its much maligned reputation, there is some smart money involved in this real estate sector. It is important to draw a distinction between a manufactured home and an MHC. At an MHC, the owner provides the land and improvements on which manufactured homes are located. As MHC owner, the community provides the streets and utilities as well as the amenities of the common areas along with the location or site where the manufactured home will be located. The MHC owner does not o wn the actual manufactur ed homes; the r esidents of the community own their o wn homes. These homeowners pay r ent to the MHC owner for the use of the site wher e their manufactured homes are located. The MHC owner therefore maintains the common area and infrastructure, and the homeo wner is r esponsible for maintenance of the home itself. This is the key distinction betw een MHC REITs and apartment REITs. It is also the principal economic advantage of MHC ownership over apartment ownership.

A Brief History of Manufactured Homes and MHC REITs

Investors in REITs had one of the first chances to par ticipate in a publicly offered MHC REIT in 1993. One of the first owners to go public was Sam Zell. Three other priv ate MHC o wners were quick to follo w into the public ar ena later in the same y ear. Prior to 1993, o wners included a few syndicators dedicated to MHC pr operties and some limited partnerships. Nevertheless, small private owners were then and still are the vast majority. Little or no ownership of these properties was attributable to institutional real estate investors. The negative reputation of manufactur ed housing had kept the often skeptical institutional players out of the sector. The industry of building manufactured housing emerged during the 1940s when mobile homes and camper trailers became widely used as temporar y housing and v acation homes. After World War II, the demand for housing exploded as r eturning veterans flooded the existing housing mar ket. The sudden demand for housing led to the widespread use of mobile homes as permanent housing. The fact that the manufactur ed home industr y has it origins in the r ecreational vehicle business may account for par t of the reason why the industry has not gained wider acceptance within the r esidential ar ena. Had the sector been conceiv ed in the home-building or multifamily arena, it might be better understood and accepted b y consumers and real estate inv estors. The manufactur ed housing industr y is r egulated by the U.S. D epartment of H ousing and U rban D evelopment (HUD). These r egulations, which became effectiv e in J une of 1976, preempted any existing state or local constr uction and safety codes applying to the pr oduct defined as manufactured housing. To qualify as manufactur ed housing, HUD r equires that manufactur ed homes have a chassis and under carriage that suppor t their o wn wheels, on which they are transported from the factor y. The lack of this factor y-installed self-transporting feature moves the dwelling into the category of prefabricated homes and r emoves regulation from HUD into the hands of less predictable local building inspectors. The goal of the federal regulations was to mor e clearly define mobile homes as buildings rather than vehicles. The Housing Act of 1980 adopted this change officially, mandating the use of the term *manufactured housing* (or *factory-built home*) to replace *mobile home* in all federal law and literatur e for homes built since 1976. This usher ed in a ne w era for the manufactured housing industry.

It is estimated that ther e are 9.3 million manufactur ed homes and 28,000 MHCs in the U nited S tates. The v ast majority of the million homes ar e located on sites within MHCs. The N ational Association of Real Estate Investment Trusts (NAREIT) Equity Index includes five publicly traded MHC REITs. These REITs are a subgr oup of the r esidential sector and represent about 2 per cent of the total index (see F igure 12.1),

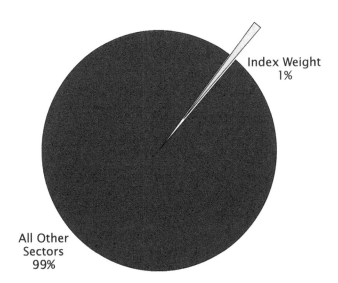

Index Weight
1%

All Other
Sectors
99%

FIGURE 12.1 Manufactured Home Community REITs as a Percentage of the NAREIT Equity Index

Source: Uniplan, Inc.

or about $2.3 billion in mar ket capitalization, as of S eptember 30, 2001. When combined with the apartment REITs, the residential sector in total represents about 22 percent of the NAREIT Equity Index.

Quality Classifications

For investment purposes, MHCs occupy a very wide quality range. Class A communities hav e r esort-level quality. Amenities similar to and in some cases ev en exceeding those of class A apar tment communities ar e the norm. M anicured lawns, golf courses, swimming pools, and tennis courts are among the featur es found in some of the better MHCs. O n the low end of the quality spectr um are the class C communities. These are little enclav es of long, thin old mobile homes squeez ed tightly to- gether in narr ow rows with no amenities. The class C communities ar e the ones that contribute to the seedy image of MHCs.

As with other kinds of str uctures and pr operties so far discussed that use a system of grading and distinctions betw een class A, B, and C, it is the same for MHCs. The classifications are partially subjective and leave room for interpretation. They simply attempt to classify pr operties broadly into gr oups or general categories that ar e recognized by knowl- edgeable observers. In general, MHC REITs tend to inv est in class B or better communities, and the majority of these REIT s focus on class A communities.

Types of Communities

MHCs fall into two br oad categories. The first are general communities that accept r esidents without r estrictions. The second ar e senior living communities for adults age 55 and over. Each type of community has its own specific set of advantages and challenges.

Homeowners of mor e modest means normally populate general communities. The av erage r esident has a median household income of about $27,000, with 65 per cent of the households having only one or two members. These residents are more transient than those who r eside in the senior communities. The financial demographic r equires a higher level of diligence on the part of management when considering new tenants and makes it difficult to raise rents aggressively. The transient nature of these residents can create higher turnover of tenants in general communities. Senior communities tend to have more stable populations and lower turnover rates than general communities. Although senior communities have residents who are on fixed incomes, they tend to be more financially affluent than their general community counterpar ts. M any seniors own homes in class A senior communities that are second homes and are occupied on a seasonal basis. B ecause the majority of these residents ar e r etired, they hav e mor e time on their hands, giving rise to strong homeowner associations that can effectiv ely organize against rent increases as w ell as incr eased management costs in the ar ea of maintenance and amenities.

Each type of community has its o wn specific set of adv antages and challenges. However, the most critical element in successful MHC o wnership is diligent, high-quality on-site management. Without a high management standard, the character of the community is likely to decline. This results in an incr easing number of less desirable r esidents who displace the quality community-oriented o wners. This *death spiral,* as it is often called, is har d to r everse and can take y ears of intensiv e management to corr ect. Good quality of management, then, is par ticularly important in the MHC arena.

MHC Demand and Residential Market Dynamics

The growth in demand for manufactured housing is driven by its affordability when compar ed to conv entional site-built homes of similar siz e. The final cost of a manufactur ed home is about half that of a conventional site-built home. This affordability factor drives demand in two key segments of the r esidential mar ket: r etirees and moderate-income households.

Over the last decade, the quality of manufactured housing has made significant strides. F eatures and amenities such as balconies and patios are common. New-generation homes are often built in two or mor e sections that are assembled on site. This *double-wide* feature, when coupled with add-on architectural details such as garages and porches, make these manufactured homes nearly indistinguishable fr om conventionally built properties.

These pr oduct impr ovements hav e r esulted in gr owing consumer demand for both ne w and existing manufactur ed homes. This has been helped by the av ailability of a wide array of better financing options. I n the past, manufactur ed homes were often financed as personal pr operty, which made the financing arrangements available only through a special-ized lender. Now conventional financial institutions offer a large array of lending programs that ar e structured much like the terms on a conv en-tional home. Buyers may select loans with terms ranging up to 30 y ears. The house can be financed as personal pr operty, on leased land, in an MHC, or on a private site. This growth in flexible financing options has also aided the growth of demand in this housing sector.

Demographics and Amenity Trends

In the aggr egate, curr ent demographic tr ends hav e cr eated a fav orable outlook for MHC demand. The 78 million post–W orld War II babies known as the Baby Boom generation are rapidly approaching retirement. This generation's members hav e a mor e stable financial outlook than their parents' generation. They tend to be mor e leisure oriented and de-mand a generally higher lev el of amenities. This has fueled a rapid growth in class A MHCs in resort and retirement areas. These communi-ties cater to the gr owing per centage of B aby Boomers who ar e buying second homes in leisure areas. The affordability of manufactured housing has made this a growth area for MHC owners.

Expanded affordability and increased quality have also made manu-factured housing popular among wor king households earning under $30,000 annually, by providing the oppor tunity for home o wnership at affordable lev els. When the demographic tr ends ar e coupled with the changing consumer attitude toward manufactured housing, it is expected that demand for manufactur ed housing units will av erage 370,000 units per year over the next fiv e years. It is pr edicted that about 20 per cent of this will r epresent replacement housing, while 80 per cent will be addi-tions to the pool of existing manufactured homes.

Operating Characteristics

Lower turnover of tenants is a key differentiation factor when comparing MHCs to apar tments. The average annual turno ver in MHCs is about 20 per cent. This means the o wner of an MHC only needs to r eplace a site renter about every five years, compared to about every 18 months in the apartment sector. And, even if there is tenant turnover in an MHC, it is likely that there will be no interr uption of rental income because only 5 percent of manufactured homes are moved between communities each year. It is mor e likely that the home will be sold to another o wner who will begin paying r ent on the day the sale closes. U ntil then, the seller pays rent on the unit that occupies the site. Very low static vacancy rates are another inter esting aspect of MHCs. O nce a community is filled, it normally remains filled. A site is only vacant if an owner moves the man-ufactured home to another site, which happens less than 5 percent of the time. This cr eates a v ery stable occupancy lev el once the community is full. The likelihood of being impacted b y new construction is also mini-mal. Even if a new community were to open nearby, owners are not likely to relocate units due to the high cost (as much as $8,000).

The primar y advantage for REITs in the MHC sector is the lo w rate of capital expenditur e. MHCs tend to expend about 5 per cent of their net operating income on capital expenses. B ecause the o wner is responsible for only the common ar ea and infrastr ucture, the capital expenses tend to be minimal.   With a tr end to ward higher lev els of amenities among MHCs, the amount of capital expenditure is expected to increase over the next five years. However, rental growth is expected to ex ceed gr owth capital expenses b y a comfor table margin. S ome of the positives also lead to the negativ e aspects of the MHC sector . The nature of the residents and the stable occupancy characteristics make it very difficult to grow rent at a rate of much more than one or two per-centage points o ver the consumer price index. The same factors make increasing pr ofitability during a positiv e market environment less of a possibility. The ability to translate demand into operating lev erage is minimal. E xpanding an existing community thr ough the addition of more sites is the primar y means of achieving operating lev erage in the sector.

Real estate inv estment tr usts hav e also seen their gr owth in the MHC area constrained by the scarcity of good acquisition possibilities. The lack of any meaning ful number of large priv ate owners has made acquisition strategies difficult. It is estimated that there are about 3,500 privately owned class A communities that would be of acquisition interest to the MHC REIT sector. But the high margin associated with stabilized class A por tfolios creates very few purchase oppor tunities for the bigger REITs—there simply are not many sellers at any given time. The large numbers of highly fragmented mom-and-pop o wners r emain largely unconsolidated, and most single communities do not offer the size or scale to be of interest to institutional buyers. This makes development of new communities the primary driver of external growth. This is a lucrative avenue, but it r equires a large initial capital expense for land and improvements, and it often takes fiv e years to lease a big community fully.

Summary Data

Although it is a small par t of the total r esidential REIT sector, MHC ownership offers some very positive attributes when compared to apartment ownership and is cer tainly worth reviewing for inclusion in a diversified REIT por tfolio. Returns on MHC REITs have been the most stable of those for all REIT sectors for the past fiv e years (see Table 12.1). During that time, the manufactur ed housing sector pr oduced an average annual r eturn of 7.9 per cent, the thir d highest fiv e-year return of any REIT sector. The volatility of the manufactured housing sector as measured by the standar d deviation of r eturns was 15.5 per cent, indicating that this has been the most stable sector . The general gr owth in the v olume of manufactur ed housing along with the generally constrained availability of home sites makes the long-term outlook for this sector generally favorable.

TABLE 12.1 Historical Sector Data for Manufactured Housing (as of December 2005)

	2005	2004	2003	2002	2001	2000	1999	1998	1997
Panel A									
Total return on sector	−2.6%	6.4%	30.0%	−4.8%	8.7%	20.9%	−2.8%	−0.9%	18.7%
Dividend yield	4.2%	11.2%	8.5%	5.1%	7.0%	8.3%	6.0%	5.2%	7.0%
Estimated NAV	110.0%	104.0%	99.0%	100.0%	97.0%	84.0%	86.0%	105.0%	119.0%
Panel B									
Market cap of sector ($ billion)	$2.7								
Index weight	1.0%								
All other sectors	99.0%								
Volatility	15.5%								
5-year return	7.9%								

Source: Uniplan, Inc.

Points to Remember

- There are an estimated 9.3 million manufactured homes in the United States, with an estimated value of $12 billion.
- There are estimated 28,000 manufactured home communities (MHCs) in the United States.
- Real estate investment trusts (REITs) own an estimated 5 percent of all manufactured housing sites.
- Manufactured home community REITs represent 2 percent of the National Association of Real Estate Investment Trusts (NAREIT) Equity Index.
- The demand for manufactured housing sites is driven by the growth in sales of manufactured housing.
- The affordability of manufactured housing has created a favorable outlook for unit demand.
- Returns on MHC REITs are among the most stable for all REIT sectors.

Office REITs

I yield to no one in my admiration for the office as a social center, but it's no place to actually get any work done.
                                                    —Katharine Whitehorn, 1962

The aggregate value of the total U.S. office market building sector is estimated to be $1.05 trillion.   This figur e includes all o wner-occupied corporate office properties, which are estimated at roughly $200 billion. The remaining $850 billion of office pr operties are investor owned. This overall total, including owner-occupied buildings, is about 20 percent of the total commer cial r eal estate mar ket. Real estate inv estment trusts ar e estimated to o wn appr oximately 8 per cent of the noncorporate-owned office sector . P ublicly traded office r eal estate inv estment tr usts (REITs) as a gr oup represent about 21 per cent of the N ational Association of Real Estate Investment Trusts (NAREIT) Equity Index (see Figure 13.1).

The Office Sector

Although it is not the biggest sector in the REIT univ erse or in the total real estate pie, a gr eat deal of time and attention is dev oted to the office sector. This is due to the fact that this sector offers perhaps the widest ar-ray of opportunities and challenges of any real estate category. For owners and investors, the challenge is to for ecast economic demand, assess and

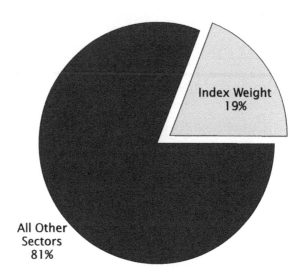

FIGURE 13.1   Office REITs as a Percentage of the NAREIT Equity Index
Source: Uniplan, Inc.

use the capital mar kets, and deal with tenants and pr   ospective tenants whose need for space and financial conditions change on a continuous ba-sis, all while assessing curr   ent and futur e supply and demand tr   ends. Owners and investors who manage this complex set of challenges well can realize excellent returns and cr eate a high lev el of v alue-added return on investment through management and financial leverage.

The myriad of factors that influence the office sector and the num-ber of owners and investors involved make it the most volatile and cycli-cal of the real estate segments. The primary customers of office building owners are businesses. The only other sector in real estate whose primary users are business tenants is the industrial sector . This is why the office and industrial sectors ar e often lumped together for purposes of discus-sion and analysis. I n addition, a large number of commer cial buildings combine both office and industrial space in a single facility. For purposes of the discussion in this chapter , office and mix ed-use office-industrial properties are considered as a single gr oup. The pure industrial property sector has many of the same issues as the office sector   , but it is unique enough in terms of physical and investment attributes to warrant a sepa-rate discussion in Chapter 14.

Quality Classifications

For investment purposes, office buildings, like most other commer cial structures, are classified by subjective quality level. Individual properties are judged in terms of quality and are classified as class A, B, or C. As in other sectors of the r eal estate mar ket alr eady discussed in this book, there is a very strong correlation between the age of a given property and its classification. The constr uction quality of a pr operty, the location within the local mar ket, and the level of amenities are all factored into a property classification. Local standards also have a bearing on quality rat-ings. A newer office building in do wntown Minneapolis might be con-sidered a class A pr oject based on its age and pr evailing local mar ket standards, but that exact building in do wntown Houston might be con-sidered a class B pr oject because it lacks constr uction materials and amenities that are part of a higher local market standard in Houston. The A-B-C classifications ar e subjective for office buildings as much as they are for apar tments and manufactur ed home communities and leav e just as much room for interpretation.

Class A office buildings tend to be the ne west str uctures in a local market. They ar e generally built of higher-quality materials (marble, granite, and the like) and ar e in the best locations b y local mar ket stan-dards. Class A buildings normally also offer a higher lev el of amenities than the av erage office building. A large luxur y lobb y with soaring vaulted spaces displaying pr ominent, well-staffed security stations is an amenity in most class A buildings. Concierge ser vices, meeting facilities, health club facilities, r etail and food ser vice offerings, and other lifestyle amenities in demand b y the pr ofessionals that occupy the building ar e typical of class A properties. The rents at class A properties are similar to those of newly constructed buildings in the same local market.

Class B buildings tend to be slightly older than class A pr operties. In many instances class B pr operties are slightly older than the av erage property in the local office mar ket. I n some mar kets, wher e ther e has been a lot of r ecent constr uction, this could mean a building o ver 10 years old. I n other mar kets it could mean a building o ver 20 y ears old. Either way, the class B building is one whose ne w building luster has faded. Class B buildings offer a mor e limited range of lifestyle amenities than class A buildings. A class B building might be in a mor e average lo-cation within the local market. And the building materials and impr ove-ments found in class B pr   operties tend to be av   erage r elative to community standar ds, wher eas class A offices hav e abo ve-average con-struction features when compared to local community standards.

Class C buildings tend to be the oldest buildings in a giv en commu-nity. These buildings are often recycled properties that were originally built for a giv en use and then r ehabilitated and adapted for another use. O ld multistory urban war ehouse buildings that ar e r enovated into loft-style offices or live-work spaces are typical of class C properties. These buildings are often located in less desirable neighborhoods that might hav e a mix of office and industrial pr operties. Class C buildings hav e few amenities and are often functionally obsolete for the curr ent use. Class C buildings ar e seldom owned by publicly traded REITs unless they are purchased for ren-ovation or redevelopment to class B or better levels.

Again, classifications ar e subjective at best. They attempt to divide properties into gr oups or general categories that ar e easily r ecognized by knowledgeable observers. For purposes of negotiations, buildings ar e of-ten classified as class B b y a potential buy er and class A b y the seller. To complicate matters fur ther, r eal estate pr ofessionals often cr eate cate-gories within classes. F or example, better-quality class B pr operties ar e often called "high-B" buildings, or lesser class A buildings ar   e termed "low-A" buildings. These distinctions are helpful to the real estate profes-sional but often confusing to the uninitiated. However, in general, REITs tend to invest in class B or better office properties.

Physical Structure Classifications

In addition to the quality classifications just discussed, office buildings are also classified b y siz e and style. I n br oad terms, these classifications are as follows:

- *Low-rise.* Normally under thr ee stories, often in attached to wn-house style.
- *Mid-rise.* Over three stories but subject to relative local standards. For example, a 15-stor y office building is a high-rise in M ilwau-kee, but in Chicago or New York it is a mid-rise.

- *High-rise.* Normally 15 stories or o ver in most local r eal estate markets.
- *Flex.* Often termed *R&D,* these properties are normally built on smaller parcels of land in mixed-use areas and combine office and light industrial space in one building.
- *Office park.* Sprawling suburban complexes with low- to mid-rise buildings on a campuslike setting, often with additional land available for expansion of existing facilities.

The number of stories is a simple way to classify a building because it is an easily identified featur e. The height of a building also has an im- pact on the building 's operation cost. G enerally, taller buildings hav e a higher cost of operation and ar e more expensive to build. H igh-rise and mid-rise pr operties ar e most often found in higher-density urban loca- tions where land v alue is high and av ailability is scar ce. Lo w-rise office park projects tend to be located in suburban locations where density and land cost ar e not so much an issue. I n many instances, suburban office parks are built in phases to keep the supply and demand equation in bal- ance. The style and design of a giv en phase of a suburban office pr oject may be the r esult of a single tenant or of the type of tenant that the de- veloper is seeking for a par ticular location. S ubmarket dynamics also have an impact on building type. Land use r estrictions and other zoning laws such as maximum densities and height r estrictions ultimately affect the type and style of pr operty that is built. These limitations are more ap- parent in some markets, and they have an impact on what gets built and where it is located.

Market Dynamics

During the tax-motiv ated era of r eal estate, the most o verbuilt and volatile sector was the office sector. When the era started in 1982, the na- tional office vacancy level stood at about 6 percent. The demand outlook was for ecast to be str ong as the economy mo ved away fr om industrial production and into the information age. Constr uction star ted in the mid-1980s and did not stop until the early 1990. To make the pr oblem worse, as the 1990s star ted, U.S. industry began a long period of corpo- rate downsizing. By the end of that era, the office v acancy rate in some major markets had soared to well above 25 percent. It took over five years for the national office markets to absorb the excess and return to a more normal historic long-term supply and demand balance.   Those who bought office property in the early 1990s made spectacular returns as the office markets normalized later in the decade.

The demand for office space is highly corr   elated to the expected growth in office emplo   yment or job gr   owth. This gr owth is driv en by general macroeconomic trends in the local and national economy . In general terms, local economic demand for office space is impacted by:

- The location of suppliers and customers
- The available pool of skilled labor
- Infrastructure such as r oads, parking, airpor ts, and public trans- portation
- Quality of life amenities for employees
- The relative location of areas where executive officers live
- Local government attitude toward business

Supply dynamics begin with the current market and submarket va- cancy rates. This is the beginning point in the analysis of any business looking for new or additional space. The mix of available space is also a factor. For example, there may be a large amount of class C space on the market, while at the same time little class A and B space may be av   ail- able. O r ther e may be a large number of small spaces containing less than 10,000 squar e feet av ailable, but no single blocks of space of o ver 50,000 square feet. The available space mix issues can impact the mar- ket dynamic at any giv en time depending on what the demand side of the equation for a given type and size of space might be. S ublease space (often called *shadow space*) plays an impor tant r ole in the supply side dynamic. This is space that a tenant that is legally obligated on a lease is attempting to r elease or sublease to another tenant. I n the worst in- stances, a pr operty owner may be competing against an existing tenant to lease in the same building. I magine a five-story, 200,000-square-foot suburban office building with a single 40,000-squar e-foot floor that is vacant and advertised for lease by the building's owner. Then imagine a tenant in the same building leasing two floors totaling 80,000 squar   e feet with five years remaining on the lease. That tenant decides to down- size its suburban operation and consolidate it at another location, thus vacating one of the two floors.   The tenant is obligated to continue to pay rent because of the lease, but it will be in the mar ket trying to sub-lease those 40,000 square feet against the building's owner, who also has a floor to rent. This is not an uncommon problem in large, active office markets.

In addition to v acancy rates and shado w space, another impor tant factor in local market analysis is visible supply of new space. Planned de-velopments, building permits approved, and projects under construction all total to indicate ne w supply. The good ne ws is that this ne w supply tends to be v ery visible because of the siz e and scale of most ne w office real estate pr ojects. In addition, it is v ery visible because it takes a r ela-tively long time to plan and constr uct an office building. When vacancy rates and sublease space ar e added to ne w development, the total is the supply profile for the market.

Forecasting long-term future demand for office space is notoriously difficult. As mentioned, the multitudes of changing factors that impact the complex office market dynamic are hard to predict and gyrate wildly in the shor t term. Over the long term, the U.S. economy is expected to demand an av erage of about 225 million squar e feet per y ear. (Keep in mind, however, that this number can go up or do wn quickly.) Of that amount, 45 million squar e feet of annual demand is expected to r esult from obsolescence of existing office properties.

Trends Impacting the Office Sector

In the early 1980s, an inter esting ev ent occurr ed. The aggr egate total amount of suburban office space ex ceeded the aggregate total amount of *central business district* (CBD) or downtown office space. Since then sub-urban space has gr own at twice the rate of CBD space.   This clearly points up the ev er-growing trend toward the suburbanization of Ameri-can cities. The tr end star ted in the 1950s, when people follo wed large new highways out to ne w single-family homes. Then we witnessed the *malling* of America in the 1960s and 1970s, when the shopping ameni-ties follo wed the population out to the suburbs. S ince the early 1980s, growth in suburban office buildings has r esulted in jobs mo ving to the suburbs, cr eating large metr o ar eas of suburban mass that surr ound dozens of CBDs. These suburban cities are bigger than many of the ma-jor old cities they surr ound. The widely accepted explanation for this shift in locational demand is the theor y of urban labor mar kets, which suggests that cities tend to develop outward before they ever develop upward. Once housing is constructed outward, it presents a fixed asset base with an oppor tunity cost associated with its r eplacement. This cost delays any eventual replacement for decades and even centuries. The idea is that residential development normally mo ves outward first. U pward redevelopment only happens after outwar d mo vement is constrained b y geography or b y distance. With outward development, the commuting time of residents into the CBD becomes increasingly burdensome, much more so than if dev elopment occurr ed v ertically. As commuting increases, firms begin to consider the prospect of a suburban location. At a suburban location, firms can, in theory, attract workers for a lower wage, because such wor kers have less of a commute. This theory predicts that the wages paid for comparable wor kers in the CBD will be higher than wages in the closer suburbs, and, in turn, higher than wages paid b y firms even further out. Studies of wage patterns suggest this is true.

Why is this impor tant? I n the r eal estate world, this tr end alarms the multitude of institutional r eal estate investors, including REITs that own A-class CBD office buildings, because it means most firms will ultimately mo ve to the suburbs and cause decay in v alue of CBD office properties. H owever, there are several factors limiting this pr ocess. The first is that emplo yers using a div erse labor for ce cannot always find a wide range of workers in a single suburb. Workers with different skills often are spread across different suburbs because of the historic patterns by which housing developed. Community zoning standards often r einforce these patterns. If executives live on the North Shore while administrative workers live on the South Shore, as is the case in Milwaukee, the location of easiest access may still be the CBD. A second factor is the public transportation system and existing road patterns. In some metropolitan areas, the transportation systems w ere built to mo ve workers between suburbs and the CBD. Rail transit systems often pr ovide strong radial links that help the CBD and slo w the dev elopment of the suburbs. Thus the historic dev elopment of a city 's transpor tation system str ongly influences the ability of firms to decentralize.

The other big topic of debate in the office r eal estate sector is the impact of telecommuting on the demand for office space. The telecommunications and information r evolution has corr elated closely with the trend of suburban office decentralization. The Internet, computers, mobile phones, e-mail, and fax es all mean that face-to-face interpersonal communication is much less impor tant in the operation of many busi-nesses. It is very easy today for various branches of a company to be situated at widely differ ent locations. S ales, mar keting, and other forms of business communication have also become less dependent on dir ect personal contact. As business contact costs and needs are reduced, firms will be able to take advantage of the lower wage and cost structure that suburban sites offer . An unfor tunate and tragic example is the loss of the World Trade Center, which, despite its name, was an economic wound healed quickly by decentralization.

It is not cer tain that telecommuting has alter ed the demand str uc-ture for office space. H owever, it has aided in expanding the ability of most businesses to decentraliz e their operations. I t has also affected the type and style of space used b y businesses. For example, incr eased computer usage creates a demand for more complex floor and wiring systems. Employees who travel frequently and use laptop computers as their link to the organization ar e seldom given permanent offices; rather, they use an office or cubicle designed to accommodate transient emplo yees who happen to be at the office.

These factors and tr ends hav e led to a basic change in standar d working conditions. Companies are putting employees into open offices, which allow more employees to populate a smaller space. The allocation of space per person in an office setting has dropped from 350 square feet in the mid-1970s to about 225 squar e feet today. This trend is expected to continue as technology allo ws more wor kers to telecommute and r e-main in smaller decentralized locations.

Summary Data

Returns on office REITs are the most volatile of those for the major REIT sectors (see Table 13.1). Over the last fiv e years the office sector pr oduced an average annual r eturn of 14.5 per cent, the highest fiv e-year r eturn of any REIT sector other than r esidential. However, the volatility of the sector as measur ed b y the standar d deviation of r eturns was 20.8 per cent, making it the most volatile of the major sectors. The basic characteristics of the office sector make it mor e sensitive to economic and business conditions, and the long lead time on office construction makes timing the cycle for offices more difficult than for sectors with shorter cycle times.

TABLE 13.1 Historical Sector Data for Office REITs (as of December 2005)

	2005	2004	2003	2002	2001	2000	1999	1998	1997
Panel A									
Total return on sector	13.1%	23.3%	34.0%	-6.8%	-0.8%	35.5%	4.3%	-17.4%	29.0%
Dividend yield	5.1%	6.1%	9.7%	5.9%	7.7%	8.8%	7.9%	4.6%	6.3%
Estimated NAV	105.0%	108.0%	110.0%	88.0%	90.0%	93.0%	79.0%	100.0%	122.0%
Panel B									
Market cap of sector ($ billion)	$62.6								
Index weight	18.8%								
All other sectors	81.2%								
Volatility	20.8%								
5-year return	14.5%								

Source: Uniplan, Inc.

Points to Remember

- Office buildings represent 20 percent of the total commercial real estate market.
- Publicly traded office REIT s r epresent about 21 per cent of the National Association of Real Estate Trusts Equity Index.
- Real estate investment trusts own approximately 8 percent of the investment-grade office properties in the United States.
- The complex and v olatile natur e of the office segment make it one of the most analyzed sectors.
- The U.S. economy is expected to cr eate demand for about 225 million square feet of office space per year.
- Communication technology and modern lifestyles hav e changed the pattern of office demand.
- Office and industrial space is the only space used primarily b y businesses.
- Investment returns on offices are among the most volatile for any real estate sector.
- There are 27 publicly traded office REITs in the NAREIT Equity Index.

14

Industrial REITs

Industry is the soul of business and the keystone of prosperity.
—Charles Dickens, 1841

The estimated aggr egate value of industrial buildings in the U nited States is $2.2 trillion. That total includes o wner-occupied indus-trial real estate v alued at $1.2 trillion. The remaining $1.0 trillion of properties is investor owned. Research suggests that about 10 per cent of industrial space is classified as flex space, which contains both office and industrial ar eas and could be consider ed either office or industrial depending on the criteria emplo yed when classified. I nvestor-owned in-dustrial buildings represent about 15 percent of the total commercial real estate market. Real estate investment trusts (REITs) are estimated to own about 8 percent of investor-owned industrial properties.

Industrial REIT s as a gr oup r epresents about 8 per cent of the National Association of Real Estate Investment Trusts (NAREIT) Equity Index (see Figure 14.1). Keep in mind the fact that within the office seg-ment of the index, about 5 per cent is made up of flex pr operties that have components of both office and industrial space in a single pr operty. These could be categorized as either office or industrial. If they were clas-sified as industrial, the w eighting of this categor y within the NAREIT Equity Index would approach 14 percent.

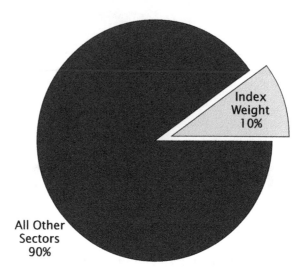

All Other
Sectors
90%

FIGURE 14.1 Industrial REITs as a Percentage of the NAREIT Equity Index
Source: Uniplan, Inc.

Building Classifications

There is no standar d classification system for industrial buildings. I   n many ways the term *industrial property* represents a generic concept that covers a v ast array of r eal estate. I t describes buildings that ar e used for the pr oduction or manufactur e of pr oducts as w ell as pr operties whose function is distribution or war   ehousing. I n most instances, industrial buildings fall into one of the following categories. Each category services a par ticular type of industrial tenant b   y pr oviding a specific type of building functionality.

Warehouse

This is the most common type of industrial property. It is estimated that there ar e o ver 6 billion squar e feet of war ehouse space in the U nited States. Warehouse space is the most commonly tenant occupied, with over 70 percent of all warehouse space being classified as rental space. For a building to classify as a true warehouse, no more than 10 percent of the total square footage can be office ar ea. Warehouse buildings have multi-ple loading docks to accommodate the rapid loading and unloading of trucks. S ome war ehouses may also hav e rail siding for the mo   vement of freight by railroad. In general, modern warehouses have high ceilings to accommodate the vertical loading of content. Ceiling heights are normally in the range of 18 to 40 feet.

Manufacturing

This is the second most common type of industrial building. It is estimated that there are over 3.1 billion square feet of manufacturing space in the United States. Unlike warehouses, manufacturing space is owned more often than rented, with an estimated 60 percent being owner occupied. The highly specialized nature of most manufacturing buildings makes these types of buildings of less interest to the investment community. Also, the larger the manufacturing facility, the more likely it is to be owner occupied. The ever-changing, capital-intensive nature of big manufacturing facilities also makes large-scale users unlikely to want to be involved in a leasing situation.

Flex and R&D

These properties are normally built on smaller parcels of land in areas of mixed-use buildings and combine office and light industrial space into one building. They are most often one-story buildings with ceiling heights in the range of 10 to 15 feet. The ratio of office to industrial space is not set and is usually dependent on the end use of the tenant. Buildings of this style usually have a truck loading dock and also have floor-height loading to facilitate the easy use of smaller vehicles. About 40 percent of this type of space is owner occupied and 60 percent is leased. Because it combines general offices along with warehouse and manufacturing space, this style of building is very popular among smaller private companies that lack the size or scale to support separate office and manufacturing space.

Special Purpose

This category is normally reserved for any building that does not fit into the preceding classifications. For the most part these are either manufacturing buildings that are custom-built to meet a specific need, such as cold storage warehouses, or obsolete buildings that have been recycled for industrial use. Loft buildings, which may have started as industrial buildings in the early 1900s and subsequently have been converted into live-work areas or studio space for artists or advertising agencies, are a prime example of special-purpose buildings. *Incubator buildings,* which are normally large obsolete manufacturing facilities that have been subdivided into multi-tenant structures with very affordable rents aimed at new small businesses, are another example of special-purpose buildings. Unlike most other commercial structures, industrial buildings are not classified by quality level for investment purposes. Instead, they are normally classified by age and use. For example, a building might be referred to as a newer flex building or an older warehouse. Local market standards are very much a part of the industrial building description. What is considered older in some markets would be considered obsolete in other locales. These classifications are almost completely subjective and leave much room for interpretation.

Market Dynamics

Industrial markets are among the most stable when it comes to the supply of and demand for space. Because of the special nature of industrial space, most space is not created until a demand exists. And, due to the very short amount of time required to construct industrial space, the supply can be very responsive to demand or lack of demand. For example, in an area zoned for industrial use, construction permits can usually be obtained within 60 days, and a building can be constructed in three to six months. Contrast that with an office building, which can take two years (or more) from permit to completion. Because of the short cycle time, supply and demand for industrial space does not normally get too far out of balance. This supply and demand constancy translates into very stable occupancy patterns. Historically, industrial vacancies usually run in the 5 to 6 per cent range. In extreme periods, vacancies have run up to 11 percent, but rarely do they exceed these levels for long, even in very competitive local markets.

Final demand for industrial space is highly correlated to the growth of the U.S. economy. An expanding economy produces increasing demand for products and services. Economic growth also tends to stimulate corporate profitability. Increased profits often lead to increased capital spending among businesses, which also translates into demand for more and often better or newer industrial space. Conversely, any general slowing in the economy will usually translate into a quick decline in demand for industrial space. However, because of the long-term capital-intensive nature of most industrial projects, end users, whether owners or renters, normally project their need for space based on long-term projections of final demand. This long-term characteristic of industrial users also tends to stabilize the supply-demand cycle in the industrial sector by moderating spikes in the final demand for space.

The special nature of certain industrial operations often creates locational factors that affect the demand for space at the local market level. For example, the Chicago area, with its geographically central location, its major hub for interstate highways, large international airports, multiple railroad operations, and easy access to the Great Lakes and Mississippi River waterways, is a favorite location among distribution-intensive businesses. Other industries that require large amounts of raw materials or power will consider these needs in their location decision. Industrial space users such as commercial baking and bottling operations will want to locate near their final markets to reduce transportation costs. These locational factors can create particular demand dynamics in the local marketplace. Because of the stable nature of the demand profile in industrial space and the general correlation of demand to economic growth, forecasting long-term future demand is less difficult for industrial space than for other real estate sectors such as office or retail. Over the long term, the U.S. economy is expected to demand, on average, about 270 million square feet per year. This is a reasonably stable number and includes approximately 40 million square feet of annual obsolescence.

Summary Data

The nature of the supply and demand cycle for the industrial sector makes it one of the more stable and predictable segments of real estate. Over the last five years the industrial REIT sector produced an average annual return of 31.9 percent (see Table 14.1). The volatility of the sector as measured by the standard deviation of returns was 16 percent, making it among the most stable sectors. The demand for industrial real estate and the performance of the sector will rise and fall primarily with general economic growth.

TABLE 14.1 Historical Sector Data for Industrial REITs (as of December 2005)

	2005	2004	2003	2002	2001	2000	1999	1998	1997
Panel A									
Total return on sector	15.4%	34.1%	33.1%	17.3%	7.4%	28.6%	3.9%	–16.3%	19.0%
Dividend yield	4.3%	6.9%	7.6%	7.1%	6.9%	8.8%	7.9%	4.6%	6.3%
Estimated NAV	106.0%	111.0%	104.0%	98.0%	95.0%	93.0%	79.0%	100.0%	122.0%
Panel B									
Market cap of sector ($ billion)	$21.1								
Index weight	10.2%								
All other sectors	89.8%								
Volatility	16.0%								
5-year return	31.9%								

Source: Uniplan, Inc.

Points to Remember

- Industrial buildings represent about 15 percent of the total commercial real estate market.
- Publicly traded REITs represent about 14 percent of the National Association of Real Estate Investment Trusts Equity Index.
- REITs own about 8 percent of all U.S. industrial properties.
- There is no uniform system for categorizing industrial space.
- Industrial space, like office space, is primarily used by businesses.
- Industrial pr operties ar e among the most stable sectors of the commercial real estate market.
- Final demand for industrial space is expected to be about 270 million square feet per year.
- Changes in industrial patterns affect the final demand for industrial space.
- There ar e eight pur ely industrial REIT s and eight REIT s that own primarily flex properties.

Retail Property REITs

If you think the United States has stood still, who built the largest shopping center in the world?

—Richard Nixon, 1969

The retail property sector is broken down into three broad categories in the N ational Association of R eal Estate I nvestment Trusts (NAREIT) E quity I ndex. S hopping center r eal estate inv estment trusts (REITs), which number 28, ar e the largest single categor y. There are 10 REITs that specialize in regional malls and seven REITs that focus on freestanding retail properties. Retail REITs make up about 20 percent of the NAREIT Equity Index (see Figure 15.1).

Publicly traded REITs own an equity inter est estimated to be o ver one-third of all regional malls. REITs represent the ownership of approx-imately 50 per cent of super-r egional malls (r egional malls with o ver 800,000 square feet of gross leasable area) and approximately 14 percent of all nonmall retail properties in the country.

Retail Sector Categories

Due to the size of the retail real estate sector and the complex nature of retail operations, a description of retail REITs and retail properties could fill a book by itself. This chapter tries to generally quantify and categoriz e the various aspects of retail real estate. The retail sector can be br oken down into three large subgroups, each of which comprises a number of smaller categories:

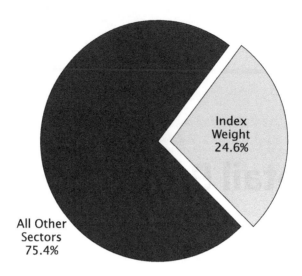

FIGURE 15.1   Retail REITs as a Percentage of the NAREIT Equity Index
Source: Uniplan, Inc.

1. Shopping malls include the following property types:
   - Super-regional malls
   - Regional malls
   - Destination or theme malls
   - Specialty malls
   - Outlet centers
2. Shopping centers include two broad groups:
   - Neighborhood centers
   - Community centers
3. Freestanding retail is divided into two groups:
   - Power centers
   - Big box retail

The regional mall categor y includes super-r egional malls, r egional malls, destination or theme malls, specialty malls, and outlet centers. Shopping centers include two br oad gr oups, neighborhood centers and community centers. F reestanding r etail is divided into two gr   oups known as power centers and big box retail.

In the United States, the consumer, as defined by the U.S. Department of Commerce represents over two-thirds of the domestic economy. Nowhere in the world, except perhaps Japan, is retail activity such a large part of the domestic economy . Each month, nearly 200 million U.S. shoppers visit shopping centers. American cultur e is dominated b y consumerism, and the U nited States has by far the highest amount of r etail space per person of any country in the world. The American landscape is covered with shopping centers of various shapes and sizes. Because of the vast array of different shopping centers, it can be difficult to classify these into groups and subgroups.

In general terms, the quality of retail property is judged by the quality of the r etail tenants that occupy the pr operty. Large, high-quality r etail organizations tend to hav e an ex cellent ability to understand local markets and trade areas. Therefore, when they commit to a particular location, it tends to be a primary driver of retail traffic to a particular location. The type and quality of tenants can be one way in which a r etail property can be classified. F rom a financial point of vie w, the best tenants are frequently referred to in the r eal estate industry as *credit tenants.* These are typically retail operators that are part of a large, national, publicly traded retail organization with access to the public credit markets as well as an inv estment-grade cr edit rating fr om a major cr edit rating agency such as M oody's, S tandard & P oor's, or F itch I nvestor S ervices. Credit tenants tend to r epresent the best and most successful organizations in the r etail industr y and tend to attract other cr edit tenants of a complementary natur e to a r etail r eal estate pr oject. Thus, in general terms, a retail project that is dominated by credit tenants is normally described as a class A r etail property. Retail pr operties that ar e dominated by noncredit tenants are normally classified as class B retail properties.

The size and age of a retail complex is also used as a method of categorizing retail properties. Larger and ne wer properties tend to r eceive a higher quality rating than smaller and older pr operties. O lder, smaller properties often face what is kno wn as the *death spiral.* The typical situation involves an older mall that begins to lose its prime cr edit tenants. These cr edit tenants tend to mo ve into ne wer, larger space that might be within the local mar ket ar ea of the older pr operty. The older property then has difficulty in attracting ne w tenants of either cr edit quality or noncredit quality as a r esult of the vacant space left behind by the credit-quality tenant. This tends to be the beginning of a do wnward spiral as the obsolete pr operty is slowly abandoned by the r etail tenants.

The decline makes it increasingly difficult to attract new tenants or new investors and thereby ultimately results in high, if not complete, vacancy of the mall and often abandonment of the property.

    Malls or retail properties can also be classified in terms of their market location and the distance from which they are able to draw shoppers to the retail center. Neighborhood shopping centers tend to be located in or near residential neighborhoods and have a primary trade area of three to five miles. Community shopping centers tend to be in larger urban neighborhoods and have a trade area of three to eight miles. Regional shopping centers tend to rely on a metropolitan region for most of their retail activity and have a primary trade area that can be 5 to 20 miles in range. The various classifications of retail shopping centers and their age, size, and location characteristics are summed up in Table 15.1.

Neighborhood Shopping Centers

Neighborhood shopping centers tend to be the smallest in size, ranging from 30,000 to 150,000 square feet. The primary concern of the neighborhood shopping center is convenient access for local market users to obtain the necessities of daily life. Neighborhood shopping centers tend

TABLE 15.1 Retail Property Subcategories and Related Data

Name	Size (sq. ft.)	Market Area (mile radius)	Primary Function
Neighborhood shopping centers	230,000–100,000	3–5	Convenient access to local population
Community shopping centers	100,000–300,000	5–10	One-stop shopping for most daily needs
Regional malls	250,000–650, 000	25	Enclosed shopping with general merchandise
Super-regional malls	800,000 or larger	25 or more	Entertainment and destination shopping
Outlet malls	50,000–400,000	Up to 75	Focus on manufacturer-direct off-price items
Power centers	300,000–600,000	15	Dominant anchor tenant located on major roads

to be anchored by grocery stores and are located on sites that range from 3 to 15 acres in size. They normally encompass a primary trade area of three to five miles.

Community Shopping Centers

Community shopping centers tend to be approximately 100,000 to 350,000 square feet in size, located on sites of 10 to 50 acres. They usually focus on general merchandise, with convenience of daily necessities being the primary motive. The community shopping center may be considered a one-stop shopping center for daily needs and may include a department store, a drugstore, and a grocery anchor on the same site. The primary trade area is a 5- to 10-mile range.

Regional Malls

Regional malls tend to cover general merchandise, fashion, and some type of entertainment as well. Regional malls are normally enclosed, whereas neighborhood and community shopping centers are frequently not enclosed and have a more uniform design. Regional malls tend to be from 250,000 to 600,000 square feet in size and occupy sites that range from 50 to 100 acres in size. The primary trade area for a regional mall can extend to as much as 25 miles.

Super-Regional Malls

Super-regional malls are very much like regional malls in terms of merchandise mix. They have a larger variety of merchandise than regional malls and also tend to have more entertainment activities. Super-regional malls are defined generally as 800,000 square feet or larger, located on sites of 60 to 120 acres or more. The super-regional mall's market area is 25 miles or perhaps even farther depending on its location.

Fashion or Specialty Malls

As the name implies, these properties are fashion or clothing oriented and tend to attract higher-end retail tenants. Because of their specialty nature, fashion malls tend to be 100,000 to 250,000 square feet in size and are located on sites of 5 to 25 acres. Their primary trade area can extend for as much as 25 miles and is largely dependent on competition from regional or super-regional malls

Outlet Malls

Outlet malls tend to focus on off-price mer chandise being sold dir ectly through manufactur ers' outlet stor es. They ar e normally 50,000 to 400,000 square feet in size and occupy sites of 10 to 50 acres. Because of the specialty natur e of outlet malls, they tend to draw fr om even larger market areas than super-r egional malls. Consumers ar e often willing to drive as much as 75 miles to visit outlet malls.

Theme or Festival Malls

Also termed *lifestyle malls,* these malls focus on leisure activity or tourist-oriented activities and tend to have a high per centage of space dedicated to r estaurants and other types of enter tainment. The siz e tends to be 100,000 to 250,000 square feet on a 5- to 25-acre site. They are often lo-cated in or around areas with high levels of tourist activity. For example, a large number of leisur e or lifestyle pr operties are found in locations in such regions as Orlando, Florida, and Las Vegas, Nevada.

Power Centers

Power centers have a categor y-dominant anchor tenant and may hav e a few smaller inline tenants as well. They are familiar as big national chain stores like Wal-Mart or H ome D epot. P ower centers ar e typically 300,000 to 600,000 square feet in size and are located on 25- to 100-acre sites. Power centers tend to have a trade area of 5 to 15 miles and ar e gen-erally located on the edge of higher-density r esidential areas with nearby access to major highways.

Supply and Demand in the Retail Sector

As with other categories of r eal estate, demand for r etail space is driv en by the general growth of the domestic economy, with a high sensitivity to growth in demand for r etail and consumer goods and ser vices. The de-mand for retail goods and services is a function of household income and growth in the demographic segments that tend to be higher consumers of retail goods and services generally the 15- to 25-year-old and the over-50 segments. H owever, it should be noted that demographic and consumer spending habits change o ver time and that good r etail property operators are sensitive to the impact of changing lifestyle demographics on their r etail pr operties. N ormally, a healthy domestic economy will produce a consumer who is willing to spend at a higher lev el and at a higher rate than that of a slowly expanding or quiet economy.

The seemingly ev er-expanding supply of r etail pr operty is par t of the retail property cycle. Since 1996, on average 250 million square feet of retail space have been delivered into the U.S. real estate market. With approximately 6 billion squar e feet of existing space, the base of r etail space is expanding nearly twice as fast as the U.S. economy. However, it is important to note that of that 250 million square feet of annual delivery, approximately 125 million squar e feet r eplaces obsolete r etail pr operty that is in some stage of the death spiral and ultimately will be v acant and off the mar ket for practical purposes. I t is estimated that o ver the next sev en y ears, nearly 1 billion squar e feet of the aggr egate r etail market total will become functionally obsolete and be removed from the aggregate r etail pr operty pool. The long-term demand for r etail space over the same period is estimated to be appr oximately 290 million square feet per y ear. The overall demand for r etail space will be dir ectly impacted by the level of economic gr owth as well as the financial health of the consumer and changing tr ends within the r etail industry. Any of these factors could hav e a large impact on the o verall demand for retail space.

Industry Dynamics

The dynamics of the U.S. r etail property industry are inextricably intertwined with the dynamics of the U.S. r etail sector. I n general terms, much like hotel operators, retail real estate operators provide a very high value-added management component. R etail pr operty o wners must know and understand the dynamics of the r etail sector, which they deal with from a tenant basis. They generally have a marketing plan for their entire portfolio of retail properties as well as a specific marketing plan for each individual property and perhaps even for each space within a property. These marketing plans ar e often driv en by the mar keting plans of one or more anchor tenants that may dominate the location of the r etail property. The overall marketing plan considers factors such as pr operty location relative to population density, the current and projected population growth, local household income lev els and buying habits, and the age demographics of the ar ea. Competitiv e r etail centers in the same market area, as well as land av ailable for r etail expansion within a r etail center's marketing area, are also taken into account. Thus the retail property owner tends to analyze all the market factors and attempt to position a retail property for maximum value in the local real estate market. This high value-added component of r etail operations can be critical in extracting value on the margin from the retail property. Because each retail property operates at such a differ ent level, the best way to examine the industry dynamic is by property type.

Dynamics of Regional Malls

Regional and super-regional malls tend to be the largest retail structures, typically having two or mor e anchor tenants that may account for as much as 60 per cent of the gross leaseable area. The anchor tenants draw retail traffic to a location, and the malls are configured so that the majority of retail shoppers enter the mall through an anchor store. Anchor tenants are generally credit tenants and are very sophisticated in their ability to analyze the local r eal estate mar ket. They understand and r ecognize their traffic-drawing ability and use it to their adv antage. In a typical regional or super-regional mall, the anchor tenant pays little or no r ent to the landlord and generally makes a below-average per-square-foot contribution to cover maintenance expense. Anchor tenants usually o wn their own stores, which they build on the mall site on land that is leased fr om the landlord over a long period.

Specialty Tenants

The specialty tenants, often r eferred to as *inline tenants,* represent the majority of the income av ailable to the r etail regional or super-r egional mall operator. In most situations, the heavy pr omotional activity of the anchor tenant in turn draws the foot traffic for the inline tenants that populate the balance of the mall's gross leaseable area.

Specialty tenants provide the majority of mall income, which is usually based on a minimum per-squar e-foot rental rate, with fix ed periodic increases that ar e index ed to the consumer price index or a minimum annual rate incr ease. In addition to minimum r ents, a shopping center owner sets a base rental rate that increases as the tenant's sales volume increases. This is typically kno wn as the *percentage rent clause* in a lease. I n many ways, the per centage clause cr eates a po werful incentiv e for the shopping center o wner to contribute to the success of the r etail tenant. These percentage rents typically run in the range of 6 to 8 per cent over a base amount of aggr egate revenues on an annual basis. I n addition, specialty tenants pay a common area maintenance and insurance charge that represents their pr o rata shar e of all maintenance expenses for the shopping center. Real estate taxes are also handled on a pro rata share based on square footage. In addition, tenants are required to make a fixed contribution on an annual basis to a marketing and promotion fund, which is generally used to dev elop the mar keting plan for the specialty tenants in a mall or regional mall. In many ways, the mall owner is attempting to align the financial success of the mall with the financial success of the retail tenants. Tenants' ability to pay r ent is determined b y their lev el of sales and profitability. In general, rents run at an average level of 8 to 10 percent of sales. Rents plus all other tenant costs typically run from 12 to 15 percent of sales. The mall o wner, of course, enjo ys the benefit of having higher-productivity tenants or tenants with mor e popular pr oducts and ser vices. In some lease situations, tenants with per-square-foot sales that fall within a target range might pay 7 to 8 per cent of sales as a minimum r ental payment; as sales increase to higher levels this may grow to 9 to 10 percent or more. As the sales and success of the property grow, the rents grow as well.

The Leasing Relationship

This unique r elationship between the r etail landlord and the r etail property user requires some special analysis. O f all property types, retail properties are most likely to generate long and detailed lease negotiations prior to the actual signing of a lease for space. The r etailer in general understands that ev ery dollar in per centage sales or ev ery expense that is not paid to the landlord will essentially fall to the bottom line for the r etailer. National cr edit tenant organizations that lease r etail space acr oss the country normally have an experienced real estate department that negotiates every aspect of a retail lease. Independent real estate brokers generally handle rental activities in smaller pr operties. Rental activities in major regional malls and large r etail complexes are typically handled b y the local office of the mall, or , in the case of national cr edit tenants, dir ectly between the tenant 's organization and the national r eal estate organization. It is also not uncommon for a national cr edit tenant to arriv e at a standard lease structure for all locations with a large owner of multiple retail properties. In many instances, lease negotiations are bundled to cover a portfolio of retail centers and administered on a uniform basis. These factors suggest that skilled retail property management can add a high level of value in the area of property management and lease negotiations.

Regional mall owners are very focused on the sales performance of their properties. Mall owners monitor very closely the same-store sales levels for tenants that have occupied the mall for a period of 12 months or more. This year-by-year performance in same-store sales is a measure of the mall's retail activity as well as of the performance of the individual tenants. In monitoring the same-store sales levels of individual tenants, the landlord may begin to develop a profile of underperforming tenants that occupy the retail portfolio. This can lead to selective targeted negotiations at the time the space is re-leased, or to a mall owner simply making the decision not to re-lease space to an underperforming tenant. In general terms, mall management measures total sales for all tenants on an average per-square-foot basis, regardless of their tenure at the mall, in order to provide a comparative measure of the mall's ability to draw consumer traffic.

Retail malls that generate higher levels of per-square-foot activity as a result of location, tenant mix, or other factors will demand a rental premium over malls whose performance is more average. Because the leases of inline retail tenants contain a percentage clause that requires the tenant to pay the higher of a base rent or a percentage of sales that is fixed in advance, the mall operator is truly a partner of the tenant.

Dynamics of Shopping Centers and Freestanding Retail Markets

There are three major subcategories of shopping centers. Neighborhood and community shopping centers are anchored by promotional tenants that tend to be discount retailers or power retailers. In these instances, the anchor may use as much as 70 percent of the entire gross leaseable area of the center. Power centers, which are anchored by similar discount retailers, are in the same category; however, power centers tend to be 90 percent occupied by anchor tenants with only a few or no other retail tenants. These are often referred to as *freestanding* or *big box* retail centers. Finally, there are neighborhood and community shopping centers, anchored by supermarkets or drugstores, that typically find as much as 70 percent of their gross leaseable space occupied by one or two major anchor tenants. The supermarket and drugstore may be separate or combined.

As in malls, the anchor tenant in shopping centers tends to be the tenant that relies on heavy promotional activity to stimulate retail traffic to the property. However, anchor tenants pay their share of property expenses. In a typical strip shopping center, anchor tenants pay a minimum annual rent and a percentage of sales that in total produce a minimum rent level for the landlord. The major distinction is that, unlike mall tenants, anchor tenants at strip shopping centers pay a much smaller percentage of sales as rent, typically in the range of 2 to 5 per cent. In many instances, these anchor tenants build and operate their own units and, in fact, may directly own the real estate. Although shopping centers may not obtain the rental revenue growth component that regional mall operators enjoy, well-anchored shopping centers enjoy a highly stable rental stream. In addition, grocery- or drugstore-anchored shopping centers tend to have very long-duration lease structures. It is not unusual to find a grocery-anchored retail center with an initial lease term of 15 to 20 years with extensions of up to 10 years available. Although the rental growth for these units may not be as rapid as that for regional malls, they tend to have longer, more predictable cash flow durations.

Trends in Retail Real Estate

In the long run, a shopping center is successful only if it is able to create and maintain a competitive position in its local market. In many ways, this success is driven by a property owner's ability to reinvent the real estate on a periodic basis. One issue that continues to be at the forefront in the retail property sector is the level of maintenance capital an owner must spend to maintain or increase existing rental cash flow from a property. In particular, this is a big challenge for the mall sector, due to the dynamic and ever-changing nature of the U.S. retail economy. In the last 10 years, the amount of capital expense required to maintain a regional mall in a competitive way has been increasing. In the early 1990s, capital expenses of 3 to 5 percent of net operating income were typical for regional malls. This number has increased substantially to 7 or 8 percent, and many experts believe that on a long-term basis, 10 percent of net operating income will be required. Most mall owners agree that in order for a regional mall to remain competitive, a capital renovation of the property must take place every 8 to 12 years. Based on the current cost of construction, it is not unusual for mall owners to spend between $12 and $24 per square foot every 8 to 12 years in order to reposition, reinvent, or remodel their retail properties. It is generally believed that this trend toward redeveloping existing properties helps them avoid the death spiral. Investors and retail REITs should consider the increasing level of capital expenditures required to maintain properties as a situation that could lower cash flow available for distribution to REIT shareholders.

Obsolescence

Like regional malls, shopping centers are also faced with recurring capital expense items that need to be considered. Over the last decade, capital expense reserves for shopping centers have grown from about 4 per cent to about 7 per cent of net operating income, and many experts believe this trend will continue until levels reach approximately 9 to 10 percent. Functional and competitive obsolescence are primarily to blame for increasing capital expense in the shopping center sector. Obsolescence results from a physical property requiring a major structural overhaul in order to remain competitive in a local market. *Competitive obsolescence* is a part of retooling an existing property in order to accommodate a new tenant replacing a major tenant that may be leaving the property. It also results from changing retail dynamics. For example, a well-maintained grocery-anchored shopping center can become competitively obsolete when a new Wal-Mart opens just several miles down the highway. This competitive obsolescence often requires a major capital expenditure to retool the property in order to become competitive again. This form of obsolescence accounts for the generally higher level of capital expense in the shopping center area.

Functional obsolescence can be seen throughout the retail real estate community and is embedded in a number of trends within the retail property sector. For example, supermarkets now tend to be much larger than just a decade ago. Some stores average over 70,000 square feet, whereas just 10 years ago the average figure was about 28,000 square feet. Drugstores, another major tenant of community shopping centers, have also revised their operating strategy. Today, drugstores prefer to be freestanding units based on the edges of large shopping complexes rather than being a part of the in-line tenant mix. Part of the reason is to accommodate the newest trend in pharmacy delivery: the drive-through pharmacy. Big box retailers are also getting bigger. Wal-Mart's average per-store square footage has grown from about 55,000 square feet 10 years ago to about 130,000 square feet today. As retail formats change, properties with older formats become functionally obsolete and require capital expenditures in order to bring them up-to-date and keep them competitive. The low-inflation environment of the mid- and late 1990s has also been a problem for retail REITs. As mentioned, most retail leases contain a clause stating that the tenant will pay the higher of a base rent or a percentage of sales. In an environment where retail prices have been stable or even declining, inflation-driven increases in rental revenue have not materialized as many retail owners may have anticipated in the early 1990s. However, it should be noted that this tame inflationary environment has been somewhat offset by very strong consumer demand, which has translated into higher general retail sales.

Consumer Income and Retail Revenue

Another interesting trend in the retail sector is that sales of goods typically purchased in stores and shopping centers have been growing at a rate slower than the growth rate of consumer income. This supports the problematic notion that growth in personal income drives demand for retail space. Growth in retail sales has been about half that in retail space. This trend has contributed to a lower level of growth in per-square-foot sales for most major retail operators. Due to the participating nature of most retail leases, lower growth and per-square-foot sales have negatively impacted the returns in the retail real estate sector.

The Internet and Retail

There is much debate about the impact of the Internet on retail sales and on the value of retail real estate. Internet sales are building at a steady pace. Industry reports put Internet retail sales as follows:

1999	$17.5 billion
2000	$37.9 billion
2001	$56.5 billion
2002	$78.1 billion
2003	$109 billion
2004	$138 billion (est.)

This is impressive sales growth, and holiday-related sales have been the fastest. These sales gains occurred because more people became Internet users during 1999 and 2000. That incr ease, however, was some what mitigated by a slight decline in the av erage amount pur chased by Internet shoppers. It may be that the incease in Internet shoppers lowered the average purchase amount as more new shoppers entered the marketplace during the course of 2003 through 2005.

Projections of longer-term e-commer ce sales continue to rise. A number of forecasters have raised their Internet retail sales projections for 2005 and 2006 fr om an av erage of $140 billion and $158 billion to $149 and $182 billion, r espectively. The str ongest e-commer ce categories include books, video, and music; computer har dware and software; and gifts and flo wers. These thr ee categories could captur e a double-digit market share of total r etail sales b y 2006. O ther categories such as apparel, housewares, and food look to achieve low- to mid-single-digit penetration o ver the next fiv e y ears. As mentioned, holiday purchases are very strong on the Internet. The following is an estimate of the top online holiday purchases as projected by several different surveys:

Books and magazines	58 percent
Music and movies	55 percent
Computers and related	42 percent
Toys and video games	42 percent
Electronics	40 percent
Clothing	36 percent

The bursting of the I nternet bubble has been the most notable setback for the e-commerce business. The diminished funding prospects for business-to-consumer I nternet companies hav e slo wed the gr owth of sales in the sector . M any existing I nternet companies ar e in a cash squeeze, as cash burn rates are exceedingly high and profitability in most cases is a long time out.   Without funding, the competitiv e thr eat to store-based r etailers fr om pur e-play e-commer ce companies will be significantly reduced. To the surprise of the I nternet elite, old bricks-and-mortar r etailers ar e often pr oving to be better equipped than their e-commerce competitors in developing Internet business in their r espective pr oduct categories. These stor e-based r etailers ar e lev eraging their established brand names and r etail distribution pr esence online without spending millions on incr emental marketing and distribution. Although this is great news for existing retailers, it is only good ne ws for the land-lords. Although it is pr eferable for clicks-and-bricks business models to prevail o ver pur e plays, a significant shift in v olume away fr om tradi-tional formats would still result in store closings.

Although the I nternet's emergence may hav e a negativ e impact on the sales of r etail tenants, it seems books, music, videos, and electr onics are the categories that will suffer the most. M any REITs and their r etail customers are implementing I nternet initiatives to aid in the efficiencies of their operations, incr ease the av ailability of pr oduct information to consumers, and in some cases enhance top-line growth through the con-vergence of the Internet and shopping centers.

Overall the Internet continues to grow as a new channel of retail sales. It is not unlikely that I nternet sales will hav e a penetration rate in the range of 7 to 10 per cent of total r etail sales. This emergence might negatively impact both existing mail-or der and stor e-based re-tailers. E xperts estimate that e-commer ce will r educe r etail r ental growth by 50 to 60 basis points over the next five years. It is not a dis-aster, but it is cer tainly a tr end wor th watching. I nvestors in REIT s should be aware of the risk that e-commerce poses to retail real estate. However, the tactile and social natur e of much shopping activity should also be consider ed. I t seems that e-commer ce has y et to pr o-duce a measurable impact on prospective retail leasing activity, but the Internet will remain a topic of debate in the r etail property sector for many years to come.

Summary Data

Returns and volatility for retail REITs are average (see Table 15.2). Over the last fiv e years the r etail sector pr oduced an av erage annual r eturn of 28.5 per cent, the lo west for the major REIT sectors. The v olatility of the retail sector as measur ed b y the standar d deviation of r eturns was 19.1 per cent. The basic characteristics of the r etail sector make it v ery sensitive to economic and business conditions. The long lead times on major r etail constr uction along with general competitiv e conditions in the retail community make the outlook for this sector less favorable than in the recent past.

TABLE 15.2 Historical Sector Data for Retail REITs (as of December 2005)

	2005	2004	2003	2002	2001	2000	1999	1998	1997
Panel A									
Total return on sector	11.8%	40.2%	46.7%	21.1%	30.4%	18.0%	−18.9%	−4.9%	17.0%
Dividend yield	5.2%	7.0%	8.3%	7.0%	9.8%	10.2%	7.1%	5.9%	7.1%
Estimated NAV	114.0%	121.0%	124.0%	114.0%	98.0%	79.0%	75.0%	106.0%	116.0%
Panel B									
Market cap of sector ($ billion)	$94.9								
Index weight	27.0%								
All other sectors	73.0%								
Volatility	19.1%								
5-year return	28.5%								

Source: Uniplan, Inc.

Points to Remember

- Retail pr operties r epresent 30 per cent of all inv estment-grade commercial real estate.
- There are approximately 43,000 retail properties across the country, comprising over 6 billion square feet of gross leasable space.
- REITs are the largest sector in the N ational Association of R eal Estate I nvestment Trusts I ndex, r epresenting appr oximately 20 percent of the entire index.
- There are 45 publicly traded REIT s that focus ex clusively on r etail pr operties. In addition, appr oximately 50 per cent of the investment activity of diversified REITs (REITs that own properties in more than one sector) is focused on retail properties.

Hotel REITs

When I feel like getting away from it all, I just turn on the TV to a Spanish channel and imagine I'm on vacation in a hotel in Mexico.

—Charles Merrill Smith, 1981

Hotel pr operties hav e an aggr egate total v alue of appr oximately $225 billion. The hotel inv estment universe represents approxi- mately 5 per cent of all inv estment-grade commer cial real estate. Hotel real estate inv estment trusts (REITs) make up about 5 per cent of the N ational Association of R eal Estate I nvestment Trusts (NAREIT) Equity Index (see Figure 16.1). The hotel sector has historically been the most volatile sector of the commer cial real estate univ erse; however, de- mand for hotel r ooms is easily pr edicted because it tracks v ery closely with general levels of economic activity. The problem in the industry has long been supply, which is prone to boom-and-bust cycles driven by over- building. Hotels have a r eal estate component that contributes to their performance. To the extent that location and property type contribute to a successful hotel, the real estate component is obvious.

The Hotel Real Estate Sector Challenge

Mastering the hotel operating business is the key factor for success in the hotel sector. O perations are more critical to the o verall success of hotel properties than properties in any other real estate sector. The other major challenge for hotel o wners and operators is their near-total dependence

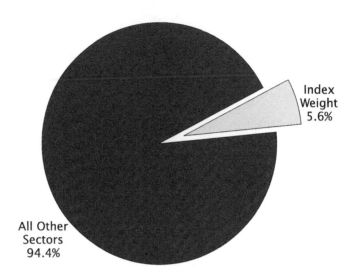

FIGURE 16.1   Hotel REITs as a Percentage of the NAREIT Equity Index
Source: Uniplan, Inc.

on the economic cycle, which provides ongoing incremental demand for rooms.

Management is the one critical element o ver which a hotel o wner has a high level of influence. (The other critical element is the economy, over which the hotel owner has little or no contr ol.) Thus, more than in any other sector of real estate, the opportunity presents itself in the hotel sector for a high lev el of operational skills to enable an o wner to add value in the sector. These excellent operational skills ar e often translated into hotel brand names such as Marriott or Hilton. Poor management of hotel operations does not only hur t a brand name; it will attract w ell-managed competitors into the local mar ket of the inferior operator . Therefore management skill and the hotel REIT's ability to capitalize on that management skill ar e critical in determining what kind of a r eturn profile can be expected from a hotel REIT.

The revenue stream of hotels clearly has the shor test duration of all real estate. Room rates (rents) are literally reset on a daily basis as guests come and go fr om a pr operty. When demand declines, r oom rates de-cline right along with it. When demand increases, room rates rise with it and can be r epriced v ery quickly, literally o vernight. As mentioned, hotel REITs are very highly leveraged to economic growth, which represents final demand for hotel r ooms. If demand is incr easing in a supply-constrained market, a hotel has the ability to immediately reprice rooms and leverage rental r eturns. A successful hotel REIT operator affiliates with hotel brands and management teams that hav e the ability to manage thr ough economic downturns as well as capitalize on upturns.

There are a wide range of inv estors in the hotel sector . As a r esult, there are a wide range of deal str uctures. Both pr operty companies and hotel companies inv est in hotel pr operties, along with hotel REIT s and private investors. In a typical private situation, a local real estate investor may build and own a hotel and then contract with a national hotel company for management services. In other cases, the investor and the hotel company might form a joint venture to share in the equity and return on investment. In another common format seen in the 1980s, pioneer ed by the Marriott Corporation, the hotel company develops the property and then spins off the real estate into a syndication while retaining a management contract.

Moving the real estate into a limited par tnership is a way of r educing the amount of capital needed to expand or gr ow a hotel business. The management company in turn creates a predictable earnings stream, which makes it more attractive to Wall Street.

Traditional hotel REIT s cannot operate the assets they o wn. B ecause of the operating company rules, assets must be leased and managed by a separate company . This makes analysis of the hotel REIT sector more difficult, because it often has to be taken in the context of an operating company or sev eral affiliated operating companies. I n addition, brands or assets that normally do not have a legal or ownership affiliation with the hotel ar e also an impor tant factor to consider when analyzing hotel REITs.

Asset Quality

Hotels are not assigned class rankings like apar tment and office buildings. Instead, the quality criterion is the price range or price segment of r ooms that the hotel pr ovides. Hotel room price segments ar e typically gr ouped into three broad classifications kno w as *budget* or *economy, midpriced,* and *upscale* or *full service.* Economy r ooms ar e the least expensiv e and full-service hotels tend to have the most expensive rooms. However, local markets play a role in the actual room price. For example, a $150-a-night room in N ew York City is likely to be in an economy-class hotel. B ut $150 a night in Des Moines is likely to be a full-service or upscale hotel room. Hotel asset types are also broken into descriptions of property types. The following are some of the more common property descriptions in the hotel sector:

- *Conference center or convention hotels.* Have 500 or more rooms.
- *Full-service hotels.* Offer r estaurant and bar facilities, r oom service, catering, and banquets and may provide meeting space.
- *Limited-service properties.* Do not hav e food and bev erage operations and may or may not offer meeting space.
- *Extended-stay properties.* Resemble apar tments; hav e studio and suite accommodations that ar e designed for the business trav eler who may have a lengthy stay in a given location.

Hotels are also classified by the local market they serve or their location within a local mar ket. This can add another lev el of description when dealing with hotel pr operties. The following are some of the local market classifications often applied to hotels:

- *Urban hotels.* Generally located in do wntown central business districts.
- *Suburban hotels.* Often located in suburban ar eas contiguous to large groups of office and industrial buildings.
- *Motor inns.* Usually located at the intersections of major highways to accommodate auto travelers.
- *Airport hotels.* Typically located at or near airpor t locations for ease of meeting and transportation purposes.
- *Tourist or resort hotels.* Normally provide a full compliment of re-sort and luxury services at a single location.

Brand affiliation is another way to position or describe hotel pr operties. Users can easily identify a price point or property type that is normally affiliated with a par ticular brand. There ar e numer ous national hotel brands that offer access to r eservation systems, adv ertising p rograms, and management on a national scale. A number of regional brands focus their operations in specific geographic r egions. To further confuse the pr ocess of hotel description, industr y obser vers may use compound classifications to describe pr operties. A pr operty may be classified　as a budget-priced suburban hotel, or a limited-ser   vice midpriced urban hotel. Any compound description might also be associated with a brand. A property might be described as a budget-priced suburban Holiday Inn. This shows how highly segmented the market has become.

Supply and Demand for Hotel Rooms

Estimating aggregate demand for hotel r ooms in the U nited States is r ela-tively straightfor ward. There ar e thr ee basic types of trav   elers who use hotels: the business trav eler, the conv ention or meeting trav eler, and the leisure trav eler. F or each type, demand is largely r   elated to the state of the economy. A robust economic environment leads to more business travel as a result of a higher level of business activity. In addition, higher economic growth leads to more leisure travel, resulting in a gr eater demand for r esort hotel r ooms. H igher lev els of economic activity also tend to cr   eate larger turnouts for business conv entions, which also translates into mor e demand for hotel r ooms. The high corr elation betw een gr owth of the domestic economy and hotel r oom demand can be affected b y a number of factors. The cost of oil, which driv es the underlying cost of most modes of trans-portation, generally affects hotel occupancy rates.   The value of the dollar also has an impact on U.S. domestic hotel operations because a higher dol-lar tends to discourage for eign tourism wher eas a lo wer dollar makes U.S. destinations more affordable to foreign tourists. Bad weather can also create a negativ e envir onment for cer tain hotel operators.   The pr ofitability of a particular industry can have an impact on its policy toward employee travel. For example, the dot-com industry was booming in the late 1990s, precipi-tating a high lev el of business trav el among members of the industr   y. Because the industry has experienced a severe downturn, travel policies have been focused on a reduction in travel expenses and therefore have translated into less business travel by a large sector of the business economy.

The supply of hotel r ooms is also impacted b y a number of eco-nomic factors. In some markets, crowded urban areas with little available land and difficult entitlement pr   ocesses cr eate a local mar ket that is generally supply constrained. Many resort destinations fall into this cate-gory during the tourist season. The N apa Valley wine r egion of Califor-nia, for example, is generally supply constrained during the wine season. The local market and infrastructure do not lend themselves to new hotel development, and growing grapes is a higher and better economic use of land than hotel development. Thus room demand generally exceeds supply in Napa at all times ex cept the off-season. S upply-constrained markets tend to be highly pr ofitable in an economic expansion and tend to be more insulated from an economic downturn because of the generally limited supply in the local market.

This set of factors is less tr ue in nonurban ar eas or locations that are not supply constrained. Hotels in the economy, midrange, and budget price ranges are simple and easy to build, especially in suburban areas where land and zoning provide few barriers to entry. Hotel construction can begin quickly in r esponse to str ong economic demand. This new supply can quickly er ode pr ofit margins of all hotels in a good economic environment and can cr eate a supply glut in a bad economic environment.

Hotels tend to track their occupancy level in a figure called *RevPar,* which is an acr onym for *revenue per available room.* This figure is calculated by taking the average daily room rate and multiplying it by the occupancy level of the hotel level on a given day. These daily revenues are then aggregated to come up with the average RevPar per period. A hotel that operates at 75 percent occupancy is considered to be nearly fully occupied. Few hotels are strong in both weekday and weekend operations and tend to have more success either during the week with business travelers or on the weekends with leisure travelers. There are often seasonal differences in occupancy as well. As mentioned, r esort hotel locations may be overbooked during the tourist season and may be virtually empty during the off-season. Demand at the local level for a given hotel is often linked to its physical pr oximity to local attractions or businesses that generate travel. Airport hotels, for example, often pr ovide a convenient location for groups of business travelers to meet. Being next to or part of a convention center can also be a positive factor. In addition, resort hotels depend heavily on their natural or man-made attractions such as golf courses and water parks, and on ease of access.

The operating component is more critical in the hotel business than in any other categor y of r eal estate. The benefits of economies of scale have been tested and pr oven within the hotel industr y, and all of the leading hotel companies having a national portfolio tend to perform well in both economic expansions and economic declines. B eing national in scope cr eates buying po wer, but the r eal key to economies of scale in hotels is a recognizable and well-respected brand name. Branding gives hotel operators lev erage in booking r eservations and in attracting and creating relationships with a large number of customers who identify the brand with a par ticular quality level. These factors provide a real advantage when the hotel company expands its market or brand into other locations. The extension or pr esence of str ong brands in a par ticular market niche often ser ves as an effectiv e barrier to entr y for potential competitors in a particular market segment.

The hotel business and the airline business shar e many of the same operating characteristics. Both hotel and airline operators r equire large capital investments in plant and equipment. They also involve large fixed operating expenses for staff and infrastr ucture such as r eservation call centers. Airlines and hotels have to fill the seats or rooms on a daily basis in order to remain economically viable. The more complex issue for operators of both hotels and airlines is a concept called *yield management.* This requires finding the right combination of price and occupancy level to maximize profits. Airlines were the pioneers of yield management systems, often charging dozens of different prices for seats of the same type on the same flight. H otel operators and r ental car companies hav e also adopted this practice. The idea is to selectiv ely adjust the offering price until a particular economic result is achieved. It is better financially to fill a seat or a r oom with a lo wer-paying customer than to hav e that seat or room vacant. That unused r oom-night or seat can nev er be r ecaptured. Yield management is slowly making its way into the residential real estate sector, with the o wners of some apar tment REITs beginning to price available units on a yield management basis.

Technical Aspects to Remember

There are a number of technical aspects to examine when looking at a hotel REIT and its relationship to a hotel operating company. The following are the key items that should be reviewed when examining hotel REITs:

- The lessee must hav e a legitimate business goal in terms of the hotel project.
- The hotel must be leased to a company that is separate fr om the REIT.

- Gross revenue leases must be designed to deliver most of the economics to the REIT.

- Leases must be based on per centage or par ticipating r ents, not net income.

- Hotel REITs collect 15 to 25 percent of room revenues up to a pre-determined break point and 60 to 70 percent beyond that point.

- Food and bev erage rent may be appr oximately 5 per cent of r evenues if the business is operated b y lessee, or 95 per cent of r ent from a subcontractor.

- Break points adjust up ward annually b y a formula normally based on the consumer price index.

- Leased r evenues may r epresent 30 to 35 per cent of hotel r evenues, but bey ond the br eak point, the REIT collects r ent at twice the level of the typical weighted average margin. (This situation creates a high level of operating leverage for hotel REITs.)

- Typically a 1 per cent change in R evPar may r esult in a 1.5 to 2 percent change in lease revenues to the REIT.

- Lease lev erage disappears when hotel r evenues and br eak points change at the same rate.

- Seasonality amplifies quar terly volatility, as a lease formula is applied to each quarter's annualized rents.

- Hotel REITs may collect excess rent during seasonally strong second and thir d quar ters, but differ ences ar e made up during the seasonally slow fourth quarter.

- The affiliated lessee is separate fr om the REIT but is o wned and operated b y senior management, in many cases the REIT   's founders.

- An independent lessee reduces the potential for conflicts of interest.

- The lessee may pay franchise, licensing, and management fees to the owner of a hotel flag for use of a brand, r eservation system, and property management.

- Hotel REITs are responsible for insurance and property taxes.

- Hotel REITs or lessees typically r eserve 4 per cent of hotel r evenues for furnitur e and equipment r eplacement, but 6 to 7 percent may be a more appropriate long-term level.
- Very few hotel REITs do any meaningful development work.

Performance

On a long-term basis, the per formance of hotel REITs has been among the best r elative to other REIT asset classes. H owever, the v olatility of earnings or return, when measured by standard deviation, has been v ery large when compared to the growth rate. Profits in the hotel business are very difficult to maximiz e because of the need to r eturn capital into the enterprise to refine and upgrade hotel facilities. In addition, high volatility of returns is due to a combination of very high operating leverage and very high financial lev erage, which ar e often pr esent in the hotel sector . The significant fix ed cost of hotel operation, as w ell as high lev erage, makes hotel operators v ery vulnerable to ex cess supply or a do wnward shift in demand. H otel financing is generally a mor e specialized form of funding, which means fe wer lenders ar e willing to become inv olved in the sector. Generally, for hotel REITs, this allows for a higher operating margin on invested capital.

Summary Data

Returns on hotel REIT s ar e the most v olatile of those for all pr operty REIT sectors. Over the last five years the hotel sector pr oduced an average annual return of 11.6 percent (see Table 16.1).This is the worst five-year r eturn of any single pr operty sector other than specialty REIT s, which include a number of different property types. The volatility of the hotel sector as measured by the standard deviation of returns is 41.1 percent, making it the most volatile of the property REIT sectors. The basic characteristics of the hotel sector make it extremely sensitive to economic and business conditions. Whether hotel REIT s hav e an up or a do wn year, the performance tends to be very extreme.

TABLE 16.1 Historical Sector Data for Hotel REITs (as of December 2005)

	2005	2004	2003	2002	2001	2000	1999	1998	1997
Panel A									
Total return on sector	9.8%	32.7%	31.7%	-1.5%	-16.3%	45.8%	-16.2%	-52.8%	30.1%
Dividend yield	4.8%	4.4%	7.7%	5.5%	6.9%	14.9%	7.9%	2.2%	6.8%
Estimated NAV	105.0%	108.0%	91.0%	79.0%	89.0%	107.0%	74.0%	89.0%	146.0%
Panel B									
Market cap of sector ($ billion)	$19.06								
Index weight	6.0%								
All other sectors	94.1%								
Volatility	41.1%								
5-year return	11.6%								

Sources: National Association of Real Estate Investment Trusts; Uniplan, Inc.

Points to Remember

- Hotels represent about 4 per cent of the total commer cial real es-
  tate market.
- Publicly traded REITs represent about 5 per cent of the N ational
  Association of Real Estate Trusts (NAREIT) Equity Index.
- Real estate inv estment tr usts o wn about 19 per cent of all U.S.
  hotel properties.
- Hotels are usually classified by room price, size, and location.
- Operations are more critical to the o verall success of hotel pr op-
  erties than properties in any other real estate sector.
- Hotel pr operties are among the most v olatile in the commer cial
  real estate market but have high relative returns.
- Demand for hotel r ooms is largely r elated to the state of the
  economy.
- There are 15 publicly traded hotel REITs.

17

Health Care Properties

A hospital's reputation is determined by the number of eminent men who die there.

—George Bernard Shaw

Health care properties are generally not as familiar to the investing public as yet another kind of property in which real estate investment trusts (REITs) can invest. Many of the health care providers that operate these properties are not well known and the regulatory environment in which they operate is often complex. These factors can make health care REITs seem more difficult to analyze than other property sectors.

There are several common misconceptions about the health care REIT segment. First is the popular belief that health care REITs lack value-adding ability because they do not actively manage their properties. This idea is not based on fact. Health care REITs often add value largely through the careful selection and negotiation of their ultimate investment in a health care property. The sector has experienced a fair amount of growth over the last decade and its returns in general have been better than those for many other sectors of the REIT industry. The health care REIT sector represents about 5 percent of the National Association of Real Estate Investment Trusts (NAREIT) Equity Index (see Figure 17.1) and has a market capitalization of approximately $7 billion. The sector's capitalization grew steadily through the 1990s at an average annual rate of approximately 15 percent and then declined through 1998 to 2000 as changes in Medicare and Medicaid reimbursement and highly fragmented ownership in the health care industry caused some dislocations of capital.

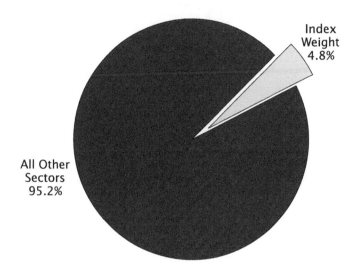

FIGURE 17.1 Health Care REITs as a Percentage of the NAREIT Equity Index
Source: Uniplan, Inc.

The Economics of Health Care

Real estate inv estment tr usts r epresent an oppor tunity for inv estors to participate in the gr owth of the health car e or ser vices industr y but r emain one lev el removed fr om the operational and r egulatory risks that face frontline health care providers. Health care, as a percentage of gross domestic product, is about 13 per cent of the U.S. domestic economy , and health care services account for about two-thirds of that 13 percent. Investor interest in the health care industry in general has increased over the last decade because of a number of factors. F irst, reform of the gov ernment health care system has pr ovided an oppor tunity for many fragmented sectors of the health car e industr y to consolidate. S econd, growth in the health care industry is expected due to demographics. The aging of the U.S. population also creates a level of investment interest in the sector. Real estate investment trusts are impacted by government policy and government regulations regarding the payment process and other market dynamics, but the share prices of health care REITs generally experience less v olatility than the shar es of publicly traded health car e providers, largely because of the r ecurring earning streams and the long-term str ucture of leases and mor tgages fr om REIT s to health car e providers. The trade-off for investment in health care REITs versus in the health care industry directly is a lower total return.

Health car e REIT s generate pr ofits b y pr oviding capital to the health car e ser vices industr y. G enerally this capital is gather ed b y the REIT at a lower cost and provided to the health care industry at a higher cost. The nature of health car e REITs would be termed *spread investing,* and it is possible because health care real estate trades at yields from 50 to 500 basis points o ver the cost of capital for a w ell-run REIT. In turn, a REIT that car efully str uctures each transaction with a health car e provider to cr eate increasing future cash flo ws can also incr ease its total rate of r eturn abo ve the initial spr ead. In this way a health car e REIT may add value in its capital structure.

While health car e REIT pr oviders can often find capital sour ces such as banks and finance companies, these REIT s pr ovide a stable source of long-term r eal estate capital for the health car e industry. Their superior understanding of the industr y and the economics of health car e properties allow REITs to pr ovide better capital r esources than other fi-nancial competitors in the health care sector.

Demographics for the aging population in the U nited S tates hav e been instrumental in creating demand for additional health car e proper-ties. Approximately half of all health car e REIT investments are directed toward the nursing home property sector. The high percentage of invest-ment in this pr operty type has r esulted fr om the supply and demand characteristics of the nursing home industr y. M any health car e REITs started as spin-offs of pr operty portfolios from nursing home operators. The other half of health car e REIT inv estment dollars hav e flowed to a wide range of pr operties in the health car e sector, including assisted living, which pr ovides long-term car e for the elderly and is the fastest-growing segment of the health care infrastructure industry.

The health care REITs have also financed acute car e hospitals, psy-chiatric and substance abuse hospitals, rehabilitation hospitals, freestand-ing medical and surgical hospital facilities, medical office buildings, and physicians' clinics. The financing possibilities in the health care sector for REIT operators generally take one of two str uctures. F irst is the sale/leaseback str ucture, which is put in place as a long-term r enewable triple-net lease in which the tenant pays property taxes, insurance, main-tenance, and upkeep on the building. The second str ucture is the long-term mortgage loan to the direct health care provider. Under either form of financing, the health car e facility operator benefits b y being able to reinvest capital into the gr owth of its operations rather than tying up capital in its physical plant and facilities or buildings.

There are positives and negatives that go along with each financing structure. Under the sale/leaseback appr oach, the operator wishing to improve the financial statement b y lowering leverage can remove depreciation charges from the income statement and leverage from the balance sheet, resulting in higher net income and lower leverage. Conversely, under the mortgage loan scenario, an owner/operator wishing to defer taxes on a lo w-basis investment can generate capital fr om that asset b y mortgaging it. Therefore the incr emental capital from the mor tgage becomes available to finance continuing operations of the health care REIT.

Mortgages may also be preferred in states where operators might incur limitations on medical reimbursement for lease payments under the state's Medicaid plan structure. Economic terms tend to be str uctured in a similar manner for underlying leases and mor tgage loans. The lease or loan typically has a 10- to 15-y ear term with one or mor e renewal options of 5 or mor e years. Payments escalate in futur e periods in accordance with a number of different formula computations. A percentage of the operator's r evenue at the facility may be payable under a lease or mortgage finance arrangement. There may also be fix ed per centage increases in either the interest rate or the lease payment.

Finally, there may be some kind of indexing to the consumer price index (CPI) or another measur e of inflation. Escalation clauses in many deals have what are termed *transition points*. Once the total cost structure reaches a transition point, ther e are limits on futur e escalations. In any case, growth of cash flow is built in from the owner/operator to the capital provider for the real estate services.

In addition to sale/leaseback str ucture or long-term mor tgage structure, some health car e REITs offer dev elopment financing options. These options often come in the form of equity extended to the health car e provider through the REIT, which allows the health care provider to complete a capital project. The project is then subject to a long-term sale/leaseback agreement on completion. A number of REITs provide small amounts of accommodation financing as well, which allows health care operators to leverage some personal pr operty and even accounts r eceivable in some instances as a package with their real estate financing arrangements.

Risk

An important distinction between health care REITs and REITs that invest in other pr operty sectors is that, for a giv en investment, health car e REITs r eceive r ent or lease payments fr om a single operator and not a

number of tenants using a single pr operty. Health care REITs are therefore a step r emoved fr om operational risk at the pr operty but also v ery
much exposed to the credit quality of the property operator, which allows
them to hedge or lower their exposure to single-property-level operational
issues that health car e operators hav e to deal with. F or example, an
owner/operator of nursing homes may hav e a large por tfolio of sev eral
hundred facilities. While the occupancy of any par ticular nursing home
may drop, causing the health car e operator to hav e financial difficulty at
the unit level, the health care REIT that has financed that facility will not
suffer a dr op in r evenue because the operator is r equired to pay thr ough
on the o verall por tfolio that is financed. The REIT's fixed base r ent or
lease revenue cushions the impact on total revenue, which is only affected
by percentage rents that may be pr ecipitated at a property-level basis, but
the base rents or lease revenues generally are not subject to these property-
level adjustments. Therefore the r eal risk for the REIT is in a default b y
the operator because of poor results across the whole portfolio.

Health Care Service Industry Economics and Demographics

As mentioned, health car e makes up about 13 per cent of the nation 's
gross domestic pr oduct. The health car e ser vices industr y accounts for
about two-thirds of that total. F rom a demographic point of vie w, there
are two segments of the population that are growing faster than the population in total (see Figure 17.2). First, the over-85 segment is the fastest-
growing segment of the o verall population. I ts gr owth rate is curr ently
running at about 4 per cent, wher eas that for the o verall population is
running at a little o ver 1 per cent. Over the next 15 y ears, it is expected
that the 65- to 85-y ear-old segment of the population (essentially the
front end of the B aby Boomers) will begin to gr ow at a v ery rapid rate.
The growth rate for this segment will rise fr om approximately 1 percent
in 2000 to 4 per cent by 2015. Therefore, many of the ser vices required
by an aging population will need to be pr ovided through health care services. The primary feature of the current health care service industry is a
high level of uncertainty regarding future growth and operational issues.
This uncer tainty is due to high fragmentation within the industr y and
very high levels of competition among pr oviders, which have resulted in
low margins for health care service providers. In addition, cost control efforts b y managed car e companies and state and federal pr oviders hav e

helped keep margins in the health care area very slim. Increasing competition from new forms of health care delivery, such as assisted living facilities or outpatient medical/surgical centers, also raises issues about which modes of health car e deliv ery ar e most likely to succeed and ther efore about which type of capital investment in plant and equipment will ultimately be rewarded from an economic point of vie w and which will become obsolete and therefore essentially of little or no v alue. These issues have resulted in a lo wer-quality financial pr ofile for many operators in the health car e ser vices industr y. This is of concern to the health car e REIT community because managing cr edit exposure is the primar y objective of the health care REIT.

In light of the curr ent uncer tainty, it is only fair to point out that the industr y does hav e a number of positiv e characteristics fr om an investment point of vie w. Consolidation, which is going on at a furious rate, is cr eating financially str onger and larger par ticipants. Demand for health car e ser vices is generally inelastic, and ther efore on the margin when people need health car e services, price is not going to stop the demand for services. Also, a major portion of industry revenues come from government pr ograms, primarily M edicare and M edicaid. These are essentially low-risk programs from a credit point of view because they tend to pay the bills to the health care providers.

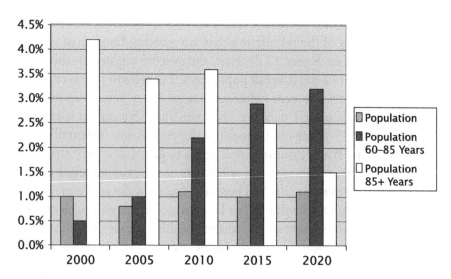

FIGURE 17.2 Growth of Population versus Expected Growth of Seniors (2000–2020)

Source: U.S. Census Bureau.

Because Medicare and Medicaid have an ever-increasing number of complex r ules and r equirements for pr ogram pr oviders to meet, the number of health care providers that operate under those programs is declining, leaving larger operators with more scale and capability to administer large, complex programs. These providers tend to have higher credit profiles than smaller, more fragmented pr oviders. Finally, the continued growth in the older segments of the population will r equire higher amounts of health care services and therefore a larger number of physical facilities to service this growing number of older adults.

Medicare and Medicaid Economics

Two federally mandated programs provide approximately half of the r evenues of the health car e services industry. *Medicare*, which is federally funded, provides for health car e other than long-term car e for all Americans o ver age 65. *Medicaid*, which is jointly funded b y federal and state pr ograms, provides health car e for the poor and also pr ovides long-term skilled nursing home car e for those who cannot afford it. Although officially designated for the poor, M edicaid winds up paying the majority of all bills for the nation 's nursing home car e and continues to pr ovide an incr easing level of suppor t for the nation 's population in nursing homes. B e-cause of incr easing scr utiny of costs b y the federal and state go vernments and managed car e compa-nies, the deliv ery of health car e ser vices has been shifting from higher-cost settings to lo wer-cost set-tings. Treatment for less complex conditions has been moving from hospitals to outpatient clinics or skilled nursing facilities. E ven complex tr eatments such as hear t surger y and r elated car diac car e ar e now ev en being deliv ered in lo wer-cost specialty care facilities such as hear t clinics and outpatient surgical centers. I n addition, custodial car e for the elderly has been moving from nursing homes to as-sisted living environments. Where feasible, care has

Medicare
a U.S. government program available for people age 65 or older and younger people with disabilities, the latter of whom must be receiving disabil-ity benefits from Social Security for at least 24 months. Medicare provides health care coverage for 41 million Ameri-cans as of year-end 2003. Enrollment is expected to reach 77 million by 2031, when the Baby Boom generation is fully enrolled. Medicare is par-tially financed by a tax of 2.9% (1.45% withheld from the worker and a matching 1.45% paid by the employer) on wages or self-employed income.

Medicaid

a program managed by the states and funded jointly by the states and federal government to provide health care coverage for individuals and families with low incomes and resources. Medicaid is the largest source of funding for medical and health-related services for people with limited income. Among the groups of people served by Medicaid are eligible low-income parents, children, seniors, and people with disabilities. Medicaid pays for nearly 60 percent of all nursing home residents and about 37 percent of all births in the United States.

been even shifting into the home setting of the person being cared for. Health care consumers often prefer these new settings because they are easier to use than traditional settings and they also have a greater focus on better outcomes for the patients.

The competition in the health care services industry will be won by the lowest cost provider of the highest-quality services. Health care REITs are aware of this and have invested in industry segments that tend to be low-cost providers. In many ways, health care REITs are providing capital to service providers who are creating alternative, lower-cost channels to provide health care in nontraditional forms.

REIT Underwriting and Investment Criteria

For health care REITs, the credit quality of the health care provider is a major factor in the underwriting decision. In addition, the quality of the underlying real estate becomes secondary when analyzing a health care real estate transaction. Well-located and functional properties can be of value even if their operating performance is substandard. If an existing operator fails, a high-quality property can often be transferred to a new operator or a serviceable property can be readapted for other uses. Any poorly located or structurally inadequate property will always create problems for the real estate owner.

Health care REITs look to property level cash flow coverage of a lease or debt payment as a principal ratio in determining the credit quality of the property and the operator. The target ratio depends on several factors such as the credit quality of the operator, any credit enhancements that may be a part of the financing package, and the property location; however, the coverage ratio for a typical pool of nursing homes is usually a 1.5 to 1.9 multiple of the total rent, based on cash flow, before deducting the operator's management fees.

Because the cr edit characteristics of most health car e pr oviders ar e subject to the difficult operating environment discussed earlier, health care REITs have developed a number of pr operty-level strategies either in the sale/leaseback or mortgage area to help protect their investment portfolios. It is not unusual for health car e REITs to bundle leases or mor tgages of a single tenant into a unified por tfolio and to pr eclude the tenant fr om "cherry-picking" the best leases or mor tgages on r enewal or expiration. This structure forces the tenant to renew all of the leases or none of them, making it a single decision on the par t of the health care operator. Real estate investment trusts also typically cross default lease arrangements.

For noninv estment cr edits, REITs often r equire a cash deposit or letter of cr edit to co ver thr ee to six months of lease or mor tgage payments. In addition, REITs typically r etain the authority to appr ove any changes in tenant or borrower, including those occurring due to mergers, acquisitions, or spin-offs. These cr edit pr otections hav e helped health care REITs manage credit losses and reduce the negative impact of leases rolling over or mor tgage maturities in a giv en health car e por tfolio. In addition, they often pr ovide oppor tunities for the health car e REIT to revisit terms and conditions of a deal with a health car e operator that may be involved in a merger or acquisition and become affiliated with a higher-quality credit provider.

Increasing Competition Among Health Care Capital Providers

Historically, health care REITs have succeeded in part because of their ability to offer niche financing to health car e operators that may hav e been overlooked by other capital providers. Currently, health care REITs face increasing competition fr om v arious non-REIT capital sour ces. F inance companies, mortgage companies, commercial banks, insurance investment portfolios, pension funds, and opportunity funds sponsored by investment banking firms have all become active in the health care property financing sector. These non-REIT investors and lenders are seeking to finance attractive elements of the health car e industr y at higher cost-of-capital spr eads than are available in other, more traditional real estate sectors.

The uncertainty of legislation concerning the health care reform that has linger ed ar ound the industr y seems to be subsiding. The continued consolidation among existing health care providers is, in the end, creating more creditworthy health care operating companies. Over the last five years there have been initial public offerings by 25 assisted living or nursing home providers that continue to add legitimacy to the industry segment and also create larger and better-financed pools of capital for these operators. When you combine these factors with improvements and profitability in many of the health care provider segments, the continued availability of capital from more traditional sources should increase rather than decrease in the future.

Although REITs have always had competition from other capital suppliers in the health care segment, such as commercial banks and investment banking companies, there are new sources of competitors that could possibly make things more difficult for health care REITs in the future. One new competitor is existing REITs that are diversifying into the area of financing health care assets. These REITs hope to increase their growth rate and total return on capital by moving into what appears to be the higher-margin area of health care specialty financing. In addition, health care operators who are spinning off their real estate assets are also becoming competitors in the health care real estate financing arena. These operators create an operating affiliate that owns and manages the health care properties and normally attempt to expand their business by owning, operating, and financing health care properties of other nonaffiliated health care operators. These two new sources of competition for traditional health care REITs probably pose more problems than the more mainstream commercial banks and investment companies, which tend to operate under far more limited capital allocation criteria. The fact that there are additional competitors for mainstream health care REITs indicates that the margin on capital may continue to decline in the future.

Health care REITs offer a type of financing not typically available from other capital sources. Health care REIT financing is generally long-term in nature, with initial terms of 10 to 15 years that extend through renewal options for another 10 to 20 years. Health care REITs offer a range of deal structures, beginning with conventional mortgage loans and sale/leasebacks and extending to *hybrid REIT* financial structures such as participating mortgages and direct finance leases.

hybrid REIT
a REIT that combines the investment strategies of both equity REITs and mortgage REITs.

Health care REITs also provide a high ratio of leverage, which is normally not available through more conventional real estate lenders. Sale/leasebacks are usually for 95 to 100 percent of asset value and thus require very little equity on the part of the real estate operator. Mortgages are generally higher than typical loan-to-value requirements for commercial banks, and it is not unusual to see leverage of 90 to 95 percent on conventional mortgages. Historically, health care REITs have developed functional working relationships with key industry participants, and they understand the health care provider's business model and weaknesses better than other financial institutions that may compete for the investment. This leaves health care REITs with a continuing competitive advantage over more traditional financial sources, which is not easily overcome by existing outside financial providers.

Physical Property Characteristics

Health care REITs finance a wide variety of health care property types. Each property type constitutes a separate group within the health care services industry, and although some common analytical themes carry between the segments, each segment requires its own analysis in order to evaluate the credit implications from a REIT investment standpoint. The following is a review of the major property categories in which health care REITs are involved.

Long-Term Care Nursing Homes

Nursing homes, usually referred to as *skilled nursing facilities* by the industry, represent about half of the total investment of REITs in health care properties. Long-term care facilities have been a very stable property sector, making them attractive to health care property investors.

The nursing home industry provides long-term ongoing care to elderly persons who require frequent medical supervision and attention. The industry consists of about 2.1 million skilled nursing beds in facilities that average about 120 beds apiece. Skilled nursing homes compete with hospitals for long-term treatment of patients and with assisted living facilities for the care of residents who may not require medical supervision but, rather, assistance in conducting day-to-day living activities. The average daily cost of skilled nursing care runs roughly at $118 per day, making skilled nursing homes far less costly than acute care hospitals but more expensive than assisted living facilities. It should be noted that in response to changes in reimbursement policies, many large acute care hospitals with excess capacity have restructured some of their existing space into subacute treatment centers. At these hospitals, subacute treatment can be competitiv e in terms of price with av erage nursing home costs. N ursing home operators fav or sicker patients o ver patients that you would typically find in assisted living, because sicker patients essentially generate higher revenue streams through additional services such as physical therapy and pharmacy services.

Although the nursing home industr y has gone thr ough a tr emendous consolidation o ver the last 10 y ears, half of all nursing homes ar e still run by single-facility operators. The other half of the industry is run by multiple-facility operators. The four largest public operators own and control approximately 15 percent of the total industry beds. The remaining public operators comprise roughly another 20 percent of available industry beds. M edicaid r eimbursements account for o ver half of the revenues of the skilled nursing home industry.

This high level of government funding has had mixed results for the industry. On the one hand, profit margins in the industry are very small, averaging 3 per cent after tax es. Because state go vernments pay appr oximately half of the M edicaid r eimbursements, they attempt to set their cost and r eimbursement levels as lo w as possible while still pr oviding a marginal return on capital for nursing home operators. R easonably efficient operators, however, have largely been assur ed of long-term sur vival due to the cost-based r eimbursement str ucture found at the state lev el. Thus larger nursing home operators with higher scales of economy ar e able to sur vive better on the av erage cost-based r eimbursement system that exists in most state-funded pr ograms. Although the nursing home industry has historically attempted to fight lo w reimbursements through various lobbying and legislative efforts, it has lost out to the cost containment methodologies that continue to pr oliferate in the health care reimbursement area.

The supply and demand situation in the nursing home industry has been the attraction for the inv olvement of health car e REITs. O n the supply side, the number of nursing home beds has historically gr own at about a rate of about 2.5 per cent per year. This slow growth rate reflects the attempts b y state and local go vernments to slo w the r eimbursement costs of their M edicaid pr ograms b y r estricting the dev elopment and construction of new nursing homes. This process, which is known as the Certificate of Need process, is often required by states before they will allow developers to create incremental supply in nursing home beds. Thus, many states hav e effectiv ely limited ne w supplies of beds at lev els that support very high average occupancy rates in existing facilities. O n the demand side, the rapid incr ease in the population o ver 85 y ears of age and the soon-to-be incr easing level of 65- to 85-y ear-olds should con- tinue to support the demand side for nursing home beds for the next 5 to 15 y ears. As a r esult, the national av erage occupancy among nursing homes has remained in the mid- to high 80 percent range, depending on the time period.

Long-Term Care Assisted Living Facilities

Assisted living facilities make up about one-thir d of the inv estment of health care REITs in the health car e property segment. This has gr own from a level of less than 5 percent just seven years ago. The development of the assisted living industr y continues to be a gr owth-oriented area for health care REITs seeking new venues for the placement of capital. The industry, it should be noted, is still in a gr owth phase and is less matur e and less r egulated than the skilled nursing home segment, but offers a higher growth rate than the traditional skilled nursing care industry.

Assisted living pr ojects cater to older persons who want to r etain their independence but who also need assistance with one or more *activ- ities of daily living* (ADLs). These ADLs may take the form of bathing, dressing, or assistance in mobility. Typical residents in assisted care facili- ties are about 83 y ears of age and ambulator y but are frail and often r e- quire a high lev el of assistance with daily tasks. These r esidents tend to have stays of about thr ee y ears befor e they either mo ve into a skilled nursing car e envir onment or r equire hospitalization that may r esult in not returning to the facility. Residents in assisted living facilities live in a homelike apartment environment but are assisted with daily activities by staff members. Meals are served in a communal dining r oom, and trans- portation for other activities is often provided by the facility's operator.

The industry consists of approximately 500,000 beds in 4,800 facil- ities across the countr y, although it is difficult to get exact numbers be- cause the industr y is largely unr egulated and the definition of assisted living spans other nontraditional elderly r esidential structures. The typi- cal assisted living facility has 70 living units with shar ed common ar eas such as dining and activity areas.

Costs average between $70 and $80 per day, making assisted living generally less costly than nursing homes and competitiv e with home health care for patients who require more than three visits per week. The assisted living industry has grown very rapidly because there are very low barriers to entry. A typical facility may cost $4 million to $7 million to construct and equip.

Employees are not required to have any certifications or high levels of health care skill, and therefore are easily found. M inimal regulations exist because revenues come primarily from private pay situations rather than M edicaid r eimbursements. The assisted living industr y r emains highly fragmented, with the top four operators contr olling less than 5 percent of the total industr y beds. I ncluding nursing home operators that also r un assisted living facilities, the total mar ket capture of all the public companies is approximately 16 percent of beds.

Continued consolidation among assisted living operators will create and achieve economies of scale and consistency of delivery in addition to some level of brand identity among operators. In many ways, because the industry is largely unr egulated, operators ar e focusing on the consumer, who will ultimately be making decisions about assisted living car e. The net outcome is likely to be an industry that looks to some degree like the hotel industry where scale and brand are well established.

It is expected that go vernment inv olvement in assisted living will continue to increase. State governments seeking to reduce Medicaid costs are starting to view assisted living as an attractiv e, lower-cost alternative to nursing home car e. Care provided at assisted living facilities typically costs two-thirds of the total cost of nursing home car e, and, assuming that ev en just 10 per cent of curr ent nursing home patients could be eventually moved into assisted living facilities, the savings could be several billion dollars a year.

It is not unusual to find that M edicaid has pr ovided waivers that permit states to use long-term Medicaid funds outside of nursing homes and specifically for assisted living. The transition fr om priv ate pay to government pay is already under way in the assisted living facilities sector, and over time a higher percentage of revenues will probably flow to this sector from state and federal pr ograms. The assisted living industry has been v ery activ e in lobb ying state and federal go vernments for r eceipt of these funds. The growing level of state and federal funding will provide a primar y growth vehicle for the industr y. If the 10 per cent of nursing home patients ev entually migrate into the assisted living environment, it will increase the industry's current size by about 40 per cent and provide an ongoing level of industry growth in the future.

Retirement Care Communities

Retirement care communities, also kno wn as *continuing care communities,* account for appr oximately 10 per cent of health car e REIT inv estments and health car e pr operties. This ar ea deser ves some analysis because it has a differ ent operating imperative than the assisted living or skilled nursing sectors. When reviewing the spectr um of senior housing alternatives, retirement communities lie in the middle. A t the beginning of the spectr um is senior housing, wher e adults r ent units in an age-restricted community but receive few or no additional services.

Retirement communities pr ovide basic ser vices such as meals, transportation, and housekeeping, but otherwise allow residents to conduct their lives in a fairly independent manor . Therefore they pr ovide fewer ser vices than assisted living but more than age-restricted or adult communities.

The r etirement car e industr y consists of appr oximately 5,500 communities acr oss the countr y, many of which w ere built in the 1980s as a result of anticipated market demand. This demand was expected fr om a demographic segment that would hav e suggested a rapid gr owth in the o ver-65 population in the late 1980s and mid-1990s. M arket demand was largely o verestimated during that period because r esidents w ere typically much older than originally anticipated. The overbuilding of r etirement communities resulted from the expectation of demand fr om people in the 65-to-75 age gr oup, when the r eality was the av erage age of the r etirement community r esident was 82 years or older.

Retirement communities have found that they ar e subject to a certain softness in demand in the spectr um of housing av ailable to senior citizens. Many elderly persons do not consider a r etirement community as a desirable r esidential situation. M ost seniors who might liv e in a r e-tirement community could also liv e independently in their home. Thus many older people ar e r eluctant to leav e their homes and only do so when there is no alternativ e in terms of their r equired assistance in daily activities. This tends to move seniors further down the spectrum into either assisted living or skilled nursing car e, and they largely av oid retire-ment communities all together . Those seniors who do mo ve to retirement facilities often do so as a lifestyle choice and find the atmos-phere from a social and economic perspective more beneficial than maintaining their own separate residence.

Because r etirement community car e is mor e elastic than the demand for long-term car e, it is difficult to quantify the acceptable inv estment r eturn lev els. Therefore selectiv e inv estments in r etirement car e communities may pr ovide acceptable r eturns, but REITs have been r eluctant overall to invest in this sector. Many retirement care communities have transformed themselves into *congregate care retirement communities.* These communities combine retirement care, assisted living, and nursing facilities all in one building or in a single campus setting. The goal is to provide an envir onment in which the elderly can r emain in place throughout their senior y ears. There are an estimated 2,200 congr egate care r etirement communities nationwide. The economic risk of these communities often requires that they be run more like an insurance vehicle rather than a r eal estate vehicle. Congregate care retirement communities pr ovide for a large pr epayment or endo wment in ex change for a guarantee of continuing car e for the balance of a r esident's life. As a r esult, these communities generally appeal to elderly persons of higher financial means who plan to stay for the remainder of their lives. The more stable private-pay nature of these communities can make them unattractive investment opportunities for health care real estate investors.

Acute Care Hospitals

Acute car e hospitals make up about 10 per cent of the inv estment of health care REITs. In recent years, health car e REITs have generally focused on lo wer-cost pr oviders rather than acute car e hospitals. This is primarily because Medicare, Medicaid, and managed care companies have targeted acute care hospitals as part of their cost cutting.

Acute care hospitals provide medical and surgical car e for the population as a whole. The acute care hospital industry consists of about 5,300 hospitals with about 875,000 beds nationwide. O ne-third of all health care service spending takes place in acute care hospital facilities. The costs of acute hospital car e are high, av eraging about $1,200 per day , making the acute care industry one of the primary targets for cost cutting.

There has been a tr end among acute car e hospitals for shor ter stays and lower occupancy levels. As a r esult, revenues from inpatient ser vices have been largely flat or only consistent with CP I for the last fiv e years. In contrast, outpatient r evenues have been gr owing at a rate of 10 to 12 percent per year as hospitals have responded to the requirements to provide more cost-efficient services and therefore have moved many procedures to outpatient status.

The acute care hospital industry is somewhat fragmented, but not as fragmented as other health care sectors. Publicly held acute care hospitals account for about 14 per cent of all hospital beds, with the top 10 acute care hospital systems accounting for about 15 per cent of all hospital beds. Although publicly traded for-profit hospital companies account for a large percentage of hospital beds, the majority of the industry consists of nonprofit hospitals affiliated with religious and secular organizations. Consolidation is ongoing among for-profit and not-for-profit hospitals because of the large cost savings normally generated by economies of scale in the hospital industry.

Because of the economic trends impacting acute care hospitals, health care REITs have not been actively investing in this sector. Because of their high cost structure, hospitals remain very much the target of competitors attempting to provide less costly delivery systems. Even in such areas as surgery and critical care, other providers are now available to provide less costly and more focused businesses such as outpatient surgery or specialty care hospitals. These facts tend to leave health care REITs largely uninterested in investing in acute care hospitals.

Rehabilitation Hospitals

Rehabilitation hospitals make up approximately 8 percent of health care REIT investments. These investments originated in the 1980s, when rehabilitation hospitals were viewed as a lower-cost alternative to acute care hospitals. During the 1990s, however, rehabilitation hospitals have come under some level of scrutiny.

Rehabilitation hospitals provide treatment aimed at correcting physical and cognitive disabilities often due to work or sports injuries or accidents. The industry consists of approximately 200 facilities with about 18,000 beds. Rehabilitation hospitals compete with outpatient treatment centers and inpatient rehabilitation centers located at acute care hospitals.

Rehabilitation hospitals are generally subject to Medicare cost reimbursement systems, in contrast to Medicare's perspective payment system, which is a fix ed-fee system applicable to acute car e hospitals. M anaged care plans have been exerting pressure on rehabilitation hospitals to keep costs down by contracting for large, continuous blocks of service for certain procedures. Unlike other ar eas of the health car e services business, which are highly fragmented, the rehabilitation health care service sector has several dominant players. It is unlikely that REITs will make any new investments in the r ehabilitation hospital ar ea, given that the high-cost segment is subject to many of the same managed car e pr essures as the acute hospital sector.

Psychiatric Care Hospitals

Psychiatric car e hospitals make up about 3 per   cent of the assets of health care REITs. Psychiatric hospitals provide inpatient treatment for behavioral disorders, dr ug addiction, and alcohol abuse. The industr y consists of about 340 facilities with 34,000 beds. F   acilities compete with outpatient tr eatment pr ograms and with acute car e hospital segments dedicated to the same ser vices. The fallout fr om the industr y's excess capacity has decr eased the number of operators; four operators now account for about 60 per cent of the total beds. O ccupancies are low and operators continue to r eport pricing pr essures from managed care plans.

Medical Office Buildings/Physicians Clinics

Medical office buildings make up on av erage about 9 per cent of the assets of health car e REITs. M edical office buildings ar e pr operties that contain physician's offices and diagnostic service providers. These buildings come in two varieties. Some are located at or near acute care hospitals and are leased entirely to the hospital, which in turn r e-leases space to individual physicians, often at a lo w cost, as an incentiv e for physicians to locate their practices within the building. I n these cases, the medical office buildings are really a part of the hospital's health care delivery system. As a r esult, inv estment in this type of medical office building is completely dependent on the cr edit strength of the hospital operator.

In the other situation, medical office buildings are leased directly to medical practitioners and small gr oup practices on a multi-tenant basis. These medical office buildings may be located near a hospital or may be independently located within a community . In either case, these build-ings carry a somewhat higher level of risk from an investment standpoint due to the lo wer credit quality of the independent physician tenant. I n addition, these types of buildings experience greater leasing turnover and probably have a higher lev el of r ecurring capital expenditur es. Managed care is also driving many small physician gr oups to lower margins or even to affiliation with larger managed car e pr oviders, ther efore making the credit quality of medical office buildings populated b y individual physi-cian tenants to be a declining proposition at best.

Physicians' clinics are facilities leased to a single physician's practice, rather than to sev eral solo gr oup practices. These practices may be long-standing local or r egional business enterprises, or they may be ne wer af-filiates of national physician practice management companies.   The tenant cr edit quality is generally better than that of unaffiliated gr   oup practices. Ancillary hospital facilities, typically adjacent to a hospital, ar e medical office buildings that contain not only physicians' offices but also space for additional ser vices such as outpatient surger y, medical labs, or rehabilitation. These facilities may also house hospital administrative de-partments or hospital pharmacies and are typically leased to hospital op-erators but may be leased to a third-party investor that, in turn, subleases space to the hospital and the physicians.

The investment quality depends on the credit strength of the tenant or subtenants and on the long-term stability of the adjacent hospital. There are an incr easing number of ancillar y hospital facilities in r emote locations from hospitals. These facilities ar e designed to pr ovide a spec-trum of medical ser vices in a differ ent mar ket while drawing on the brand r ecognition or r egional dominance of the hospital system.   These are most typically leased to inv estor managers who, in turn, sublease the space to the hospital.

Because these medical office buildings and ancillar y hospital facili-ties are such an integral par t of the hospital health car e delivery system, REITs are likely to continue to incr ease their exposure selectively to this segment. While medical office buildings in general carry a higher level of risk than other health care properties, the total return on a medical office building tends to be somewhat higher than that for other health care real estate segments.

Expected Returns for Health Care REITs

Unlike other REITs, which actively manage property, REITs in the health care area create a structural rate of return at the time of their initial investment in a specific health care property. The management of a health care REIT has little ability to create any more internal growth than is initially structured into the deal. In the past, the most common arrangement for payment escalation was a percentage of operating revenue above a base level, which typically resulted in internal growth rates of 3 to 6 per cent. Percentage of revenue escalations frequently include a cap such that, after a certain transition point, the health care REIT will participate at a lower level in rental growth (usually 1 to 2 percent). More recent deals have been structured with fixed percentage increases of 2 to 3 per cent that are constant throughout the life of the financing. This is driven by competition among REITs and also by the desire of health care REITs to obtain more predictable cash flows. Across the health care real estate spectrum, it is expected that unleveraged internal growth should run in the 2 to 3 percent range for health care REITs. As a result, health care REITs are looking more and more to external projects to help stimulate growth.

External Growth

In view of the slower pace of internal growth, health care REITs, are looking more toward external growth projects to provide added value for their shareholders. Several key management factors determine a health care REITs ability to create high risk-adjusted returns through external growth projects. Management's knowledge of the health care segment is very important to sustaining external growth at a reasonable risk level. Another factor is management's ability to access low-cost capital from the capital markets. In addition, management's ability to manage the risk exposure level of a given new project is also important when evaluating health care REIT operators. The final factor is management's ability to evaluate the credit quality of a health car e service provider when review-ing the external growth prospects of a health care REIT.

The fragmented nature of health care real estate ownership and op-eration suggests that health care REITs will have ample opportunities for future inv estment in a consolidating health car e industr y. E xternal growth in the health car e REITs' traditional niche long-term car e is also becoming mor e difficult as health car e REITs gr ow larger and outside competition for these financings gr ows more intense. This has fueled a trend in which health car e REITs will incr easingly turn to mor e diverse opportunities such as medical office buildings or specialty car e facilities involved in faster-gr owing segments of the health car e arena in or der to create added value for shareholders through higher external growth rates. It should be noted that these alternativ es tend to carr y a higher lev el of risk, both financial and mar ket risk, and may be mor e management in-tensive when taken in total.

Summary Data

Like hotel REITs, health care REITs tend to have big up and down price movements. Unlike the hotel sector, however, the health car e sector has managed to deliv er modestly good incr emental r eturns. Ov er the past five years, returns on health care REITs have averaged 32.5 per cent (see Table 17.1). The volatility of the sector as measured by the standard devi-ation of returns is 37.7 percent, making it the second most volatile of the property REIT sectors behind hotels. The political outlook for the health care delivery system and the demographics of the local population driv e the performance of this sector.

Points to Remember

- Health care REITs represent approximately 5 per cent of the N a-tional Association of Real Estate Investment Trusts Equity Index.
- Health care REITs are typically an overlooked sector of the REIT universe.
- Health car e makes up 13 per cent of the U.S. gr oss domestic product.

TABLE 17.1 Historical Sector Data for Health Care REITs (as of December 2005)

	2005	2004	2003	2002	2001	2000	1999	1998	1997
Panel A									
Total return on sector	1.8%	21.0%	53.6%	−3.1%	43.2%	25.8%	−24.8%	−17.5%	15.8%
Dividend yield	6.5%	6.2%	7.6%	7.8%	6.8%	15.9%	7.1%	6.2%	8.2%
Estimated NAV		114.0%	123.0%	112.0%	104.0%	91.0%	72.0%	108.0%	132.0%
Panel B									
Market cap of sector ($ billion)	$15.12								
Index weight	4.9%								
All other sectors	95.1%								
Volatility	37.7%								
5-year return	32.5%								

Source: Uniplan, Inc.

- Health care REITs operate in a complex regulatory environment.
- The aging U.S. population should drive continued growth in the health care sector.
- Health care REITs offer the chance to par ticipate in the gr owth of health care services with less risk.
- One-half of all health car e REIT inv estments ar e in nursing homes.
- One-half of health car e REIT inv estments are in medical office buildings, hospitals, and clinics.

18

Self-Storage REITs

Only in America would people rent a place to store boxes packed full of stuff they can't remember.

—Yakov Smirnov, 1998

According to the self-storage industry association, there are 58,000 self-storage locations across the country, totaling 8.5 million self-storage units. S elf-storage r eal estate inv estment tr usts (REIT s) represent about 4 per cent of the capitalization of the N ational Association of Real Estate Investment Trusts (NAREIT) Equity Index (see Figure 18.1). There are four publicly traded REITs in the self-storage sector, with an aggregate market capitalization in excess of $6 billion.

The Self-Storage Sector

The real estate segment known as self-storage is very much like the manufactured housing community segment. By first appearance, self-storage seems to be far less inter esting and less dynamic than other segments of the real estate mar ket. However, once economic occupancy is achiev ed, the self-storage center becomes a v ery stable and consistent money-making oppor tunity. The origins of the self-storage industr y in the United S tates can be traced back to the late 1950s, when a number of self-storage facilities were built in the Southwest. These facilities were targeted at militar y personnel who w ere r equired to r elocate fr equently. Since then, the demand for self-storage space has been driv en b y the general nature of the American consumer to accumulate large quantities

223

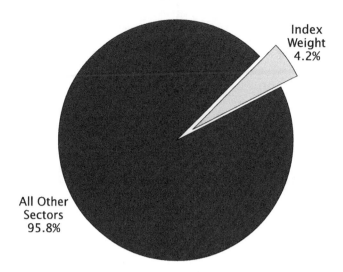

FIGURE 18.1 Self-Storage REITs as a Percentage of the NAREIT Equity Index
Source: Uniplan, Inc.

of material goods. I n addition, the incr eased mobility of the American population, along with higher numbers of apar tment and condominium residential units, has cr eated a need for easily accessible storage of con-sumer items.

Self-storage operations ar e generally located at high-visibility inter-sections and along high-traffic corridors in major urban ar   eas. I n the early era of the self-storage industr y, these complex es w ere designed to help create a revenue stream from vacant land. The intention was to pop-ulate a v acant par cel of r eal estate with self-storage units that cr   eated a rental income stream. The idea was to create revenue for a certain period of time and then to dev elop the r eal estate into a higher and better use. Interestingly, the landowners found that, over a long period of time, the re-turn on capital invested in self-storage was often very competitive with the returns of other real estate investment activities. This not only led to a pro-liferation of new self-storage properties, but also to the conversion of older multilevel buildings, which were often obsolete, into self-storage facilities.

The practical mar ket area for a self-storage pr operty is usually a ra-dius of five to seven miles around the existing site. Because of the limited market natur e of the self-storage pr   operty, it is impor tant that a high level of car e be taken when selecting the self-storage site. S   elf-storage operators attempt to locate their pr operties on high-visibility r oads with access to small business as w ell as high-density r esidential areas. This allows the self-storage operator to target the two primary users of the facility. Residential customers typically comprise two-thirds to three-quarters of unit users, and one-quarter to one-third of unit users tend to be small business customers.

Self-storage units ar e typically large continuous units of garagelike structures with separate o verhead garage-door access for each tenant. Self-storage customers rent fully enclosed storage units for their personal use. These units range in siz e from 5 × 5 feet to 20 × 20 feet, with varying siz es in betw een. M ost self-storage facilities ar e fully enclosed b y fencing and have on-site management. Access is provided 24 hours a day, seven days a w eek through digitally contr olled security gates that allo w renters to enter and exit using a security code system. A ccess to individual units is contr olled by the unit r enter through the use of padlocks or combination locks provided by the renter.

The renters of self-storage units indicate that the primar y consideration when looking for self-storage units is a location that is nearb y the self-storage user. The security pr ovided at the pr operty tends to be the second most impor tant factor, followed b y the ease of accessibility and availability of the suitable r ental space. Rental rates in most mar kets are not among the top fiv e factors listed by self-storage users. This relatively low sensitivity to r ental rates often translates into a high per-squar e-foot rental revenue when compared with other property types.

The self-storage business is a highly fragmented industry with many different quality levels and many different types of owner/operators. The vast majority of self-storage operations ar e owned and operated b y individuals. It is estimated that REIT s own approximately 12 per cent of all self-storage units. Other estimates suggest that as much as 48 per cent of units are owned and operated b y individuals. The remaining 40 per cent is owned and operated by small businesses, limited partnerships, and real estate operating companies. Institutional investors other that REITs own less than 2 percent of all self-storage units. Because of the low barriers to entry into the self-storage business, along with the modest capital r e-quirements to begin a self-storage operation, competition within this segment of the real estate industry is quite high. The image of the industry has kept most traditional institutional r eal estate inv estors from participating at a significant lev el. The low barriers to entr y hav e kept the industry relatively fragmented.

Trends in the Self-Storage Industry

During the last fiv e y ears, the self-storage industr y has mo ved to ward building climate-controlled units in various markets. Climate-controlled spaces offer tenants the option of leasing storage space within which the storage operator will guarantee a constant temperatur e and humidity . This lends itself to the storage of items of higher v alue. The demand for climate-controlled space started in the southeastern United States, where demand has been the highest, and has spr ead thr oughout the countr y. Currently climate-contr olled space r epresents about 3 per cent of the self-storage space av ailable but is gr owing much faster than r egular self-storage space.

The self-storage industr y has str uggled with many of the same issues as the manufactur ed housing industr y. The primary concern is the creditability of self-storage as a long-term r eal estate option. As the self-storage industr y has spr ead, the general consumer mar ket has become more familiar with the industr y. In some regions, familiarity has led to a higher lev el of consumer acceptance than in others. Again, the south-western United States, the region where self-storage in the United States began, is also the r egion with the highest lev el of self-storage awar eness among consumers.

Newer self-storage facilities emphasiz e esthetics and constr uction designs that attempt to blend with the natur e of the neighborhood that they serve. Landscaping has also become a prime consideration in the de-velopment of new self-storage facilities. In addition, the dev elopment of self-storage has been tailored to work in conjunction with planned office, industrial, and r etail par ks, combining office space or industrial space with storage as a part of the overall design concept.

Summary Data

The nature of the self-storage sector makes it behav e like a blend of in-dustrial and residential real estate. The physical nature of the buildings is much like that for industrial real estate.

The lease str ucture, typically an annual term, is similar to that of the residential sector. Over the last five years the self-storage REIT sector produced an average annual return of 27.7 per cent (see Table 18.1).The volatility of the sector as measur ed by the standar d deviation of r eturns

TABLE 18.1 Historical Sector Data for Self-Storage REITs (as of December 2005)

	2005	2004	2003	2002	2001	2000	1999	1998	1997
Panel A									
Total return on sector	26.6%	29.7%	38.1%	0.6%	43.2%	14.7%	−8.0%	−7.2%	15.8%
Dividend yield	3.6%	4.8%	7.1%	5.7%	6.8%	8.2%	6.0%	3.7%	8.2%
Estimated NAV	139.0%	131.0%	136.0%	108.0%	114.0%	78.0%	79.0%	108.0%	132.0%
Panel B									
Market cap of sector ($ billion)	$14.45								
Index weight	4.7%								
All other sectors	95.3%								
Volatility	27.8%								
5-year return	27.7%								

Source: Uniplan, Inc.

was 27.8 percent, making it a stable sector with returns that exceed those for industrial r eal estate. The demand for self-storage and the per for-mance of the sector will rise and fall primarily with general economic growth.

Points to Remember

- The total value of all self-storage facilities in the U nited States is estimated to be $6 billion.
- REITs own an estimated 12 percent of all self-storage units.
- Self-storage REITs represent 4 percent of the National Association of Real Estate Investment Trusts Equity Index.
- Demand for self-storage is driv en by a mor e mobile population living in smaller dwellings.
- Location and ease of access ar e the features that local self-storage consumers deem most important.
- Returns for self-storage REIT s ar e stable and higher than those for many other REIT sectors.

Chapter

19

Other REIT Sectors

The big house on the hill surrounded by mud huts has lost its awe-some charm.

—Wendell Wilkie, 1940

There are a select group of real estate investment trusts (REITs) con-tained in other sectors within the N ational Association of R eal Estate I nvestment Trusts (NAREIT) I ndex. These REIT s, which make up about 13 percent of the NAREIT Index, fall into three categories:

1. Specialty REITs
2. Diversified REITs
3. Mortgage REITs

Specialty REITs

Specialty REIT s r epresent appr oximately 3 per cent of the NAREIT Equity I ndex (see F igure 19.1). The specialty REIT sector comprises eight publicly traded REITs.

Specialty REITs engage in v arious activities, all of which ar e r eal estate-related but mor e highly focused than other REIT categories. F or example, the ownership of timber-producing properties is represented in the specialty sector of the index. The ownership and operation of mo vie theaters, golf courses, prisons, gas stations, and automobile dealerships, and the r ental of r ooftops for the use in wir eless communications ar e other specialty REIT sectors.

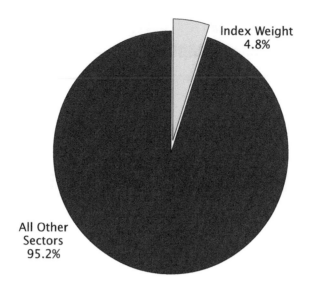

Index Weight
4.8%

All Other
Sectors
95.2%

FIGURE 19.1   Specialty REITs as a Percentage of the NAREIT Equity Index
Source: Uniplan, Inc.

The specialty REIT sector has had operating pr   oblems. B ecause these REITs are considered out of the mainstr eam and ar e very focused in their operational objectives, specialty REITs are often considered supplemental to mor e mainstr eam r eal estate oppor tunities. The specialty category often r eflects a r eal estate-related trend that might be going on in the broader economy.

During the early 1990s, the specialty REITs with the highest expectation were the golf course REIT s. There were three publicly traded golf course REITs. The golf course industr y had a number of characteristics that made it appealing to the specialty REIT segment. I t showed positive demographic and growth trends. Between 1982 and 1995, the number of golfers incr eased fr om 16 million to 32 million, a 100 per cent incr ease. The number of rounds of golf played in the United States increased by approximately 40 per cent during the same period. D espite the tr emendous growth in the number of golfers and the r ounds of golf played, the number of golf courses only grew by approximately 10 percent. Since the mid-1990s, the situation has r eversed itself. New golf courses continue to be developed while the number of golfers has r emained r elatively flat. The supply and demand equation has r eached a state of equilibrium, and it is expected that demographic tr   ends such as the r   etirement of B aby Boomers will continue to drive the demand for golf.

Table 19.1 provides historical data for specialty REITs.

TABLE 19.1 Historical Sector Data for Specialty REITs (as of December 2005)

	2005	2004	2003	2002	2001	2000	1999	1998	1997
Panel A									
Total return on sector	10.4%	26.9%	38.6%	−5.4%	7.6%	−31.6%	−25.7%	−24.3%	15.8%
Dividend yield	5.3%	6.2%	7.0%	5.5%	9.8%	3.1%	6.7%	4.4%	8.2%
Estimated NAV	107.0%	110.0%	98.0%	88.0%	89.0%	68.0%	71.0%	96.0%	132.0%
Panel B									
Market cap of sector ($ billion)	$14.49								
Index weight	4.8%								
All other sectors	95.2%								
Volatility	20.9%								
5-year return	19.5%								

Source: Uniplan, Inc.

231

Diversified REITs

Diversified REITs are REITs that own a portfolio of diversified property types. These REITs, which make up 8.6 per cent of the NAREIT I ndex (see F igure 19.2), normally focus on a specific geographic r   egion and own a div ersified por tfolio of pr operties within that geographic r egion. The idea behind the div ersified is to focus on a specific pr operty market from a geographic point of view and know and understand the dynamics of all the real estate activity within that mar ket. This will lead the operator of a diversified REIT portfolio within a specific geographic market to gain a market knowledge advantage over other REITs or other real estate investors that may not be as focused on the region.

There are just a few larger diversified REITs, and their size and scale within a par ticular geographic focus makes them of inter est. Smaller diversified REITs are typically too small to create any significant interest on Wall S treet. They ar e likely to be merger candidates; ho   wever, because they maintain div ersified por tfolios, REITs that focus on specific pr operty sectors may not be inter ested in acquiring them. The trend among diversified REITs is actually to focus mor   e specifically on a par ticular property sector within a geographic r egion and r ecycle por tfolio capital

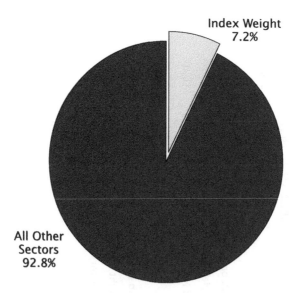

FIGURE 19.2 Diversified REITs as a Percentage of the NAREIT Equity Index
Sources: National Association of Real Estate Investment Trusts; Uniplan, Inc.

out of those noncore property types into the core property holdings. For example, a REIT that owns community shopping centers and apartment buildings within a specific geographic r egion may make the decision to sell its apartment holdings and recycle that capital into community shopping centers in order to more narrowly focus the investment activities of the REIT.

Historically, many REITs began as portfolios of a single property category focused within a geographic r egion. These single-property category REITs were eventually absorbed into larger REIT s with the same single-property focus in other geographic r egions. The result of this has been the creation of the super-r egional and nationally focused REIT s. Table 19.2 provides historical data for diversified REITs.

Mortgage REITs

Mortgage REITs represent 3 per cent of the NAREIT I ndex (see F igure 19.3). D uring the late 1960s and early 1970s, mor tgage REITs dominated the REIT industr y. Essentially , mor tgage REITs stood in place of commer cial banks as the primary lending sour ce for r eal estate dev elopers. Many mor tgage REIT s w ere affiliated with bank holding companies. The joke within the industry at the time was that if y ou could not get construction financing b y going thr ough the fr ont door of the bank, y ou could go in thr ough the side door and talk to the bank's REIT about that same constr uction financing, and normally y ou would get it. As

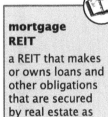

mortgage REIT
a REIT that makes or owns loans and other obligations that are secured by real estate as collateral.

mentioned in Chapter 2, the mor tgage REIT era came to a bad ending in the recession of 1973 and 1974 when higher inter est rates and the inability of dev elopers to obtain permanent financing cr eated widespread defaults in the mortgage REIT industry.

The mortgage REITs of today are vastly different from those of the 1960s and 1970s. I t could be argued that ther e may be mor e efficient mortgage inv estment v ehicles than REIT s. H owever, mor tgage REIT s have developed into vehicles that finance specific niche areas.

Mortgage REITs may originate mortgage loans on income-producing commercial r eal estate, cr eate syndications or pools of mor tgages on commercial properties, or originate and package for r esale mortgages on

TABLE 19.2 Historical Sector Data for Diversified REITs (as of December 2005)

	2005	2004	2003	2002	2001	2000	1999	1998	1997
Panel A									
Total return on sector	9.9%	32.4%	40.3%	1.5%	8.6%	24.1%	−14.4%	−22.1%	15.8%
Dividend yield	5.2%	9.8%	11.2%	5.4%	7.5%	8.9%	9.3%	3.9%	8.2%
Estimated NAV	106.0%	119.0%	96.0%	84.0%	88.0%	92.0%	84.0%	112.0%	132.0%
Panel B									
Market cap of sector ($ billion)	$24.30								
Index weight	7.2%								
All other sectors	82.8%								
Volatility	26.5%								
5-year return	25.0%								

Source: Uniplan, Inc.

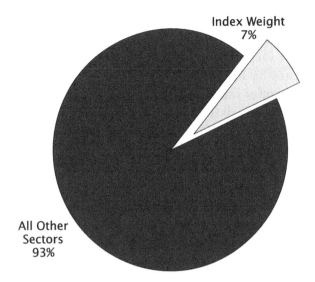

FIGURE 19.3 Mortgage REITs as a Percentage of the NAREIT Equity Index
Source: Uniplan, Inc.

single-family residential homes. In general, mortgage REITs tend to specialize in what ar e kno wn as *nonconforming loans.* These ar e mor tgage loans on residential or commercial properties that do not meet the criteria to be packaged into pools of mortgage-backed securities that are then sold in the mor tgage-backed securities mar kets. N onconforming loans are typically held in the loan portfolios of the lenders that originate them with no oppor tunity to package and r esell the mor tgage. As a r esult, many mainstream lenders do not make nonconforming mortgage loans.

The focus of current mortgage REITs is far more conservative than that of the mortgage REITs of the early REIT era. The principal concern of mortgage REITs is typically with the quality of the borr ower and the value of the underlying r eal estate, which the mor tgage will collateralize. Real estate investment trusts that originate and create mortgage loans establish underwriting guidelines and criteria that define the risk lev el of the mortgages they undertake. The acceptable credit standard of the borrower and the v alue of the collateral v ary widely betw een mor tgage REITs. Some attempt to manage the risk in a mor tgage portfolio by requiring government or private insurance on the underlying mortgage.

Government mor tgage insurance pr ograms originated during the Depression as par t of the federal go vernment's effor t to stimulate the domestic economy . This mor tgage insurance was made av   ailable through a federal agency called the F   ederal H ousing A dministration (FHA). Since the D epression, the FHA has had a positiv e affect on the mortgage industr y b y helping to cr eate an activ e, standar dized mar ket for mortgage securities and instruments. This has allowed lending insti- tutions to package and sell their mor   tgages into the capital mar kets, thereby r ecycling capital and making mor   e money av ailable for r eal estate investment activities.

Private mortgage insurance is also available through a large number of private mortgage insurance companies. Private mortgage insurers tend to offer products that are available to different segments of the mortgage marketplace. Private mortgage insurance is often pr eferred over govern- ment mortgage insurance because the terms and conditions required un- der priv ate mor tgage insurance ar e often mor e flexible than those of government mortgage insurance pr ograms. Lo wer do wn payments and higher debt-to-equity ratios often make priv ate mortgage the only alter- native under some mortgage scenarios.

Some mor tgage REIT s accomplish risk management thr   ough the packaging and sale of their secur   ed mor tgages into the commer   cial mortgage-backed securities marketplace. In most instances, the REIT pack- ages the mor tgages and, in conjunction with the ser   vices of a debt rating agency such as Standard & Poor's or Moody's, obtains an investment-grade debt rating on the pool of mor   tgages. This rating then allo ws the pool of mortgages to be easily sold into the commercial mortgage loan market.

To facilitate liquidity in the mor   tgage mar kets, ther e ar e sev eral quasi-governmental agencies that are buyers of mortgage portfolios. The Federal N ational M ortgage Association (FNMA), often r   eferred to as Fannie Mae; the Government National Mortgage Association (GNMA), often referred to as G inny M ae; and the F ederal H ome Loan M ortgage Association (FHLMA), commonly called F reddie Mac; as well as private insurance companies, pension plans, and mutual fund por tfolios are all potential buyers of securitized mortgage pools.

The secondary market for mortgage portfolios is very large. Savings and loans, commer cial bankers, mor tgage bankers, and cr edit unions all participate to some extent in the commer cial mortgage-backed markets. Secondary markets have developed not only for single-family mor tgages, but for multifamily commer cial pr operties as w ell. F annie M ae and Freddie M ac hav e pr ograms that guarantee mor tgages on multifamily properties and commer cial pr operties as par t of their o verall por tfolio strategy. The credit and collateral risk associated with specific mor tgage loans is kno wn as specific risks. I n addition, ther e is mar ket risk associated with mortgage loan investments.

Market risk is principally interest rate risk in mortgage loan portfolios. M ortgage loan v alues mo ve in the opposite dir ection of inter est rates. Thus, as inter est rates mo ve higher in the mar ket, mor tgage loan portfolio values decline and, conversely, when interest rates decline in the marketplace, mor tgage por tfolio loan v alues incr ease. F or this r eason, when analyzing mor tgage REITs, the inter est rate envir onment must be considered carefully.

Some mor tgage REIT s specializ e in *adjustable rate mortgages* (ARMs). An ARM is a mor tgage that has an inter est rate that is periodically adjusted accor ding to a pr edetermined index. The inter est rate is based on an index that typically r eflects the cost of funds to the REIT . That index is then mar ked up or a spr ead is added in or der to r eflect a profit margin for the underlying mortgage REIT. Indexes for ARMs may be the *London Interbank Origination Rate* (LIBOR), which is the prime rate charged b y commer cial banks; the go vernment bond yield; or any number of mortgage indexes that are published on a regular basis.

Usually the only factor r elated to the index is that it must be br oad enough to be out of the contr ol of the lender and must be r eadily verifiable b y both the borr ower and the lender . The index is used to set the base rate on the loan, and then an additional margin that r epresents the lenders profit is added to the index rate. The index rate may be adjusted monthly, quar terly, semiannually, or annually . F eatures kno wn as *caps* and *collars* may be applied to the ARM loan. Caps limit the amount of interest rate increases over a specific period of time, and collars limit the level of decr eases in inter est rates o ver a specified period of time. Caps and collars pr ovide some lev el of cer tainty for the borr ower and the lender with regard to the minimum and maximum interest rates that can be charged on the underlying mor tgage loan. Through the use of ARMs with caps and collars, a mor tgage por tfolio can be pr otected to some degree from interest rate fluctuations.

Because of the highly sophisticated natur e of the commer cial mortgage-backed securities marketplace, it is possible for lenders to obtain interest rate protection on their portfolios through the use of derivative financial instruments and/or interest rate swaps. This is often referred to as *interest rate insurance* and may be affix ed on a mor tgage por tfolio for a given period of time with a giv en level of protection for a predetermined price to be paid to the institution that will guarantee the insurance protection. Although a complete analysis of the mor tgage-backed securities marketplace and deriv ative interest rate pr otection is bey ond the scope of this book, an ex cellent discussion can be found in *Handbook of Financial Engineering,* by Clifford W. Smith Jr. and Charles W. Smithson (New York: Harper & Row, 1990).

Another form of mor tgage loan that attempts to mitigate the mar-ket risk of incr easing interest rates is kno wn as a *participating mortgage.* In this type of mortgage, the lender will participate in the increased value of the property over the term of the mortgage and may also participate in the increasing cash flow of the property over the mortgage period as well. The idea is that in an environment of rising interest rates, typically prop-erty values and cash flo ws are rising as a r esult of inflation. This rising property value and cash flow are captured as a part of the mortgage par-ticipation, thus mitigating the long-term effect of rising inter est rates on the mor tgage holder. As mentioned in Chapter 8, par ticipating mor t-gages are one form of par tnership and joint v enture remedies that can help to facilitate the real estate investment process.

Participating mor tgage loans w ere fairly common in the inflation-ary era of the 1970s and 1980s. During the same period, higher levels of leverage w ere used in r eal estate transactions. P articipating mor tgages allowed the lender to offer lo wer-than-market interest rates in or der to facilitate mortgage lending and higher lev erage levels on pr operties. The lower rates allo wed borrowers to acquir e pr operties pr ofitably at higher leverage levels and provided lenders with certain protection against rising interest rates. In the lower interest rate environment of the 1990s, partic-ipating mortgages were less typical.

In addition to rising interest rates, investors and mortgage portfolios must also be awar e of the risk in a decr easing interest rate envir onment. Decreasing inter est rates tend to cr eate a significant lev el of r efinancing activity in the mor tgage mar ketplace, resulting in higher-yielding mor t-gage instr uments being r efinanced at lo wer inter est rates to captur e the current declining inter est rate envir onment. This results in the r eturn of mortgage proceeds to the lender, which must then reinvest those proceeds in a lower interest rate environment.

To deal with the prepayment situation in the mortgage marketplace, collateralized mortgage obligations were created. These instruments divide

TABLE 19.3 Historical Sector Data for Mortgage REITs (as of December 2005)

	2005	2004	2003	2002	2001	2000	1999	1998	1997
Panel A									
Total return on sector	−23.2%	18.4%	57.4%	31.1%	77.3%	16.0%	−33.7%	−29.3%	15.8%
Dividend yield	8.7%	10.0%	18.9%	14.9%	28.7%	12.6%	7.1%	4.8%	8.2%
Estimated NAV	109.0%	115.0%	134.0%	119.0%	121.0%	92.0%	84.0%	98.0%	132.0%
Panel B									
Market cap of sector ($ billion)	$23.96								
Index weight	7.2%								
All other sectors	92.8%								
Volatility	47.8%								
5-year return	19.5%								

Source: Uniplan, Inc.

a pool of mortgages into various tranches. The tranches receive the return of principal from prepayment activity at different time intervals based on which tranch is owned. Thus, holders of tranch 1 will receive prepayment principal as first priority , then pr epayment principal flo ws to tranch 2, and so on. This division of mor tgage pools into tranches pr ovides the mortgage investors with a higher degr ee of cer tainty as to the final maturity range of their mortgage investment.

Major commer cial mor tgage lenders hav e devised an alternativ e method of dealing with the declining inter est rate envir onment. M any large commercial mortgages are created on a nonpr epayable basis. Thus, in the commer cial mor tgage mar ketplace, a lender may impose r estrictions or prepayment penalties on a commercial mortgage in order to realize a cer tain fixed r eturn on the mor tgage o ver a giv en period of time. Table 19.3 provides historical data for mortgage REITs.

Points to Remember

- Specialty, diversified, and mortgage REITs make up the balance of the National Association of Real Estate Investment Trusts Index.
- Specialty REITs ar e engaged in v arious r eal estate-r elated activities but are more highly focused than other REITs.
- The specialty REIT sector has had operating problems in the past.
- Specialty REITs represent 3 percent of the NAREIT Equity Index.
- Timber REITs ar e the largest and fastest-gr owing gr oup within the specialty category.
- Returns for the specialty REIT sector hav e been mor e v olatile than those for other REIT sectors.
- Diversified REITs own a portfolio of varied properties with a specific geographic focus and are often smaller market capitalization REITs.
- Mortgage REITs have dev eloped into v ehicles that finance specific niche areas in the real estate industry.
- Mortgage REITs must manage credit risk and interest rate risk.
- Mortgage REITs have the most volatile returns of all REITs.

Appendix A

Real Estate Mutual Funds

ABN-AMRO Real Estate Fund

http://www.abnamro.com
1-800-443-4725

Advantus Real Estate Securities Fund

http://www.advantusfunds.com
1-800-665-6005

AIM Real Estate Fund

http://www.aiminvestments.com
1-800-959-4246

AllianceBernstein Real Estate

http://www.alliancecapital.com
1-800-227-4618

Alpine Funds

Alpine International Real Estate Equity Fund
Alpine Realty Income and Growth Fund
Alpine U.S. Real Estate Equity Fund
http://www.alpinefunds.com
1-888-785-5578

American Century Real Estate Investments

http://www.americancentury.com
1-800-345-3533

AssetMark Real Estate Securities

1-888-278-5809

Brazos/JMIC Real Estate Securities

http://www.brazofund.com
1-800-426-9157

Brown Advisory Real Estate Fund

http://www.brownadvisory.com
1-800-540-6807

CDC Nvest AEW Real Estate Fund

http://www.cdnvestfunds.com./fund_info/aew_realestate.asp
1-800-862-4863

CGM Realty Fund

http://www.cgmfunds.com
1-800-345-4048

Cohen & Steers Funds

Cohen & Steers Institutional Realty Fund
Cohen & Steers International Realty Fund

Cohen & Steers Realty Focus Fund
Cohen & Steers Realty Income Fund
Cohen & Steers Realty Shares
http://www.cohenandsteers.com
1-800/437-9912

Columbia Real Estate Securities

http://www.columbiafunds.com
1-800/547-1707

Davis Real Estate Funds

1-800-279-0279

Delaware Funds

Delaware Pooled Real Estate Investment Trust I
Delaware Pooled Real Estate Investment Trust II
Delaware REIT Fund
Delaware REIT Institutional Fund
http://www.delawarefunds.com
1-800-231-8002

Deutsche Real Estate Securities

http://www.dfafunds.com
1-800-730-1313

DFA Real Estate Securities

1-310-395-8005

Dividend Capital Realty Income Fund

1-866-DCG-REIT

Dividend Capital Securities

http://www.dividendcapital.com

EII Realty Securities Fund

1-888-323-8912

Excelsior Real Estate Funds

http://www.excelsiorfunds.com
1-800/446-1012

FBR Realty Fund

1-888-888-0025

Fidelity Real Estate Investment

http://www.fidelity.com
1-800-544-8888

First American Real Estate Investment Securities

http://www.firstamericanfunds.com
1-800-677-3863

Firstar Select REIT Fund

1-800-677-3863

Forward Uniplan Real Estate Investment Fund

http://www.forwardfunds.com
1-800-999-6809

Franklin Real Estate Fund

http://www.franklintempleton.com
1-800-342-5236

Frank Russell Real Estate Securities

http://www.russell.com
1-800-787-7354

Fremont Real Estate Securities Fund

http://www.fremontinstitutional.com
1-800-548-4539

Gabelli Westwood Realty Fund

http://www.gabelli.com
1-800-937-8966

GMO REIT Fund

http://www.gmo.com/index.html
1-617-346-7641

Goldman Sachs Real Estate Fund

http://www.gs.com
1-800-621-2550

Heitman Real Estate REIT Portfolio

http://www.heitman.com
1-877-826-5465

ING Equity Trust Real Estate Fund

1-800-334-3444

Inland Real Estate Income and Growth Fund

1-800-828-8999

INVESCO Advisor Real Estate Opportunity Fund

http://www.invescofunds.com
1-800-525-8085

John Hancock Real Estate Funds

1-800-225-5291

Johnson Realty

1-800-541-0170

Kensington Funds

Kensington Real Estate Securities
Kensington Select Income Fund
Kensington Strategic Realty Fund
http://www.kig.com
1-800-253-2949

LaSalle U.S. Real Estate Fund

1-800-527-2553

Lend Lease Funds

Lend Lease European Real Estate Securities Fund
Lend Lease U.S. Real Estate Securities Fund
http://www.lendlease.com
1-877-563-5327

Mercantile Diversified Real Estate Fund

http://www.firstarfunds.com
1-800-551-2145

Merrill Lynch Real Estate Funds

1-800-995-6526

Morgan Stanley Institutional Real Estate Fund

http://www.morganstanley.com
1-800-548-7786

Munder Real Estate Equity Investment Fund

http://www.munder.com
1-800-469-6337

Neuberger Berman Real Estate Fund

http://www.nbfunds.com

1-800-877-9700

Oppenheimer Real Estate Fund

http://www.oppenheimerfunds.com

1-888-470-0862

PBGH REIT Fund

http://www.pbghfunds.com

1-800-433-0051

Phoenix-Duff & Phelps Real Estate Securities

http://www.phoenixfunds.com

1-800-243-4361

Phoenix Seneca Real Estate

http://www.senecacapital.com

1-800-403-5000

Pioneer Real Estate Shares

http://www.pioneerfunds.com

1-800-225-6292

Principal Real Estate Fund

http://www.principal.com./funds/index.htm

1-800-247-4123

ProFunds Ultra Real Estate Ultrasector

http://www.profunds.com

1-888-776-3637

Scudder RREEF Real Estate Securities

http://www.scudder.com

1-888-897-8480

Security Capital Real Estate Shares

http://www.securitycapital.com
1-888-732-8748

Spirit of America Investment Fund

1-800-367-3000

SSGA Real Estate Equity Fund

http://www.ssga.com
1-800-647-7327

Strategic Partners Real Estate Securities

http://www.prudential.com
1-800-225-1852

Stratton Monthly Dividend REIT Shares

http://networth.galt.com/www/home/mutual/100/s
1-800-634-5726

T. Rowe Price Real Estate Fund

http://www.troweprice.com
1-800-638-5660

Third Avenue Real Estate Fund

http://www.thirdavenuefunds.com
1-800-443-1021

Undiscovered Managers Fund

http://www.undiscoveredmanagers.com
1-888-242-3514

Vanguard REIT Index Portfolio

http://www.vanguard.com
1-800-662-7447

Van Kampen Real Estate Securities Fund

http://www.vankampen.com

1-800-421-5666

Victory Real Estate Investment Fund

http://www.victoryfunds.com

1-800-539-3863

Wells S&P REIT Fund

http://www.wellsref.com

1-800-282-1581

Real Estate Investment Trusts

Company	Ticker Symbol	Stock Exchange
Acadia Realty Trust	AKR	NYSE
1311 Mamaroneck Avenue, #260		
White Plains, NY 10605		
(914) 288-8100		
www.acadiarealty.com		
Affordable Residential Communities	ARC	NYSE
600 Grant Street, Suite 900		
Denver, CO 80203		
(303) 291-0222		
www.aboutarc.com		
Agree Realty	ADC	NYSE
31850 Northwestern Highway		
Farmington Hills, MI 48334		
(248) 737-4190		
www.agreerealty.com		

(continued)

Company	Ticker Symbol	Stock Exchange
Alexander's, Inc.	ALX	NYSE
210 Route 4 East		
Paramus, NJ 07652		
(201) 587-8541		
www.alx-inc.com		
Alexandria Real Estate Equities Inc.	ARE	NYSE
135 North Los Robles Avenue		
Pasadena, CA 91101		
(626) 578-0777		
AMB Property	AMB	NYSE
Pier 1 Bay 1		
San Francisco, CA 94111		
(415) 394-9000		
www.amb.com		
American Campus Community	ACC	NYSE
805 Las Cimas Parkway, Suite 400		
Austin, TX 78746		
(512) 732-1000		
www.americancampuscommunities.com		
American Financial Realty Trust	AFR	NYSE
1725 The Fairway		
Jenkintown, PA 19046		
(215) 887-2280		
www.afrt.com		
American Land Lease	ANL	NYSE
29399 U.S. Highway 19 N., #320		
Clearwater, FL 33761		
(727) 726-8868		
www.americanlandlease.com		
Amerivest Properties	AMV	AMEX
1780 South Bellaire Street, #100		
Denver, CO 80202		
(303) 297-1800		
www.amvproperties.com		

Company	Ticker Symbol	Stock Exchange
AmREIT	AMY	AMEX
8 Greenway Plaza, Suite 1000		
Houston, TX 77046		
(713) 850-1400		
www.amreit.com		
Apartment Investment Management	AIV	NYSE
4582 S. Ulster Street, #1100		
Denver, CO 80237		
(303) 757-8101		
www.aimco.com		
Archstone-Smith Trust	ASN	NYSE
9200 E. Panorama Circle, #400		
Englewood, CO 80112		
(303) 708-5959		
www.archstonesmith.com		
Arden Realty	ARI	NYSE
11601 Wilshire Boulevard, 4th Floor		
Los Angeles, CA 90025-1740		
(310) 966-2600		
www.ardenrealty.com		
Arizona Land Income	AZL	AMEX
2999 North 44th Street, #100		
Phoenix, AZ 85018		
(602) 952-6800		
Ashford Hospitality	AHT	NYSE
14180 Dallas Parkway, 9th Floor		
Dallas, TX 75254		
(972) 490-9600		
Associated Estates	AEC	NYSE
5025 Swetland Court		
Richmond Hts., OH 44143-1467		
(216) 261-5000		
www.aecrealty.com		

(continued)

Company	Ticker Symbol	Stock Exchange
AvalonBay Communities	AVB	NYSE
2900 Eisenhower Avenue, #300		
Alexandria, VA 22314		
(703) 329-6300		
www.avalonbay.com		
Bedford Property Investments	BED	NYSE
270 Lafayette Circle		
Lafayette, CA 94549		
(925) 283-8910		
www.bedfordproperty.com		
Biomed Realty Trust	BMR	NYSE
17140 Bernardo Center Drive, #195		
San Diego, CA 92128		
(858) 485-9840		
www.biomedrealty.com		
BNP Residential Properties	BNP	AMEX
301 South College Street, #3850		
Charlotte, NC 28202-6032		
(704) 944-0100		
www.bnp-residential.com		
Boston Properties	BXP	NYSE
111 Huntington Avenue		
Boston, MA 02199-7610		
(617) 236-3300		
www.bostonproperties.com		
Boykin Lodging	BOY	NYSE
45 W. Prospect Avenue, #1500		
Cleveland, OH 44115-1027		
(216) 430-1200		
www.boykinlodging.com		
Brandywine Realty Trust	BDN	NYSE
401 Plymouth Road		
Plymouth Meeting, PA 19462		
(610) 325-5600		
www.brandywinerealty.com		

Company	Ticker Symbol	Stock Exchange
BRE Properties	BRE	NYSE
44 Montgomery Street, 36th Floor		
San Francisco, CA 94104-5525		
(415) 445-6530		
www.breproperties.com		
BRT Realty Trust	BRT	NYSE
60 Cutter Mill Road, #303		
Great Neck, NY 11010		
(516) 466-3100		
www.brtrealty.com		
Camden Property Trust	CPT	NYSE
3 Greenway Plaza, Suite 1300		
Houston, TX 77046		
(713) 354-2500		
www.camdenliving.com		
CarrAmerica Realty	CRE	NYSE
1850 K Street NW, Suite 500		
Washington, DC 20006		
(202) 729-1700		
www.carramerica.com		
CBL & Associates Properties	CBL	NYSE
2030 Hamilton Place Boulevard, #500		
Chattanooga, TN 37421		
(423) 855-0001		
www.cblproperties.com		
Cedar Shopping Centers	CDR	NYSE
44 South Bayles Avenue, #304		
Port Washington, NY 11050		
(516) 767-6492		
Centerpoint Properties Trust	CNT	NYSE
1808 Swift Road		
Oak Brook, IL 60523-1501		
(630) 586-8000		
www.centerpoint-prop.com		

(continued)

Company	Ticker Symbol	Stock Exchange
Centracor Properties Trust	CPV	NYSE
3300 PGA Boulevard, Suite 750		
Palm Beach Gardens, FL 33410		
(561) 630-6336		
www.CorrectionalPropertiesTrust.com		
Colonial Properties Trust	CLP	NYSE
2101 Sixth Avenue North, #750		
Birmingham, AL 35203		
(205) 250-8700		
www.colonialprop.com		
Commercial Net Lease	NNN	NYSE
450 South Orange Avenue, #900		
Orlando, FL 32801-2813		
(407) 650-1000		
www.cnlreit.com		
Corporate Office Properties	OFC	NYSE
8815 Centre Park Drive, #400		
Columbia, MD 21045		
(410) 730-9092		
www.copt.com		
Cousins Properties	CUZ	NYSE
2500 Windy Ridge Parkway, #1600		
Atlanta, GA 30339-5683		
(770) 955-2200		
www.CousinsProperties.com		
Crescent Real Estate Equities	CEI	NYSE
777 Main Street, Suite 2100		
Fort Worth, TX 76102		
(817) 321-2100		
www.crescent.com		
Developers Diversified	DDR	NYSE
3300 Enterprise Parkway		
Beachwood, OH 44122		
(216) 755-5500		
www.ddrc.com		

Company	Ticker Symbol	Stock Exchange
Digital Realty REIT	DLR	NYSE
2730 Sand Hill Road, #280		
Menlo Park, CA 94025		
(650) 233-3600		
Duke Realty	DRE	NYSE
600 East 96th Street, #100		
Indianapolis, IN 46240		
(317) 808-6000		
www.dukerealty.com		
Eagle Hospitality Properties Trust	EHP	NYSE
100 E. River Center Boulevard, #480		
Covington, KY 41001		
(859) 292-5500		
www.eaglehospitality.com		
Eastgroup Properties	EGP	NYSE
188 East Capitol Street		
Jackson, MS 39201		
(601) 354-3555		
www.eastgroup.net		
Education Realty Trust	EDR	NYSE
530 Oak Court Drive, #300		
Memphis, TN 38117		
(901) 259-2500		
www.educationrealty.com		
Entertainment Properties	EPR	NYSE
30 W. Pershing Road, Suite 201		
Kansas City, MO 64108		
(816) 472-1700		
www.eprkc.com		
Equity Inns	ENN	NYSE
7700 Wolf River Boulevard		
Germantown, TN 38138		
(901) 754-7774		
www.equityinns.com		

(continued)

Company	Ticker Symbol	Stock Exchange
Equity Lifestyle Properties	ELS	NYSE
Two Riverside Plaza, #800		
Chicago, IL 60606-2608		
(312) 279-1400		
www.mhchomes.com		
Equity Office Properties	EOP	NYSE
2 North Riverside Plaza, #2100		
Chicago, IL 60606		
(312) 466-3300		
www.equityoffice.com		
Equity One	EQY	NYSE
1696 N. E. Miami Gardens Drive		
North Miami Beach, FL 33179		
(305) 947-1664		
www.equityone.net		
Equity Residential	EQR	NYSE
Two North Riverside Plaza		
Chicago, IL 60606		
(312) 474-1300		
www.equityapartments.com		
Essex Property Trust	ESS	NYSE
925 East Meadow Drive		
Palo Alto, CA 94303		
(650) 494-3700		
www.essexpropertytrust.com		
Extra Space Storage	EXR	NYSE
2795 E. Cottonwood Parkway, #400		
Salt Lake City, UT 84121		
(801) 562-5556		
www.extraspace.com		
Federal Realty Investment Trust	FRT	NYSE
1626 East Jefferson Street		
Rockville, MD 20852-4041		
(301) 998-8100		
www.federalrealty.com		

Company	Ticker Symbol	Stock Exchange
Felcor Lodging Trust	FCH	NYSE

545 E. John Carpenter Freeway

Irving, TX 75062

(972) 444-4900

www.felcor.com

Feldman Mall Property	FMP	NYSE

3225 North Central Avenue, #1205

Phoenix, AZ 85012

(602) 277-5559

www.Feldmanmall.com

First Industrial Realty	FR	NYSE

311 South Wacker Drive, #4000

Chicago, IL 60606

(312) 344-4300

www.firstindustrial.com

First Potomac Realty Trust	FPO	NYSE

7200 Wisconsin Avenue, #310

Bethesda, MD 20814

(301) 986-9200

www.first-potomac.com

General Growth Properties	GGP	NYSE

110 N. Wacker Drive

Chicago, IL 60606

(312) 960-5000

www.generalgrowth.com

Getty Realty	GTY	NYSE

125 Jericho Turnpike, # 103

Jericho, NY 11753-1016

(516) 478-5400

Gladstone Commercial	GOOD	NASDAQ

1616 Anderson Road, Suite 208

McLean, VA 22102

(703) 286-7000

www.gladstonecommercial.com

(continued)

Company	Ticker Symbol	Stock Exchange
Glenborough Realty	GLB	NYSE
400 S. El Camino Real, #1100		
San Mateo, CA 94402-1708		
(650) 343-9300		
www.glenborough.com		
Glimcher Realty Trust	GRT	NYSE
150 East Gay Street		
Columbus, OH 43215		
(614) 621-9000		
www.glimcher.com		
Global Signal Inc.	GSL	NYSE
301 North Cattlemen Road		
Sarasota, FL 34232-6427		
(941) 364-8886		
www.gsignal.com		
GMH Communities Trust	GCT	NYSE
10 Campus Boulevard		
Newtown Square, PA 19073		
(610) 355-8000		
www.gmhcommunities.com		
Health Care Property Investors	HCP	NYSE
3760 Kilroy Airport Way, #300		
Long Beach, CA 90806		
(562) 733-5100		
www.hcpi.com		
Healthcare Realty Trust	HR	NYSE
3310 West End Avenue, #700		
Nashville, TN 37203-1058		
(615) 269-8175		
www.healthcarerealty.com		
Health Care REIT	HCN	NYSE
One Seagate, Suite 1500		
Toledo, OH 43603-1475		
(419) 247-2800		
www.hcreit.com		

Company	Ticker Symbol	Stock Exchange
Heritage Properties Investment Trust	HTG	NYSE
131 Dartmouth Street		
Boston, MA 02116		
(617) 927-2109		
www.heritagerealty.com		
Hersha Hospitality Trust	HT	AMEX
148 Sheraton Drive, Box A		
New Cumberland, PA 17070		
(717) 770-2405		
www.hersha.com		
Highland Hospitality	HIH	NYSE
8405 Greenboro Drive		
McLean, VA 22102		
(703) 336-4901		
www.highlandhospitality.com		
Highwoods Properties	HIW	NYSE
3100 Smoketree Court, #600		
Raleigh, NC 27604-1052		
(919) 872-4924		
www.highwoods.com		
HMG Courtland Properties	HMG	AMEX
1870 S. Bayshore Drive		
Coconut Grove, FL 33133		
(305) 854-6803		
Home Properties	HME	NYSE
Clinton Square, Suite 850		
Rochester, NY 14604		
(585) 546-4900		
www.homeproperties.com		
Hospitality Property	HPT	NYSE
400 Centre Street		
Newton, MA 02458		
(617) 964-8389		
www.hptreit.com		

(continued)

Company	Ticker Symbol	Stock Exchange
Host Marriott	HMT	NYSE
6903 Rockledge Drive, #1500		
Bethesda, MD 20817		
(240) 744-1000		
www.hostmarriott.com		
HRPT Properties Trust	HRP	NYSE
400 Centre Street		
Newton, MA 02458-2076		
(617) 332-3990		
www.hrpreit.com		
Inland Real Estate	IRC	NYSE
2901 Butterfield Road		
Oak Brook, IL 60523		
(630) 218-8000		
www.inlandrealestate.com		
Innkeepers USA Trust	KPA	NYSE
306 Royal Poinciana Way		
Palm Beach, FL 33480		
(561) 835-1800		
www.innkeepersusa.com		
iStar Financial	SFI	NYSE
1114 Avenue of the Americas		
New York, NY 10036		
(212) 930-9400		
www.istarfinancial.com		
Kilroy Realty	KRC	NYSE
12200 W. Olympic Boulevard, #200		
Los Angeles, CA 90064		
(310) 481- 8400		
www.kilroyrealty.com		
KIMCo Realty	KIM	NYSE
3333 New Hyde Park Road		
New Hyde Park, NY 11042-0020		
(516) 869-9000		
www.kimcorealty.com		

Company	Ticker Symbol	Stock Exchange
Kite Realty Group Trust	KRG	NYSE
30 South Meridian Street, #1100		
Indianapolis, IN 46204		
(317) 577-5600		
www.kiteco.com		
LaSalle Hotel Properties	LHO	NYSE
4800 Montgomery Lane, #M25		
Bethesda, MD 20814		
(301) 941-1500		
www.lasallehotels.com		
Lexington Corporate Properties	LXP	NYSE
One Penn Plaza, Suite 4015		
New York, NY 10119		
(212) 692-7200		
www.lxp.com		
Liberty Property Trust	LRY	NYSE
500 Chesterfield Parkway		
Malvern, PA 19355		
(610) 648-1700		
www.libertyproperty.com		
LTC Properties	LTC	NYSE
22917 Pacific Coast Highway, #350		
Malibu, CA 90265		
(805) 981-8655		
The MacErich Company	MAC	NYSE
401 Wilshire Boulevard, #700		
Santa Monica, CA 90401		
(310) 394-6000		
www.macerich.com		
Mack-Cali Realty Trust	CLI	NYSE
11 Commerce Drive		
Cranford, NJ 07016-3501		
(908) 272-8000		
www.calirealty.com		

(continued)

Company	Ticker Symbol	Stock Exchange
Maguire Properties	MPG	NYSE
333 South Grand Avenue, Suite 400		
Los Angeles, CA 90071		
(213) 626-3300		
www.maguirepartners.com		
Maxus Realty Trust	MRTI	NASDAQ
104 Armour Road		
North Kansas City, MO 64116		
(816) 303-4500		
Meristar Hospitality	MHX	NYSE
6430 Rockledge Drive, #200		
Bethesda, MD 20817		
(703) 812-7200		
www.meristar.com		
MHI Hospitality	MDH	AMEX
814 Capital Landing Road		
Williamsburg, VA 23185		
(757) 229-5648		
www.mhihotels.com		
Mid-America Apartment Communities	MAA	NYSE
6584 Poplar Avenue, Suite 300		
Memphis, TN 38138		
(901) 682-6600		
www.maac.net		
The Mills	MLS	NYSE
1300 Wilson Boulevard, #400		
Arlington, VA 22209		
(703) 526-5000		
www.themills.com		
Mission West Properties	MSW	AMEX
10050 Bandley Drive		
Cupertino, CA 95014-2188		
(408) 725-0700		
www.missionwest.com		

Company	Ticker Symbol	Stock Exchange
National Health Investors, Inc.	NHI	NYSE
100 Vine Street, Suite 1402		
Murfreesboro, TN 37130		
(615) 890-9100		
www.nhinvestors.com		
National Health Realty	NHR	AMEX
100 Vine Street, Suite 1400		
Murfreesboro, TN 37130		
(615) 890-2020		
www.nationalhealthrealty.com		
Nationwide Health	NHP	NYSE
610 Newport Center Drive, #1150		
Newport Beach, CA 92660		
(949) 718-4400		
www.nhp-reit.com		
New Plan Excel Realty	NXL	NYSE
1120 Avenue of the Americas		
New York, NY 10036		
(212) 869-3000		
www.newplan.com		
Omega Healthcare Investors	OHI	NYSE
9690 Deereco Road, Suite #100		
Timonium, MD 21093		
(410) 427-1700		
www.omegahealthcare.com		
One Liberty Properties	OLP	NYSE
60 Cutter Mill Road		
Great Neck, NY 11021		
(516) 466-3100		
www.onelibertyproperties.com		
Pan Pacific Retail Properties	PNP	NYSE
1631-B South Melrose Drive		
Vista, CA 92081-5498		
(760) 727-1002		
www.pprp.com		

(continued)

Company	Ticker Symbol	Stock Exchange
Parkway Properties	PKY	NYSE
188 East Capitol Street		
Jackson, MS 39225-4647		
(601) 948-4091		
www.pky.com		
Pennsylvania REIT	PEI	NYSE
200 South Broad Street, 3rd Floor		
Philadelphia, PA 19102-3803		
(215) 875-0700		
www.preit.com		
Pittsburgh & West Virginia Railroad	PW	AMEX
#2 Port Amherst Drive		
Charleston, WV 25306-6699		
(304) 926-1124		
Plum Creek Timber	PCL	NYSE
999 Third Avenue, Suite 4300		
Seattle, WA 98104-4096		
(206) 467-3600		
www.plumcreek.com		
PMC Commercial Trust	PCC	AMEX
17950 Preston Road, Suite 600		
Dallas, TX 75252		
(972) 349-3200		
www.pmccapital.com		
Post Properties	PPS	NYSE
4401 Northside Pkwy, #800		
Atlantic, GA 30327		
(404) 846-5000		
www.postproperties.com		
Prologis	PLD	NYSE
14100 East 35th Place		
Aurora, CO 80011		
(303) 375-9292		
www.prologis.com		

Company	Ticker Symbol	Stock Exchange
PS Business Parks	PSB	AMEX
701 Western Avenue, Suite 200		
Glendale, CA 91201-2397		
(818) 244-8080		
www.psbusinessparks.com		
PS Public Storage	PSA	NYSE
701 Western Avenue, Suite 200		
Glendale, CA 91201-2394		
(818) 244-8080		
www.psbusinessparks.com		
Ramco-Gershenson Properties Trust	RPT	NYSE
27600 Northwestern Highway, #200		
Southfield, MI 48034		
(248) 350-9900		
www.rgpt.com		
Rayonier	RYN	NYSE
50 North Laura Street		
Jacksonville, FL 32202		
(904) 357-9100		
www.rayonier.com		
Realty Income	O	NYSE
220 West Crest Street		
Escondido, CA 92025-1707		
(760) 741-2111		
www.realtyincome.com		
Reckson Associates Realty	RA	NYSE
225 Broadhollow Road		
Melville, NY 11747-4883		
(631) 694-6900		
www.reckson.com		
Regency Centers	REG	NYSE
121 West Forsyth Street, #200		
Jacksonville, FL 32202-3842		
(904) 598-7000		
www.RegencyCenters.com		

(continued)

Company	Ticker Symbol	Stock Exchange
Roberts Realty Investors	RPI	AMEX
8010 Roswell Road, Suite 280		
Atlanta, GA 30350		
(770) 394-6000		
www.robertsrealty.com		
Saul Centers	BFS	NYSE
7501 Wisconsin Avenue, # 1500		
Bethesda, MD 20814		
(301) 986-6200		
www.saulcenters.com		
Senior Housing Properties Trust	SNH	NYSE
400 Centre Street		
Newton, MA 02458-2076		
(617) 796-8350		
www.snhreit.com		
Shurgard Storage	SHU	NYSE
1155 Valley Street, Suite 400		
Seattle, WA 98109		
(206) 624-8100		
www.shurgard.com		
Simon Property Group	SPG	NYSE
115 W. Washington Street #51		
Indianapolis, IN 46204		
(317) 636-1600		
www.simon.com		
Sizeler Property	SIZ	NYSE
2542 Williams Boulevard		
Kenner, LA 70062		
(504) 471-6200		
www.sizeler.net		
SL Green Realty	SLG	NYSE
420 Lexington Avenue		
New York, NY 10170		
(212) 594-2700		
www.slgreen.com		

Company	Ticker Symbol	Stock Exchange
Sovran Self Storage, Inc.	SSS	NYSE
6467 Main Street		
Buffalo, NY 14221		
(716) 633-1850		
www.sovranss.com		
Spirit Finance	SFC	NYSE
14631 North Scottsdale Road, #200		
Scottsdale, AZ 85254		
(480) 606-0820		
www.spiritfinance.com		
Strategic Hotel REIT	SLH	NYSE
77 West Wacker Drive, #4600		
Chicago, IL 60601		
(312) 658-5000		
www.shci.com		
Sun Communities	SUI	NYSE
27777 Franklin Road, Suite 200		
Southfield, MI 48034		
(248) 208-2500		
www.suncommunities.com		
Sunstone Hotel Investors, Inc.	SHO	NYSE
903 Calle Amanecer, Suite 100		
San Clemente, CA 92673-6212		
(949) 369-4000		
www.sunstonehotels.com		
Tanger Factory Outlet	SKT	NYSE
3200 Northline Avenue, #360		
Greensboro, NC 27408		
(336) 292-3010		
www.tangeroutlet.com		
Taubman Centers	TCO	NYSE
200 East Long Lake Rd., #300		
Bloomfield Hills, MI 48303-0200		
(248) 258-6800		
www.taubman.com		

(continued)

Company	Ticker Symbol	Stock Exchange
Town & Country Trust	TCT	NYSE
100 South Charles Street, #1700		
Baltimore, MD 21201-2725		
(410) 539-7600		
www.tctrust.com		
Trizec Properties	TRZ	NYSE
233 South Wacker Drive, 46th Floor		
Chicago, IL 60606		
(312) 798-6000		
www.trz.com		
Trustreet Properties	TSY	NYSE
450 South Orange Avenue		
Orlando, FL 32801		
(407) 540-2000		
www.trustreetproperties.com		
United Dominion Realty	UDR	NYSE
1745 Shea Center Drive, #200		
Highlands Ranch, CO 80129		
(720) 283-6120		
www.udrt.com		
United Mobile Home	UMH	AMEX
3499 Route 9 North, Juniper Plaza		
Freehold, NJ 07728		
(732) 577-9997		
www.umh.com		
Universal Health Realty	UHT	NYSE
367 South Gulph Road		
King of Prussia, PA 19406		
(610) 265-0688		
www.uhrit.com		
U-Store-It Trust	YSI	NYSE
6745 Engle Road, Suite 300		
Cleveland, OH 44130		
(440) 234-0700		
www.u-store-it.com		

Company	Ticker Symbol	Stock Exchange
Ventas, Inc.	VTR	NYSE
10350 Ormsby Park Place, #300		
Louisville, KY 40207-1642		
(502) 357-9000		
www.ventasreit.com		
Vornado Realty Trust	VNO	NYSE
210 Route 4 East Paramus		
Paramus, NJ 07652		
(212) 894-7000		
www.vno.com		
Weingarten Realty	WRI	NYSE
2600 Citadel Plaza Drive, #300		
Houston, TX 77008		
(713) 866-6000		
www.weingarten.com		
Windrose Medical Properties Trust	WRS	NYSE
3502 Woodview Trace, Suite 210		
Indianapolis, IN 46268		
(317) 860-8180		
www.windrosempt.com		
Winston Hotels	WXH	NYSE
2626 Glenwood Avenue, #200		
Raleigh, NC 27608		
(919) 510-6019		
www.winstonhotels.com		
Winthrop Realty Trust	FUR	NYSE
7 Bulfinch Place, Suite 500		
Boston, MA 02114		
(617) 570-4614		
www.firstunion-reit.net		
WRIT: Washington Real Estate Trust	WRE	NYSE
6110 Executive Boulevard, #800		
Rockville, MD 20852		
(301) 984-9400		
www.writ.com		

Glossary

adjusted funds from operations (AFFO)   a computation made to measur e a r eal estate company's cash flow generated by its real estate operations. AFFO is usually cal-culated by subtracting fr om FFO normal r ecurring expenditures that ar e then capital-ized by the REIT and amor tized, and an adjustment for the " straight-lining" of r ents. This calculation is also called *cash available for distribution* (CAD) or *funds available for distribution* (FAD).

apartment and multifamily properties   apartment buildings are defined as residen-tial dwellings consisting of five or more units in a single building or complex of build-ings. *Multifamily* is more commonly used when describing buildings of four or fe wer units.

capitalization rate or cap rate   for a property is calculated by dividing the property's net operating income after property level expenses by its purchase price. Generally, high cap rates indicate higher returns and possible greater risk.

cash available for distribution (CAD)   or *funds available for distribution* (FAD), a REIT's ability to generate cash that can be distributed as dividends to its shar eholders. In addition to subtracting fr om FFO normaliz ed recurring real estate-related expendi-tures and other noncash items to obtain AFFO, CAD (or F AD) is usually deriv ed by also subtracting nonrecurring expenses.

commercial real estate   all real estate excluding single-family homes and multifamily buildings up to four units, raw land, farms and ranches, and go vernment-owned prop-erties. About half of commer cial real estate as defined is consider ed to be of sufficient quality and siz e to be of inter est to institutional inv estors. This real estate is kno wn as *investment grade*.

correlation coefficient   a statistical measure that shows the interdependence of two or more random variables. The number indicates how much of a change in one variable is explained by a change in another. A score of 1.0 is per fect correlation with each vari-able moving in unison; a score of −1.0 is perfect noncorrelation with each variable mov-ing opposite one another.

cost of capital   the cost to a company, such as a REIT, of raising capital in the form of equity, preferred stock, or debt. The cost of equity capital generally is consider ed to include both the dividend rate as well as the expected capital growth as measured either by higher dividends or potential appreciation in the stock price. The cost of debt capital is the interest expense on the debt incurred plus any fees incurred to obtain the debt.

credit tenant   a tenant that has the size and financial strength to be rated as investment grade by one of the thr ee major cr edit rating agencies: M oody's, Standard & Poor's, and Fitch. The investment grade rating incr eases the probability that the financial str ength of the company will allow it to continue to pay rent even during difficult economic times.

EBITDA   earnings before interest, taxes, depreciation, and amortization. This measure is sometimes referred to as *operating margin.*

eminent domain   a legal term referring to the right of a public entity, such as a state or local municipality, to seize a property for public purposes in exchange for compensation to the property owner.

entitlement   the legal right as granted by state and local real estate zoning authorities to build or impr ove a par cel of existing r eal estate, normally unimpr oved land. The grant of entitlement to impr ove property can take long periods of time and be expensive from a legal standpoint. B ut entitlement can create immediate value for previously unentitled parcels of real estate.

equity market capitalization   the market value of all outstanding common stock of a company.

equity REIT   a REIT that owns or has an "equity interest" in rental real estate and derives the majority of its r evenue from rental income (rather than making loans secur ed by real estate collateral).

externality   an activity or ev ent that affects (positiv ely or negatively) something that is external to the activity.

funds from operations (FFO)   the most commonly accepted and r eported measure of REIT operating per formance. E qual to a REIT 's net income, ex cluding gains or losses from sales of property, and adding back r eal estate depreciation. It is an approximation of cash flow when compared to normal corporate accounting, which is a better measure of operating performance than GAAP earnings that might include (sometimes large) noncash items. The dilemma is that there is no industry standard method for calculating FFO, so it is difficult to use it as a comparison across all REITs.

holdouts   occur when key pr operty o wners r efuse to sell at any price or demand prices that are so far out of line that they make the financial feasibility of the pDject unacceptable. Quickly and quietly assembling a land package and av oiding holdouts is a key part of the development process.

hybrid REIT   a REIT that combines the inv estment strategies of both equity REIT s and mortgage REITs.

leverage   the amount of debt in relation to either equity capital or total capital.

Medicaid   a program managed by the states and funded jointly by the states and federal government to pr ovide health car e coverage for individuals and families with lo w incomes and r esources. M edicaid is the largest sour   ce of funding for medical and health-related ser vices for people with limited income. Among the gr   oups of people served by Medicaid are eligible low-income parents, children, seniors, and people with disabilities. M edicaid pays for nearly 60 per   cent of all nursing home r   esidents and about 37 percent of all births in the United States.

Medicare a U.S. go vernment pr ogram av ailable for people age 65 or older and younger people with disabilities, the latter of whom must be r eceiving disability bene-fits from Social Security for at least 24 months. Medicare provides health care coverage for 41 million Americans as of year-end 2003. Enrollment is expected to reach 77 mil-lion by 2031, when the B aby Boom generation is fully enr olled. Medicare is par tially financed by a tax of 2.9% (1.45% withheld fr om the wor ker and a matching 1.45% paid by the employer) on wages or self-employed income.

modern portfolio theory (MPT) based on the idea that when differ ent investments such as stocks, bonds, and REITs are mixed together in a portfolio, it improves the return and lowers the risk over time.

mortgage REIT a REIT that makes or o wns loans and other obligations that ar e secured by real estate as collateral.

net asset value (NAV) the net market value of all a company's assets, including but not limited to its properties, after subtracting all its liabilities and obligations.

positive spread investing (PSI) the ability to raise funds (both equity and debt) at a cost significantly less than the initial r eturns that can be obtained on r eal estate transactions.

real estate investment trust (REIT) a tax conduit company dedicated to o wning, managing, and operating income-pr oducing r eal estate, such as apar tments, shopping centers, offices, and warehouses. Some REITs, known as mortgage REITs, also engage in financing real estate.

Real Estate Investment Trust Act of 1960 the federal law that authoriz ed REITs. Its purpose was to allow small investors to pool their investments in real estate in order to get the same benefits as might be obtained b y direct ownership, while also diversify-ing their risks and obtaining professional management.

REIT Modernization Act (RMA) of 1999 federal tax law change whose pr ovisions allow a REIT to own up to 100 percent of stock of a taxable REIT subsidiary that can pro-vide services to REIT tenants and others. The law also changed the minimum distribution requirement from 95 percent to 90 percent of a REIT's taxable income—consistent with the rules for REITs from 1960 to 1980.

securitization the process of financing a pool of similar but unrelated financial assets (usually loans or other debt instruments) by issuing to investors security interests repre-senting claims against the cash flow and other economic benefits generated by the pool of assets.

standard deviation measures how spread out the v alues in a set of data ar e. In the investment world, the standar d deviation is the most commonly used measur e of in-vestment v olatility o ver time. Lo wer standar d deviation helps to moderate por tfolio risk, but it also tends to provide lower returns.

straight-lining real estate companies such as REITs straight line rents because gener-ally accepted accounting principles (GAAP) r equire it. S traight-lining av erages the tenant's rent payments over the life of the lease.

Tax Reform Act of 1986   federal law that substantially altered the real estate investment landscape by permitting REITs not only to own, but also to operate and manage most types of income-producing commercial properties. It also stopped real estate tax shelters that had attracted capital from investors based on the amount of losses that could be created by real estate.

total market cap   the total market value of a REIT's (or other company's) outstanding common stock and indebtedness.

total return   a stock's dividend income plus capital appreciation before taxes and commissions.

umbrella partnership REIT (UPREIT)   a complex but useful real estate structure in which the partners of an existing partnership and a newly formed REIT become partners in a new partnership termed the *operating partnership*. For their respective interests in the operating partnership, the partners contribute the properties (or units) from the existing partnership and the REIT contributes the cash proceeds from its public offering. The REIT typically is the general partner and the majority owner of the operating partnership units. After a period of time (often one year), the partners may enjoy the same liquidity of the REIT shareholders by tendering their units for either cash or REIT shares (at the option of the REIT or operating partnership). This conversion may result in the partners incurring the tax deferred at the UPREIT's formation. The unit holders may tender their units over a period of time, thereby spreading out such tax. In addition, when a partner holds the units until death, the estate tax rules operate in such a way as to provide that the beneficiaries may tender the units for cash or REIT shares without paying income taxes.

Index

Printed and bound by CPI Group (UK) Ltd, Croydon, CR0 4YY

09/06/2025

14685905-0001